WHERE MEDICINE FAILS

WHERE MEDICINE FAILS

Fourth Edition

Edited by
ANSELM L. STRAUSS

Transaction Books
New Brunswick (U.S.A.) and London (U.K.)

Library of Congress Catalog Number: 83-9092

ISBN: 0-87855-951-5 (paper)
Printed in the United States of America

Library of Congress Cataloging in Publication Data
Main entry under title:

Where medicine fails.

  Bibliography: p.
  1. Medical care—United States—Addresses, essays, lectures. 2. Chronically ill—Care and Treatment—United States—Addresses, essays, lectures. I. Strauss, Anselm L. [DNLM: 1. Chronic Disease—United States—Collected works. 2. Medicine—United States—Collected works. 3. Quality of health care—United States—Collected works. 4. Health policy—United States—Collected works. W 84 AA1 W52]
  RA395.A3W48 1983   362.1'0973   83-9092
  ISBN 0-87855-951-5 (pbk.)

Jmb
5-24-89

Contents

Contents

Preface to the Fourth Edition

ANSELM L. STRAUSS

The preceding edition of *Where Medicine Fails* was published in 1979. Since then there has been an economic recession—still continuing as of this writing in the spring of 1983—as well as persistent personal and national concern over the seemingly inexorable increases in health-care costs. There has also been a considerably less generous stance, on the part of the federal government, toward the medical expenses of poorer citizens; and there have been numerous alterations in legislative and agency actions at all governmental levels with regard to health care. Meanwhile the scientific and technological advances in medicine do not fail to make daily headlines, and we all wait anxiously for the ones that will really count for ourselves.

Given these changes, what relevance does this book, only somewhat revised, have for the current issues in health care? The answer is: "everything!" When asked to redo this book and to write a new preface, I wondered; but not after rereading its contents. Nothing about the American health scene has changed basically in the intervening few years since its publication: the same major health issues face Americans and are still either unsolved, unresolved, or worse yet, go unrecog-

1

nized by large segments of the responsible decision makers. Chronic illness is still our number one and most general medical problem. The health care institutions are still focused largely on, and funded for, management of acute illness. A great many Americans still do not have adequate access to good health care, medical power politics are still relatively unchanged. Medical technology still raises thorny technical, financial, ethical, and social issues. And various medical institutions — let alone their funding — still are vulnerable to the same criticisms made in the previous edition.

In this revised edition, the only change is the addition of seven new articles that have appeared in *Society* since 1979. The book opens with two articles bearing directly on health policy issues: "What Price Chronic Illness?" by Wiener et al., reviews five major policy issues, giving the pro/con arguments about them, then offers a response to all the arguments couched in terms of the implications of chronic illness prevalence. "Medicine and the Market Place," by Krizay, carefully scrutinizes the assumptions which lie behind America's deficient funding of medical care, and makes considered suggestions for that funding. There are three articles that argue the possible causative relevance of environment to cancer: "Chemicals and Cancerphobia," by Whelen; "Reducing Environmental Risks," by Harris et al., and "Cancer and Corporations," by Crawford. Guillemin's "The Price of Medical Heroics" discusses in detail some of the complex issues surrounding the development of technology and its use in intensive care units, including those for saving premature infants; while at the other end of the age range, Hochbaum and Galkin in "Discharge Planning" look at some of the problems of care given in nursing homes. These articles have been added to those published previously, adding both breadth and bite to the total critique of the national failures in health care. Let us, then, pray that by the time the next edition of this book is called for, most of these major issues will be addressed more forthrightly — and equitably.

Introduction

ANSELM L. STRAUSS

During the past years, there has been an intensive involvement of social scientists with the formulation and resolution of public issues. In this volume, the issue has to do with the health and illness of American citizens. Seemingly once far removed from the political arena, except in the agitation of New Dealers for some form of medical insurance, health care issues have become the subject of furious political debate and maneuvering at every level of government. A rising chorus of criticism from within and without the health professions has accompanied the gradual redefinition of health as a right of citizenry rather than a commodity to be purchased on a voluntary basis, when it is not actually a gift from God. Among the loudest complaints one hears are those concerning the rising costs of care and its increasing impersonality. Significantly, these criticisms are voiced mainly by people who can afford to pay for private doctors and hospitalization.

The papers in this volume represent some of this furor over health and illness. Although a few are "pure research" with no recommendations for public policy, most are directed toward reform of some feature of health care or practices, whether it be the characteristics of chronic hospitals, the attitude of the public toward the mentally ill, or the sometimes dreadful consequences of advanced medical technology. All, or almost all, of the papers are based directly on the author's research or that of colleagues, yet a reformist intention brings them directly into the arena of public controversy.

I have grouped the articles into four sections: Main Stream Medicine and Americans Marginal to It; How Medical Institutions Handle Chronicity; Chronic Illness and the Technological Imperative; and Queries about Medical Competence and Morality. The articles included under these rubrics reflect the dominant concerns about health issues prevalent in *Society* magazine during the last decade. There has been some shift in focus lately, but certainly this does not mean that the issues raised earlier have been solved. They are still with us, even though additional issues are now appearing on the national stage.

For instance, the issue of inequity in people's accessibility to medical care and in the "quality" of their care: although many Americans — physicians included — probably assume Blacks and other poor minority citizens now receive more or less "equal" care, that is not at all the truth. Neither is the same assumption which is made about that other minority group, the more destitute (or less affluent) of the elderly. A quotation from a recent review of facts and figures on income and disease will help to dispel this illusion of medical equality:

> When the Medicare and Medicaid programs were inaugurated they were hailed as great social and humanitarian gains. Poverty as a bar to decent medical care was going to be banished. The aged . . . were now going to be protected.

Unfortunately, it has not turned out that way . . . . Persons with low incomes have not been able to purchase health insurance, and drastically raised premiums have made it difficult for even those who are employed to have adequate health insurance . . . only about a third of the poor is covered by any kind of health insurance . . . . It is not easy, either, for the urban poor to get a physician because physicians are not likely to locate in the slums . . . . Even when such residents go to a clinic in a general hospital for tests or relatively inexpensive care, it is a time-consuming trip, and they will lose their wages in addition to the cost involved in getting to the clinic and paying for the care.*

The poor (and the poorer) Americans are still with us; so are their illnesses and sickness-related disabilities.

It was after Harrington's revelation in the 1960s to the middle class about genuine poverty in America, and after the OEO programs, that the voice of the poor began to be heard among the critics of American medicine—later joined by some portion of medical and nursing students, and then by representatives of the elderly like the Gray Panthers. Paradoxically, this highly industrialized nation has evolved a complex and often effective medical technology, housed and employed partly in physicians' offices, but more massively in hospitals, clinics, and medical centers. The poor and their advocates point out that this technology and the accompanying medical services are principally for the rich and relatively affluent. The argument is a bit oversimplified, but there is a good deal of truth to it. Blame for this situation is variously assigned: to the vested interests of the health professions, to the professionals as representatives of middle-class indifference or arrogance, and to the inequalities of

* H.A. Weeks, "Income and Disease—the Pathology of Poverty," in L. Corey, M. Epstein, and S. Saltman, eds., *Medicine in a Changing Society*, 2nd ed. (St. Louis: Mosby, 1977) pp. 60, 62.

the country's industrial system itself. The causes of inequities in the distribution of health care are probably quite complex, but certainly we will not get very far in readjusting the inequities on the basis of slogans. Careful research into specific types of inequity is needed as well as a continuing assessment of how whatever plans that may evolve for reduction of the inequities will actually work out when implemented.

However the health-related issues which lately have appeared in *Society* seem to be linked closely with the increasingly visible problem of chronicity. Even a short while ago, chronic illness predominantly aroused images of unfortunate people relegated to nursing homes and state mental hospitals. The shift in the public imagery of chronicity is dramatic: it is beginning to stand for cancer, heart disease, kidney disease, and so on. Yet medical institutions and their staffs are still functioning mainly in terms of an imagery inherited from the days of "acute disease" and curable illness. In contrast, virtually every page in this book reflects a major change in the kinds of illnesses prevalent now as compared with those not very many years ago. The illnesses that bring people to medical facilities and sometimes kill them are no longer the communicable or acute diseases; predominantly they are the chronic or long-term illnesses. Community and research hospitals are full of patients suffering from the acute phases of their chronic diseases — heart, cancer, emphysema, diabetes, arthritis, asthma, colitis, multiple sclerosis, alcoholism, and some kinds of drug addiction. At the end of the road, when and if the body wears out or the money runs out (or both), the chronic hospital or the nursing home receives the invalid. For the less disabled and their families, there are severe problems that characteristically accompany the immediate post-hospitalization period. Some suffering people shuttle back and forth between home and the hospital, with only the length of their cycle in question. For the poor, chronicity is even more

of a problem, and for their families a burden. Census figures show clearly that the poor average more chronic diseases and get them earlier in life than middle-class people. Thus, although medical technology is improving and most Americans can afford better medical care—and probably are getting it—the health care system is slow in adjusting to the prevalence of chronic disease. Nowhere is this more in evidence than in our chronic hospitals and in the almost complete lack of concern of health professionals for what happens to chronically ill patients after the immediate period of post-hospitalization, when they and their families are very much on their own, coping with the medical and psychological effects that follow the worsening of symptoms and the requirements of medical regimens. Add to this picture some of the untoward and possibly inevitable effects of the technology used by physicians and their helpers to handle the various chronic illness: whether the patients are in the hospital or subject to the technology at home (kidney dialysis for instance). The so-called technological imperative seemingly built into modern medicine saves lives and extends the life span of many individuals, but raises difficult problems pertaining to the "quality of life," to values, and to ethics.

One of the chief virtues of the articles that follow, written as they are by social scientists, is that they focus attention on the organizational, social, economic, and social psychological aspects of chronic illness. These articles have implications for broad issues of policy and politics. Thus, the author of "Medical Ghettos" asserts bluntly that medical organization requires a radical overhauling (not merely more money and personnel) if the poor are to receive anything like equality of medical care— and several years later he would still assert that. The paper by David Smith and his associates is still as relevant as the day it was written, pointing as it does to other kinds of Americans marginal to mainstream medicine. Albee's paper on the needed revolution in care for the retarded suggests how the acute-care orientation of medicine leads to a misreading of what is probably the major issue pertaining to the retarded. "Professionalization and Poverty in a Community Hospital" by Charles and Jacqueline Nanry points to the mismatch between certain features of professionalism and the perspectives of lay (and poor) clients. Roth's and Markson's essays on the public hospital raise profound questions about what our country does to, with, and for its chronically disabled and poorer citizens. In the nineteenth century, they were hidden away in the state mental hospitals; in the twentieth century, we have more institutions to put them into, but their fate is not much less grim, and the associated moral issues no less profound. When we urge them out of those hospitals without adequate recognition of what life will be like without proper familial or communal support, then as Dorothy Miller puts it, there will be "worlds that fail." Further, the failure of public health nursing, built on earlier conceptions of illness, when handling clients with chronic illnesses, is suggested by Irma Zuckermann's article. The standard medical view of the grossly overweight is likewise suggested by Natalie Allon's discussion of group dieting rituals.

The article by Etzioni moves us into consideration of the profound impacts of scientific research and the technological imperative upon illness, health, and social values. Suczek's portrayal of the consequences of dialysis makes those issues dramatically poignant, as does Bard's article on the plight of many cancer patients kept alive by modern technology—and scarcely helped by even the most compassionate of physicians who work, after all, within a context of overwhelmingly biological considerations. "Drugs, Doctors and Junkies," by Bernstein and Lennard, further suggests the broad social context of drug taking and drug addiction, and the health professionals relatively ineffective—and inadequate—view of those matters.

Finally, a paper by Makofsky directs severe criticism at physicians for their frequent incompetence, while another by Sudnow strongly suggests issues of dubious morality attendant on hospital staffs' "caring for" patients who are dying.

Health and medicine are not merely matters for the professionals to worry about or be challenged by; they are as genuinely political as the dreadfully contrasting mortality rates for white and black Americans, or as the decisions about who is to be dialyzed and why, or the recent challenges by women to the quite possible superabundance of mastectomy operations. It is not only the health professionals whose conceptions and vision are at fault: the chronically ill will, I hope, soon effectively teach us that our man-made environments (streets, buildings, elevators, furniture, temperatures) and arrangements (legal, financial, social) are deeply punishing for them—as well as for "normal" people, because unwittingly constructed for normal people. There are increasingly fewer Americans with no chronic illnesses at all; there will be fewer still in the next decade.

Part I
Major Health Policy Issues

What Price Chronic Illness?

CAROLYN WIENER, SHIZUKO FAGERHAUGH,
ANSELM STRAUSS, AND BARBARA SUCZEK

In recent years, the myth of the scientist-Magus has taken certain twists in the health-care arena. While some people still consider modern technology a Faustian bargain—new knowledge resulting in huge costs—others are looking elsewhere for villains. Our reimbursement system, the tendency of physicians to practice "defensive medicine," consumer demand, extravagant claims made by the media, the emphasis in medical education on specialization, the unwillingness of people to take responsibility for their own health—all of these come in for their share of the blame regarding the rising cost of medical care. A closer look at this debate reveals that participants are circling around a major issue, but not directly grappling with it. That major issue is the increasingly *chronic* and unresolved character of illness. By focusing on chronic illness, we hope to demonstrate how contained is the current debate over cost.

To understand the explosive growth in medical technology, we need first to understand that its source lies not only in greatly increased knowledge, but in the changed nature of illness. Since the 1940s, industrially developed nations everywhere have manifested the same patterns of illness: as infectious and parasitic diseases have come under control, the prevalence of various chronic illnesses has increased. The latter include such highly visible illnesses as the cancers, cardiovascular illnesses, renal diseases, respiratory diseases, diabetes, arthritis—some dramatized by heart transplant surgery, the use of pacemakers and dialysis machines, chemotherapy and X-ray therapy for cancer, the "scanner" and so on.

Lewis Thomas, in *The Lives of a Cell*, has popularized a term for these procedures, drugs, and machines, calling them "halfway technologies," meaning medical intervention applied after the fact in an attempt to compensate for the incapacitating effects of disease whose course one is unable to do much about. They are technologies designed to make up for the disease or postpone death. The outstanding example of this is the transplanting of organs. Thomas argues that this level of technology is by its nature highly sophisticated and at the same time primitive, continuing only until there is a genuine understanding of the mechanism involved in disease. (In caring for heart disease, for example, the technology that is involved is enormous: it involves specialized ambulances, specialized diagnostic services, specialized patient-care units, all kinds of electronic gadgets, plus an array of new skilled health professionals to maintain the machines and care for the patients on the machines.) Enormous cost, the continuing expansion of health facilities, and a need for more and more highly trained personnel are characteristic of this type of technology. Until the basic questions about the mechanisms of disease in the various chronic illnesses are answered, Thomas argues—correctly we believe—we must put up with halfway technologies.

That these illnesses cannot be "cured" but must be "managed" makes them different in many respects from acute illnesses, the model around which health care was traditionally built. A brief look at the salient qualities of chronic illness makes the differences apparent. Chronic illnesses are uncertain:

their phases are unpredictable as to intensity, duration, and degree of incapacity. Chronic illnesses are episodic: acute flare-ups are followed by remissions, in many ways restricting a "normal" life. Chronic illnesses require large palliative efforts: symptomatic relief (from pain, dizziness, nausea, etc.) is often as necessary as the overall progress of treatment. Chronic illnesses are often multiple: long-term breakdown of one organ or physical system leads to involvement of others. One fact becomes obvious: halfway technologies are not only prolonging life but are stretching out the illness trajectories. By trajectories we mean not just the physical course of illness but all the work that patients, staff, and kin do to deal with the illness, and all the social/psychological consequences that encircle the illness course (its intrusiveness on relationships, temperament, and so forth).

This medical technology is found in doctors' offices, hospitals, clinics, and increasingly in the homes of the chronically ill. It has prolonged life but has also made patients dependent on technology throughout the long years of their chronic illnesses. They cycle through the hospital, then go to the clinic or doctor's office, return home, go back to the hospital during acute episodes, and again back to their homes. The problems of coordinating the care given in the hospital, clinic, and home become immense. Accordingly, the explosion of technology has had a profound effect on the organization of health care and on the work of the implicated health professionals.

A special feature of medical specialization and technological innovation is that the two are parallel and interactive. If one looks at medical specialization, it is clear that it leads to technological innovation, which then involves industrial development, production, and distribution. In turn, this process creates further sophisticated specialization and associated medical work, and the establishing of associated organizations for medical work. We see this, for example, in the growth of intensive care units (ICUs), or critical care units. When first developed they were general ICUs, in which a variety of very ill patients, including cardiac patients, were cared for. Then, with further refinement of cardiovascular monitors and respirators, aided by large research funds for cardiac disease, separate intensive care cardiac units evolved. Simultaneously, specialized diagnostic cardiac units were developed, becoming further differentiated according to patient age—adult or pediatric. Corresponding with these developments, heart surgeons invented a sophisticated cardiac surgical technology. In large medical centers one finds that each specialty has begun to have its own intensive care unit—neurological ICUs, respiratory ICUs, and so on.

Discussion of indirect costs due to chronic illness rarely goes beyond suggesting loss of work time and restriction of activity. There are, however, other costs, equally hard to measure (and many borne principally by patients and their families):

- Help in the home for patients who are incapacitated, as, for instance, stroke patients.
- Transportation to and from clinics, hospitals, and physicians' offices.
- Increased burden on middle-aged, middle-class working tax payers (for Medicare, Medicaid, and increased insurance premiums).
- Counseling to cope with disease-induced stress.
- Tutoring for children with chronic illness.
- Technical services (in the use and maintenance of home equipment, such as dialysis machines and respiratory equipment).
- Inflationary cost of products as employers respond to increased benefit packages offered employees.

The impact of specialization is also greater than the most extravagant criticism of it. An example on the research level is the burgeoning field called neuroscience, which blends specialists in biochemistry, anatomy, psychology, and pharmacology in an international effort to chart the brain, thereby to discover means to suppress pain and treat mental illness. Each aspect of this effort requires highly specialized knowledge and skill and is dependent on highly specialized equipment. While the neuroanatomist is exploring the limits of autoradiography — a technique of photographing slices of animal brain tissue after first treating it with radioactive substances — the biological psychiatrist is using computerized laboratory equipment to study the blood plasma of patients who are especially sensitive to pain. Similar combinations of expertise are to be found in the development of electronic prosthetic devices (an implantable electronic inner ear, electronic vision) brought about by the increased miniaturization of electronic circuitry and the combined work of engineers, chemists, and biologists. Or consider the artificial pancreas, a still nascent development dependent on all kinds of basic science: mathematical models constructed through experimentation in a metabolic research unit; enzymatic methods for measuring blood sugar; improvement of chemical films that allow immobilization of enzymes despite the risk of infection; computer analysis to measure insulin levels; production of refined bio-materials; creation of a machine which measures a patient's blood sugar over a twenty-four-hour period. This machine finally confirmed what the researchers had long suspected: that the diabetic taking insulin every day is never fully under control; that no diabetic is being treated very well. Thus, the work of specialized research scientists becomes joined to the highly specialized world of medical instrumentation.

Obviously, the expanded medical knowledge and the technology which evolves through the combined efforts of specialization are then mirrored at the level of application. Hence the emergence not only of cardiologists, nephrologists, and neurosurgeons, but of pediatric cardiologists and hematologists with a sub-specialty in leukemia—sharpening the mastery ever more finely by limiting the focus. What is more, medical knowledge is developing at such a rapid pace that many medical options are experimental, involving increasingly higher risk, which further increases the requirements of the limited focus. Thus today, pharmacologists must try to keep physicians' informed (at Stanford Hospital through a computerized system, at the University of California Hospital, San Francisco, through a periodic bulletin) regarding the harmful interactive effect of the huge number of available drugs.

Although medical specialization is usually singled out in this regard about cost, the nursing profession is also specializing at a tremendous pace—again in response to the clinical expertise demanded by specialized equipment and more problematic trajectories. There are now numerous special-interest nursing groups for nephrology, neurosurgery, emergency room, infectious-disease control, orthopedics, oncology, rehabilitation, and critical care, to name a few. Combined nursing specialties are mushrooming, again in response to perceived need, as for example the pediatric-dialysis nurse who told us she sees herself as the coordinator whom parents need when dealing with the fragmented care in their child's treatment. This process of professional and occupational specialization is bound not only to continue but to proliferate.

Thus modern technology—heart-lung machines which increase the number of candidates for surgery, hyperalimentation machines which bypass the digestive system, intricate blood chemistry tests which give instant and multiple readings on electrolyte status—has made for a variety of options which did not exist before: What technology is to be used? How? When? Where? Who decides? This intricate technology requires specialized knowledge and has led to a proliferation of experts. They are dealing not only with the uncertainty of the disease trajectory or trajectories of a particular patient, but with the risks of the use of available technology—hence all the balancing and juggling of options and the use of consultations. Often debates are going on among the physicians regarding what is the right option, or about the appropriate sequence of options. Each decision about options can be crucial, with multiple factors being weighted and balanced, often by a multitude of people who may have different perspectives and different stakes in the decision making. All along, technologies are being used to facilitate decision making: such as imaging techniques to visualize internal organs, and monitoring machines and laboratory tests for second-to-second appraisal.

In addition, at each point where options are chosen there is a possibility of a new illness trajectory as a result of the decision to apply a given option: steroid drugs often cause secondary disease in kidney transplant patients, machines and procedures can cause infections. Furthermore, the trajectory stretchout means that diseases associated with advanced age, like degenerative arthritis and arteriosclerosis, are superimposed on the major trajectory. If a patient has multiple diseases or even a major and minor trajectory (e.g., ulcerative colitis plus an allergy to sulfa drugs, or kidney disease requiring five hours of dialysis combined with chronic back problems) the options may be counteractive—increasing the balancing decisions, and increasing the need to employ more technology in the service of those decisions.

This, then, is a brief picture of the changed nature of illness and health care. It is against this backdrop that the debate about the considerable cost of medical technology has evolved.

Impact of Chronic Illness

The reality which must be faced is that:

- Costs are even greater than most estimates, and are going to increase, despite the various assumptions—and policies based on them—about the source of increased cost.
- The impact of specialization is also greater than the most extravagant criticism of it, and this process is bound not only to continue but to proliferate.
- The diffusion of medical technology will continue, and blaming specialization for this diffusion is a distortion of the issue.

■ The notion that consensus can be reached regarding the efficacy and use of medical technology is an unreachable objective.

In *Technology in Hospitals: Medical Advances and Their Diffusion*, Louise B. Russell examined available statistics for four industrialized countries—the United States, Sweden, Great Britain, and France—and found they have all assumed, until recently, that technology is beneficial for patients (in some fashion) and therefore worth having. She concludes this may reflect the fact that the problems to be addressed—the rapid growth of costs in general, and the arrival of a number of expensive new technologies in particular—are relatively recent. The third and perhaps more pressing problem is still not faced head-on: the needs of increasing numbers of chronically ill people. There is now, and will continue to be for some time, competition among the various chronic illnesses for priority. The technologies for these illnesses are at varying stages of their development—e.g., hemodialysis well established although still being refined, the artificial pancreas as yet in the development stage. "Overuse" of technology makes a convenient target, but it is much more realistic to acknowledge that costs are bound to increase because of this intertwining of new technologies with new and more problematic illness trajectories.

While it is generally assumed (even by critics of applying cost-benefit analysis to the health arena) that costs are easier to measure than benefits, the costs are even greater than the most dire estimates. A host of organizational costs are omitted from discussion:

■ Interdepartmental coordination (time spent working out strategies for coordinating and troubleshooting; since the more options, the more possibilities of coordination breakdown, unexpected contingencies, disrupted schedules, etc.).

■ New personnel to handle these contingencies: e.g., unit managers, ward clerks, material management experts.

- Body-to-machine transportation, and vice versa, within the hospital.
- Machine purchase, maintenance, repair, monitoring; bio-engineers to handle this in large hospitals, outside contracts in smaller hospitals.
- Drug purchase, storage, and handling.
- Auxiliary supplies (throwaway tubes, catheters, connections, needles) and their purchase, storage, and distribution.
- Staff to understand, monitor, and enforce regulatory compliance.
- Safety monitoring, including building and maintaining whole departments of safety engineers.
- Time, effort, and space required for backstopping of machines and drugs.
- Resource building of skills; inservice in every department, time spent working and reworking protocols as technology undergoes rapid change.
- Record keeping and reporting.
- Building and rebuilding space to accommodate continually changing needs of departments and wards.
- Non-routine trajectory decisions: meetings-debates over options, more monitoring; then the next round per phase, and the coordination of these phased decisions.
- Time spent working out the idiosyncracies of a particular machine, or assessing it for feedback to the manufacturer.
- Continuing care at home—clinic costs, technology and supplies at home, post-hospital home visits, and new personnel to handle this (e.g., discharge nurses and liaison nurses).
- Phone networks from hospital to outlying areas in less populous states.

The diffusion of medical technology will continue to increase, and to target specialization as a scapegoat for medical-technology diffusion is a misrepresentation. For instance, critics assert that a technology is more likely to be adopted, or is adopted sooner, by hospitals with residency programs. "Open-heart surgery," according to Russell, "is a striking example: medical school affiliation and an extensive program of residency training raised the probability that a hospital would adopt open-heart surgery by 0.6 (the maximum value a probability can assume is 1.0)." Steven Schroeder and Jonathan Showstack, relying on Uwe Reinhardt's study showing that use of medical technology varies directly with density of physicians, conclude, in a *New England Journal of Medicine* article: "Controls will have to contend not only with the reimbursement system as it now operates, but also with the powerful forces toward medical specialization." The California State Health Plan continues the attack. Quoted in this report is the cycle of specialty certification as delineated by Robert Chase, former president of the National Board of Medical Examiners:

1. As a result of advances in the field, a new group develops a special expertise in this area.
2. An organization or society is formed for an exchange of ideas and to display advances to one another.
3. Membership in the organization becomes a mark of distinction in the field, and, in an effort to externalize that recognition, certification of excellence in the field becomes established.
4. Institutions with responsibility for quality of health care soon accept certification as evidence of competence and limit care within that field to those certified.

A fifth step is then offered by the California report, suggesting self-interest as the sole motivating force:

5. The specialty promotes use of its own technologies and the development of new ones, thereby starting the cycle again.

Again omitted from the cycle by these critics are the needs (and demands) of the chronically ill. At a recent meeting in a metropolitan hospital, a physician reflected this as he struggled for clues in the referral process: "People are already going to the high-volume hospitals. So if we could find out why referrals are happening we could perfect the system." People go, or are referred, to oncologists because they are better at treating cancer; to pediatric cardiologists because they are more skilled at treating heart disease in children. The incidence of open-heart surgery is higher in large medical centers with medical-school affiliation, because both patients and their referring physicians know that is where the most skilled cardiologists, the best equipment and supporting staff, are to be found. True, graduates of these large research and training centers then seek opportunities to practice their skills. True also that competition among hospitals forces equipment requirements upon them. But the assumption that supply is affecting demand ignores the evidence that there is a chronically ill population "out there" on whom these skills are being practiced. Blaming specialization itself for the diffusion of medical technology is like blaming the cure for the disease.

The vision of consensus regarding the efficacy and use of medical technologies is an unattainable goal, as Russell's caveat, in "Making Rational Decisions about Medical Technology," hints:

> Finally, if the process of testing, weighing, and deciding is not to be an empty charade, the final decision must apply to all technology, not to specific institutions, and must be supported by all elements of the medical care sector. It is a waste of time to produce, after consideration of national tests, a regulation against the adoption of a technology by hospitals, only to have a financing program continue to pay for the use of that technology when it is owned by a physician as part of his office equipment or by a contractor who provides services to hospitals.

Others in this arena, such as Schroeder and Showstack, are even more ambitious, calling the decisions about what medical services we need and can afford "social decisions," requiring "political consensus." The debate takes notice of the formidable obstacle of professional stakes biasing the outcome of evaluation studies. But the discussion tends to soft-pedal the genuine diversity in assessment. Procedures such as gastrointestinal endoscopy and respiratory therapy are held up as examples of questionable use, supported by papers or discussions from professional meetings. However, these citations from the American Society of Gastrointestinal Endoscopy or a Conference on the Scientific Basis of Respiratory Therapy reflect more the internal debates than the agreement within a particular specialty, and only serve to illustrate how much more difficult it will be to get political consensus in the larger community.

A look at governmental regulatory attempts is illuminating. Although the Comprehensive Health Planning and Public Health Services Amendments of 1966 did not really get off the ground due to meager funding and unclear direction, many of the state and area agencies set up under this law evolved into the present "health systems agencies" (HSAs) mandated by the National Health Planning and Resources Development Act of 1974. There are now some two hundred health-systems agencies in the country, attempting to rationalize health care and to serve as a restraining hand on profligate spending. The principal legacy of the 1966 act is the enactment of state certificate-of-need laws, which require that the state agency review and approve investments in new health facilities (except doctors' offices), services, and expensive equipment. Not surprisingly, composed as they are of providers of care (i.e., physicians and hospital administrators) and consumers of health care (defined as citizens of the area who are not providers), HSAs are controversial forums, described by Ann Lennarson Greer as "targets of attempted suasion by those who would expand and those who would contain the particular area's health institutions," in other words, "political hotbeds." As to certificate-of-need control, Thomas Moloney and David Rogers conclude in "Medical Technology—A Different View of the Contentious Debate over costs":

At present this strategy is in great jeopardy because it was simply too costly to obtain creditable information with which to limit the distribution of big new technologies. Information about the supply, use, and costs of special equipment and services was reported as sketchy, and consistent review standards were viewed as virtually nonexistent. Thus, the goal of direct technology control is being dropped in several states in which it was attempted.

Another attempt at governmental control of costs is the establishment of Professional Standards Review Organizations (PSROs), as part of the Social Security amendments of 1972. PSROs, composed of local physicians, are mandated to determine whether care is medically necessary, of recognized quality, and provided in the proper facility or level of care. To date, the operational definition of medical necessity and recognized quality has been based on "community standards" or "current practice," and PSROs have tended to place their emphasis on assessing appropriate length of hospital stay. In fact, the hiring of PSROs by private corporations to review employees' utilization and thereby decrease average hospital stay seems to be the trend. Obviously, utilization review is a far less controversial road to follow than the thicket of peer assessment of quality care.

Yes, But

The debate about cost as it pertains to medical technology misses the mark by not focusing on the very real and central problem of an increased number of people with chronic illnesses. However, since on first consideration many of the proposals in this debate appear reasonable, it is important to emphasize just where our quarrel with them lies, by offering a series of "yes . . . but" qualifications.

Yes, inequities have evolved in the reimbursement system, suggesting that panels might be able to adjust rates of payment to provide more incentive for nontechnical services. Al-

though this will arouse opposition from some quarters, presumably a committee representative of the medical and insurance worlds could surmount the obstacles. *But*, it should not
be assumed that this will meet the problem of "over-
specialization" and diffusion of medical technologies. Nor will
legislative interventions designed to create a better balance of
primary-care physicians and specialists and a better geographic
distribution of physicians alleviate this situation. Such measures have in the past "either failed to demonstrate the desired
impact or have created secondary, almost intolerable, side effects," according to Charles Lewis, Rashi Fein, and David
Mechanic in *A Right to Health*. Furthermore, the geographical
distribution of physicians is not the prime condition explaining the use of medical technology.

Yes, offering alternative health plans is desirable in that
competition might force more comprehensive coverage. *But*, it
should not be assumed that this will deal with either equality
or quality of care. Although data released to the public from
the Health Maintenance Organization (HMO) experience is
sparse, indications are that the principal cost-control mechanism is not decreased hospital stay, but decreased number of
hospital admissions—the supposition being that these people
are being treated on an ambulatory basis. And yet it is common knowledge that those who get quality care in an HMO are
those who know how to manipulate the system (such as how to
find a trustworthy doctor and ensure assignment to him/her,
and how to circumvent the administrative barriers to ambulatory care). Furthermore, that the consumer can make an en-
lightened choice among health plan options is a questionable
assumption; buying a health plan, unlike buying a television
set, does not lend itself to consumer cost-benefit analysis.

Yes, assessing "appropriate use" of medical technology and
achieving consensus on that assessment sounds like a reasonable expectation. *But*, given all the barriers to evaluate (the in-
conclusiveness of evidence, the lack of uniform values in medi-

cal practice, the constant modification which characterizes new technologies, the variation of use from setting to setting, the long period needed for assessment, the fiscal disincentives for those doing the evaluation, and the ambiguity in the relationship between processes of care and outcomes), assessment in the aggregate is an impossible goal. This is not to say that studies confined to single hospitals or single areas would not be helpful. For example, a study by the San Francisco PSRO verified the high use of emergency room facilities at San Francisco General Hospital by patients who came there because their doctor was unavailable, or because the emergency room is open twenty-four hours a day, admission is quick, and specialists are on call—indicating the need for alternative, less expensive facilities.

Yes, building in early prevention (one of the major arguments in this arena) may reduce eventual costs. *But*, it will be a long time before the results of prevention programs become evident. In the meantime, HMOs as presently constituted sell themselves on the basis of prevention but are still based on an acute-care model: patients learn that the best way to get prompt attention is on an acute or emergency basis. Worthwhile attempts are being made to provide outpatients with testing and services that were previously available only to inpatients. A prototype is VITAL Physical and Fitness Examination Center at St. Francis Memorial Hospital in San Francisco, which offers pap smears and breast examinations for women; urethral smears, genital-urinary examinations, and tests for prostate cancer for men; procto-sigmoidoscopy to test for rectal cancer; treadmill test for heart function; and an analysis of dietary habits and a personality profile to determine stress factors. Thus far, this program is concentrating on industrial packages for the employed population. Enlarged to wider coverage, such a prevention concept is worthy of support. But it should not be presented as a "cure" for current health costs.

Yes, the cost of medical technology can be reduced through rationing devices such as prospective reimbursement, administrative barriers to treatment, explicit criteria for allocation of new techniques. *But*, such proposals fly in the face of equality of care, for it is the poor who will suffer most from rationing. Medical servicing of the lower-income groups still exhibits considerable deficiencies. And yet it is lower-income people who have the most chronic illness, who need the support and preventive work, who get cheated out of the best technology. Rationing will only mean, as it has in England, that the elite get better care—they are able to go around the system because they want and can afford the state-of-the-art. Discussion of distribution of medical technology as it pertains to cost is based on the assumption that if you decrease the supply you decrease the demand. In contrast, we are saying that the distribution should be *more* extensive—that most poor diabetics cannot afford a correct diet, often do not have the family structure to help them maintain a regimen, and delay diagnosis and treatment because of their focus on "the deadly earnest present." Far from cost containment, what are needed are additional services which *may* in the end reduce total costs. It is to this that we turn next.

Looking at Patient Work

Those who argue that the present reimbursement system encourages overuse of medical technology claim that a more discriminating use would result if the patient were forced into partnership (for instance, through copayment insurance). A more sensible variant of this argument would be to encourage "patient partnership" by recognizing and assisting the work already being done by patients. In the hospital, patients do subtle work that is taken for granted by staff (lying still, moving one's body, hearing, seeing); they are also doing considerable decision making—small, operational choices as well as major choices between preferred therapies. In some situations, too, patients connect, disconnect, position, and monitor their own machines; in a spatially controlled situation such as on a dialysis unit, they monitor not only their own physical symptoms and their own machines but also each other and each other's machines. Staff seldom think of this as "work," more often making assessment of patients as "cooperative" or "uncooperative." Even more glaring is the inattention of the health system to patient work that goes on at home. When disease was of an infectious kind, the patient was sent home after the danger period ended. The advent of widespread chronic disease, however, makes the sharp division between home and health facility far too simple a solution to the problems faced by the chronically ill. Much of chronic illness has to do with the patient taking care of his/her own body — there is a thin line between therapy and ordinary living. And yet professionals still think predominantly in terms of "adherence" and "compliance," either abjuring virtually all responsibility in guiding or even looking into the patient work that goes on at home, or expressing annoyance with patients who do not follow prescribed regimens.

Gradual recognition of the need for personnel to aid sick people and their families to cope with problems attendant on chronicity can be descerned. The California Plan calls for revision of Medicare and Medicaid to create uniform home health benefits; relaxed restrictions that permit only skilled nursing services in certain situations; permission for non-medical personal care and support services to the chronically ill and disabled at home; the inclusion of day health care and hospice care. More attention is being addressed to the expansion of "non-physician-provided services," in the realization that while diagnosis and prescription are medical responsibilities, prevention and support activities for the chronically ill are not exclusively so. Indeed, while the extension of time allotted to each hypertension patient, for example, is attributable to the many treatment options which must be weighed by the physician, it is also attributable to the intertwining of hypertension with ordinary living and body-care habits. A properly trained home health aide can guide, monitor, correct misinformation, and could offer *phased teaching*, by which we mean teaching appropriate to the present chronic illness phase. Clinics which do not treat but teach, such as the Multipurpose Arthritis Clinic at the University of California, San Francisco, where patients gather to discuss treatment options and their side effects, can be staffed by nurses and a variety of health workers.

A 1979 *Social Policy* editorial called for an expansion of new forms of services — forms which add the health consumer to the existing means for the production of health care: "With some 50 percent of health care directed to chronic illness and about 70 percent of doctors' visits for the maintenance of chronics, support function can be readily, and best, served by self-help/self-care systems." The editorial added that self-care and mutual support as a national program must be developed in concert with the professional services which complement them, and with the financial support and planning of government. Borrowing ideas from groups like Alcoholics Anonymous and Weight Watchers, health self-help groups are expanding: I Can Cope for cancer patients, Mended Hearts for heart patients, Parent to Parent for parents of intensive care nursery graduates. Aside from the valuable contribution these groups make in terms of mutual support and exchange of information, they are performing a reverse service: teaching health professionals what it means to "live with" chronic disease — knowledge the professionals can impart to future patients. Insofar as there could be a greatly supplemented guidance of patient work in the home, and greater support of self-help groups, the health consumer would be provided with enhanced ability to read signs that portend a crisis of his/her disease, improved skill in responding to the crisis of the moment, and greater motivation to establish and maintain a regimen. Certainly the health-sciences — medical, nursing, etc. —

schools and professional associations could accord greater weight to the potential of self-care in chronic disease management, and the training of students and practitioners to teach patients to use self-care. Such proposals in the end could reduce total cost: by freeing the physicians from work that other health professionals can do, by slowing up the rate of return to hospitals, by reducing the severity of disease in the population. Not insignificantly, such a course might break the vicious cycle that characterizes health care for lower-income patients — patients who delay too long in seeking treatment for themselves and their children, do not follow regimens, come back in worse condition, and are then further aliented by professionals who have not been trained with the special skills necessary to deliver quality care to these people.

Perhaps the most fruitful aspect of the consumer movement in the health field is its potential for demonstrating the force that the concept of patient work can be in increasing productivity of service. Alan Gartner and Frank Riessman make the point, in *The Service Society and the Consumer Vanguard,* that consumers are workers: they already contribute heavily to the human services through the less obvious ways in which they assist practitioners in getting "their" work done. The tie-in of health services to other service industries has been underscored by Victor Fuchs in *The Service Economy*:

> In the supermarket, laundromat, the consumer actually works, and in the doctor's office the quality of medical history the patients gives might influence significantly the productivity of the doctor. Productivity in banking is affected by whether the clerk or the customer makes out the deposit slip—and whether it is made out correctly or not. . . . Thus we see that productivity in many service industries is dependent in part on the knowledge, experience and motivation of the customer.

Modern medical care is far too complicated to allow *equal* partnership between patients and physicians in the decision making over treatment options. Both health professionals and patients could benefit, however, from a realization on the part of consumers that good medical care is not, as Norman Cousins has commented wryly, just a matter of shoving one's body onto the doctor's table.

The value of a consumer movement notwithstanding, there is always the danger of any movement being used to counter the good intentions of its designers. Berenice Fisher has warned of the danger in "The Work of Helping Others":

> Since this movement itself takes place in a context in which resources are still limited and directed by those in power, it runs the risk of being coopted by them, of doing the society's dirty work by getting the poorest and most disadvantaged people to serve themselves—to fulfill the old bourgeois admonition that they ought to be taking care of themselves anyway.

Illustrative of a variation of this risk, Undersecretary of Health, Education and Welfare Nathan J. Stark in 1980 suggested a "keep the change" approach as part of the government drive for a system in which customers—individual patients and employers who pay for health plans—use price as a major factor in choosing among doctors and hospitals. If a worker chose an HMO whose premium is less than the reimbursement for such plans offered by the government, he would either get the whole saving as a cash award, or split it with the employer—a sterling example of subverting the intent of the consumer movement and engaging the employee in self-discrimination.

Changing Perspectives

A cruel distortion of the consumer movement would be to use it as a wedge in the argument for decreasing health dollar outlay. For in the foreseeable future, despite consumer mobilization, self-help, and prevention through health screening, there will remain a need for expert professional help and massive technological resources at great financial cost. Eradication of diphtheria, smallpox, tuberculosis; control of pneumonia and bacterial infection; improved diet and sanitation—all of these together have given us more people with chronic illnesses who live longer, require medical assistance, and need support services. Americans are thus faced with the following options: we can let more people die faster, or let many people be very sick. As in most industrialized countries, we do not choose to do either of those things, for our health priorities are fairly high. There is yet another option: we can give health care even higher priority—we can make people less sick for a longer time (perhaps by building fewer bombers or nuclear submarines).

Experiments in putting hospitals and private practitioners together in more efficient ways (such as Health Maintenance Organizations and Individual Practice Associations) are all to the good, as are voluntary efforts by hospitals to produce savings through administrative decisions (e.g., group purchasing arrangements, more efficient inventory management). Likewise, studies which demonstrate the need to reorganize hospitals to include physicians in purchase decisions (and responsibility) and pleas for economic "risk-sharing" on the part of physicians should be heeded.

Withal, medical care will continue to be motivated by the "technologic imperative" which has been paraphrased by David Mechanic in *Future Issues in Health Care* as "a tendency to take action, whatever the cost, if it offers even a slight possibility of utility." As an issue of *UCSF Magazine* published in 1980 demonstrates with great force, much of the controversy over high technology in health care revolves around the premise that diagnosis has far outstripped therapy, that we are able to detect at a highly sophisticated level diseases we are still unable to treat. Yet sometimes it is impossible to distinguish where diagnosis ends and therapy begins. Ironically, endoscopy, a procedure which has come under frequent attack for diagnostic overuse, has developed into a procedure called endoscopic sphincterotomy, which is a nonsurgical alternative for removing gallstones. Following the characteristic pattern in such development, the physician who is presently using this technique at the University of California San Francisco, Dr. Howard Shapiro, worked with the manufacturer to refine the prototype. His comments are relevant to this discussion:

> We are just beginning to realize the therapeutic potential. With 20 million Americans suffering from gallbladder diseases, the eventual application and cost savings could be enormous.

Sometimes it is equally difficult to distinguish where research ends and therapy begins. A machine called the biostandard, which contributed to research on the still-developing artificial pancreas, is currently being used to take care of diabetics undergoing surgery (for reasons unrelated to their diabetes), since it both monitors blood sugar and injects insulin. While use of this machine involves add-on costs, other developments promise decreased costs—for instance, the wider distribution of continual ambulatory peritoneal dialysis, which (for appropriate patients) is expected to cut costs to half that of hemodialysis. These illustrations simply underscore the rapidly moving nature of medical technology and the impossibility of a rigid cost-benefit approach in this arena.

Physicians could, and should, be taught more about not only the value but the limitations of particular tests. Similarly, the public could, and should, be exposed to the ambiguity surrounding many technologies and procedures, rather than mostly to the glamour of technology like the CAT scanner. Without question, there are careless and greedy doctors, duplicate procedures, industries that want to make money—of course, there should be prohibitions to stop abuses of practice and the spending of too much money at inappropriate times. Nevertheless, the real Faustian bargain would be to have the chronically ill bear the cost (in terms of unnecessary suffering or earlier deaths) for the devilment of those who are guilty of excesses (whether in medical practice or in industrial promotion).

It is generally forgotten that the term "halfway technologies" appeared originally in a 1972 report of the Panel on Biological and Medical Science of the President's Science Advisory Committee. This report stressed the difference between *definitive technologies* for the prevention, cure, and control of disease, and *halfway technologies*, described as techniques for palliation or repair. Not only are these distinctions increasingly blurred, but as Dianne Hales has aptly put it, in *UCSF Magazine*, "in the fight against disease, halfway can be a long way to go."

The inability to cope with this issue stems, in part, from the standard categorical-disease perspective taken toward chronic disease in the United States, where medical and public attention and support have been directed to specific illness such as heart disease, cancer, and muscular dystrophy. Indeed, the American health structure—with its governmental health commissions and institutes, its privately funded disease-oriented associations and institutes—supports a categorical-disease approach. Certainly, this approach does stimulate public interest and support, as well as major scientific breakthroughs. The final question we raise here is whether this competition among health specialists and specialties for research funds and resources detracts from the resolution of, or at least the focusing on, the larger issue of the organization of care around a more general perspective on the major health issue in all industrialized countries: chronic illness.

FURTHER READINGS SUGGESTED BY THE AUTHORS:

"Representing Consumer Interests: Imbalanced Markets, Health Planning, and the HSAs" by Theodore R. Marmor and James A. Morone in *Milbank Memorial Fund Quarterly/HEALTH AND SOCIETY* 58(1980):125-165.

"Medical Technology—A Different View of the Contentious Debate over Costs" by Thomas W. Moloney and David E. Rogers in *The New England Journal of Medicine* 301(1979):1413-1419.

"Income and Illness" by Paul W. Newacheck et al. in *Medical Care* 18(1980):1165-1176.

"Frequency and Clinical Description of High-Cost Patients in 17 Acute-Care Hospitals" by Steven A. Schroeder, Jonathan A. Showstack, and Edith H. Roberts in *The New England Journal of Medicine* 300(1979):1306-1309.

"Patient Power: Complex Issues Need Complex Answers" by Carolyn Wiener et al. in *Social Policy* 11(1980):30-38.

Medicine and the Market Place

JOHN KRIZAY

Inflation and concern about the level of federal expenditures have damped interest in the ongoing debate over National Health Insurance. New programs that might add to the budgetary burden are not popular, and too few people are seriously affected by high medical costs in any one year to arouse much protest over the continuing delays. Eventually, the nation will have to come to grips with this issue and make it possible for every American to have some way of protecting himself against medical disaster, for this is an area where the potential for loss is virtually unlimited. One can accurately predict the full extent of potential loss when insuring a house or an automobile or decide in advance how much his beneficiaries will need in the event of his untimely demise. But there is no way one can predict how much medical care he will need in the event of illness or injury nor, in many instances, can the victim even exercise control over the quantity and variety of medical services he will receive.

While medical care clearly falls in the category of insurable

37

activities, most proponents of National Health Insurance (NHI) present their case in welfare terms rather than as an insurance issue. They do not view protection against loss as the major objective of NHI but perceive the primary goal to be an equitable distribution of medical services and a progressive distribution of its costs. They are less concerned with providing security from the financial disaster that medical treatment can sometimes entail than they are with trying to assure that everyone have "equal" access to all the medical services they want. As a populist notion, the emphasis is on covering the cost of medical services from the first dollar for the rich as well as the poor in order to avoid differentiating patients in any way that might lead to second-class medical care. The welfare approach sees no role for market forces. Cost would be controlled by fiat; i.e., by arbitrary limits on what providers could charge. The method of controlling utilization, or how the available medical services would be allocated in the likelihood that demand exceeded supply, is never clearly spelled out.

There are, indeed, welfare aspects to this issue. Society has long since recognized that some of its citizens need community support to pay for food, housing, and medical care as well. But to build an entire national health-care system around a welfare concept will not assure that everyone is treated equally, not only because of obvious administrative obstacles to distributing available medical services on the basis of "equality," but because individuals differ in their view as to the quality, quantity, and variety of medical services they consider appropriate to their own needs.

The pause in the debate, therefore, is fortuitous, for it should provide time to rethink the requirements of a universal health program in light of certain realities that have been obscured in the deliberations to date. In particular, there is a need to understand better the nature and purpose of medical services and the extent to which the delivery of medical care is subject to the influence of the market place.

Convention has it that there are virtually no effective market forces in the economics of medicine. The urgency of illness, it is generally believed, leaves no time to negotiate or reconnoiter the market. The consumer, according to common belief, has little or no understanding of the services he is buying and little knowledge of prevailing costs for specific medical services. The facts are otherwise. While the urgent episodes of medicine provide drama and pathos that make for good theater in real life as well as on network television, such moments are far from typical. On the contrary, most medical services are routine, repetitious, and do not involve serious or life-threatening illnesses. Moreover, in the majority of instances, patients have had previous exposure to the outpatient services they are buying and should be well aware of the cost. While patients are less likely to know current hospital costs, this information can easily be obtained. Few in-hospital procedures are so urgent that there is no time for the patient and his doctor to explore the most economical mode of treatment. Options do exist in many instances in terms of length of stay, choice of hospital, intensity of care, and, sometimes, even in choice of the procedure itself without affecting the eventual outcome. The hue and cry over alleged millions of "unnecessary operations" supposedly performed each year is less a reflection of the venality of surgeons than evidence that resort to surgery is frequently an optional form of treatment and one not always supported by others in the medical profession. In the same sense, length of hospital stay where similar cases are involved may vary by one or more days for reasons that do not seem to have a clinical basis.

That patients and physicians make no effort to seek the most efficient option is frequently due to the fact that third parties (government or insurance companies) are paying a major share of the cost. Third-party payment, of course, is inherent in any insurance program, but it is possible for market forces to play a far greater role in the process than is commonly believed. In fact, exploitation of the market role offers the best opportunity for controlling costs and achieving the most efficient distribution of medical services under any national health-insurance scheme.

An examination of the true nature of demand for medical services reveals the extent to which the conventional view of the role of the market place in medicine has been exaggerated. Dr. John Fry, an English practitioner, provides us with an excellent basis for such an examination in his work "Profiles of Disease: A Study in the Natural History of Common Diseases." This study, based on twenty years of patient records from his suburban London practice, revealed that, even in England, where medical care is "free," three-fourths of all incidences of illness were treated at home without professional intervention. Of those illnesses reported to the doctor, roughly 70 percent were classified as self-limiting and not serious. His records show, further, that less than 5 percent of all patient visits involved life-threatening ailments.

Similarly, the National Ambulatory Care Survey conducted in the United States by the National Center for Health Statistics (May, 1973 through April, 1974) revealed that less than 20 percent of physician visits involved medical problems judged by the physicians to be "serious" or "very serious" in terms of threat to life or potential impairment.

The National Ambulatory Care Survey also revealed that 61 percent of all physician visits concerned problems for which the same patient had been treated by the same physician previously. In 60 percent of the visits, the patient was given an appointment for a return visit. The data do not tell us how many of the repetitive visits—either prior or scheduled for future treatment or both—are part of the 80 percent of all cases considered something less than serious or very serious. However, the percentages are so large that it is a mathematical certainty that at least half of all outpatient visits involving less-than-serious ailments are part of a treatment regime where the patient is seen more than once for the same ailment. In the majority of all physician encounters, then, it would seem improbable that the patient undergoing treatment was totally ignorant of costs and lacking in knowledge of the services he was paying for.

The National Ambulatory Care Survey findings, like those of Dr. Fry, are evidence that in the vast majority of instances, the consumer of medical services is in a position to opt for more or less professional care without in any way risking life or limb. That consumers of medical services do, in fact, exercise options in purchasing medical services is strongly suggested by another, more obscure bit of data that comes to light in examining the sources of health-care financing. As is well known, the share of health-care expenditures paid by third parties has steadily increased from one-third of all personal health-care expenditures in 1950 to about two-thirds of the total today. Yet the public, throughout this period, has continued to spend approximately 3.5 percent of its disposable income "out-of-pocket" for health care. This phenomenon is all the more striking when one considers the amazing consistency of this relationship; in not one of the 29 years from 1950 through 1978 did the out-of-pocket share of disposable income devoted to health care deviate from the mean percentage share (3.56 percent) by more than a quarter of a percentage point. It seems that while the public gladly consumes the growing quantity of medical services paid for by third parties, it still reserves 3.5 percent of the personal income at its disposal for health care. One must assume that this is the measure of the value to the public of medical services relative to all other goods and services to which the average American may devote his disposable income to improve his quality of life.

None of this is to deny that life-and-death situations do occur or that threats to a person's well-being arise that require highly skilled and complex medical intervention whose cost, at times, can stagger the most fertile imagination. Science has devised medical miracles that should be denied to no one in our society simply because of income status. How then, can market forces be brought to bear in a system whose aim is to provide everyone a reasonable degree of protection against the cost of medical disaster? Clearly, any system should leave some of the burden of paying for medical services to the consumer, where possible, as the best way of exercising some degree of control via market influence on the use and allocation of resources toward health care. We have already seen that, in the aggregate, the public will spend, out of pocket, 3.5 percent of the income at its disposal for health care no matter how much is spent for this service on a collective basis. But how much shall the consumer's personal share of medical costs be, and in what manner assigned? The simplest, most straightforward proposal offering protection against major loss while still leaving the consumer with some responsibility for payment is the so-called Catastrophic Health Insurance proposal. While the proposal is appealing in its simplicity and intent, medical catastrophe is not so simple to define. Some may find an unexpected expense of $1,000 catastrophic; a few may be prepared to withstand ten times that amount without too much pain. Some flexibility is needed, and there are ways of permitting the consumer to decide how much responsibility for his own medical expenses he feels comfortable with while still inducing him to exercise a market influence.

A reasonable, fair, and effective system can be built on the basis of the myriad health-insurance coverage programs already in existence by inviting direct consumer participation, by easing restrictions which presently make it difficult to offer everyone group coverage rates, and by bringing some order to the packaging of coverage in health-insurance plans. Building on the present system, clearly, is the most workable approach. About 95 percent of the population has some protection against health costs now, counting all those covered by private health-insurance plans, Medicare, Medicaid, CHAMPUS, and various institutional arrangements. Many countries who long since instituted National Health Insurance programs have yet to achieve the extent of coverage the United States has achieved through voluntary means. To attempt radical reform of a system that has been evolving for over thirty years and now encompasses practically the entire population of the country would be extremely disruptive, affecting not only longstanding doctor-patient relationships, but an elaborate financing network, a basic structure of employment in the health-care sector, and the behavior patterns of people who have spent many years "learning" how to function under their insurance plans. Moreover, there is no need for radical reform. A few direct and relatively simple changes can bring about total coverage with adequate insurance protection and enough market influence to assure an efficient allocation of resources both within the health-care industry and between health care and other economic activities.

Building on the System

The existing network of health-insurance programs exercises only minimal market influence, largely because of three characteristics prevalent in most health-insurance plans. (1) Most large group plans—approximately 60 percent—are non-contributory plans, meaning that the group member pays no part of the insurance premium. The employer pays it all as part of the fringe-benefits package. Members of such group plans have little interest in and little knowledge of the cost of their insurance. Far from feeling restrained in their use of medical services, they occasionally feel compelled to use as much as possible to "get the most out of" this fringe benefit. (2) Since most plans are non-contributory and since nearly all contributory plans have a major share of the premium contributed by the employer, there has been a tendency for employee groups to look upon health insurance as more of an income supplement than as insurance. In these circumstances, health plans are more likely to cover common and predictable medical expenses such as maternity and dental care, while placing limits on less common and more costly services. (3) Competition— the basis of all market influence—is greatly diminished because few of the insured population have any choice of plans. The 1978 HMO Act introduced a modicum of competition in the field by requiring that where a qualified HMO (Health Maintenance Organization) exists, it must be offered by the employer as an optional plan. However, there is no requirement that the employer be given the financial benefit of choosing the least costly of these options.

Providing each insured person or family with a clearly and readily discernible economic choice among several plans is the key to activating market forces to promote an efficient health-insurance program. "Economic choice" means that the selection of plan would directly affect the subscriber's money wages; "clear and readily discernible" means that the differences in levels of coverage would be subjected to some standards easily understood by all concerned.

This approach, obviously, would require that some marketing rules be developed, a step that would no doubt be distasteful to insurance carriers, labor unions, and other group purchasers. But the total lack of rules has led to the current chaotic situation where deductibles, co-payment features, dollar limits, exclusions, time limits, and special features can be combined in such a variety of ways that it is nearly impossible for anyone to know what is covered and what is not, or which plan is the best value.

The first step, then, would be to develop some standard components of health-care coverage that all conventional plans (i.e., other than HMOs) would be required to offer, with extent of coverage differentiated only by size of a basic deductible and standard co-payment requirements where deemed appropriate. Above this deductible, the basic coverage in all plans would be the same. Thus, the most economical plan might have a family deductible of $2,500 per year; the most expensive , a deductible of $100 per year. These options would be added to the already existing HMO option. The operative feature, and the one that would bring market forces into play, would be the requirement that each insured be offered, once a year, an opportunity to choose among these different levels of conventional coverage or the HMO option, in such a way that the difference in the insurance cost would affect his take-home pay.

This would not necessitate abolishing non-contributory plans. On the contrary, each employee group or union would remain free to negotiate as large an employer contribution to the health-care package as its bargaining power permitted. For example, if an employer agreed to pay the entire premium of the most expensive coverage available, each employee would still have an economic inducement to choose a less costly plan if the difference in cost were added to his take-home pay.

The Federal Employees Health Benefits Program (FEHBP) is an example of a health-insurance program employing some of these techniques. Although it neither sets general minimum coverage requirements nor differentiates plans by variation in levels of coverage, the contribution feature is similar to what is proposed here since the employee's paycheck is affected by his choice of plan. Notwithstanding the bewildering array of choices open to federal employees (there are not over a hundred plans with at least a half dozen available to any given employee), the inducement offered by differences in cost of plan to the employee has had a noticeable effect. In recent years, as the increase in health-care costs has outpaced the rate of increase in the cost of living, an increasing number of federal employees have displayed a willingness to self-insure for a greater part of their medical services by moving to less expensive plans within the FEHBP. Thus, since 1975, the number of persons covered by the Blue Cross-Blue Shield High Option Plan—which offers almost complete coverage with low deductibles and minimal co-payment requirements—has declined by more than half a million. In the same period, the Alliance Health Benefit Plan, which is a less expensive plan offering more limited coverage, has increased its number of covered persons from 15,000 in 1975 to over 350,000 today. In 1979, the Blue Cross-Blue Shield plan cost an employee with family about $260 more annually than the Alliance plan. That a difference of $10 in the bi-weekly paycheck would induce a substantial number of workers to assume a greater share of the risk for the cost of their medical protection illustrates the strength of market forces as they affect the choice of insurance plans. Indirectly, the same market forces induce the consumer to play a more active role in the purchase of health care, for in choosing to self-insure to a greater degree, he accepts the responsibility of monitoring more carefully his use of medical services. And, undoubtedly, he will be diligent in executing this responsibility because in self-insuring more, a greater share of the cost of his medical services will come out of his own pocket.

The FEHBP would be even more effective were it not for the confusing variety of coverage arrangements offered each employee during the annual "open season" —a two-to-four-week period during which the employee can switch to a new plan if he so desires. It is impossible for anyone to know which plan is most suitable because not only are deductibles and co-payments varied in a number of ways, but each plan has its own internal limitations on coverage that can be critical in an individual case. Because of the resulting confusion, many people are unwilling to risk greater self-insurance since the reduced coverage of the less costly plan may well exclude an expensive service they will need.

Levels of Self-Insurance

The model proposed here, by distinguishing coverage principally by levels of self-insurance through a choice of a basic deduction, would provide more effective insurance protection and, at the same time, give even greater strength to the influence of the market place. The added self-insurance would come at the low end of medical expenditures through deductibles, not at the top, or through exclusions or internal limitations which often limit coverage of particularly tragic illnesses (e.g., psychiatric care or kidney transplants). Moreover, since the insurance carriers would all be required to offer a basic standard plan with the extent of the deductible being the major difference among plans, they would be forced to compete on the basis of claims-handling service, administrative efficiency, and other economy-achieving practices that would permit them either to offer the standard plan at a lower price or to offer added coverage of services beyond that required by law.

One way insurance carriers could achieve such economies would be by becoming involved in the delivery of medical services. With the possible exception of Blue Cross-Blue Shield, insurance carriers traditionally shy away from direct involvement with medical providers. With basic coverage options standardized, however, each carrier would have to seek other ways to attract a larger share of the market. Direct involvement with the providers might be appealing, and one could envisage insurers investing some of their assets in organizing physician groups, arranging a more efficient division of responsibilities among hospitals, and offering providers various incentives to economize. Economies that have been noted in HMO operations stem ultimately from the fact that, in these organizations, the insurer and provider are integrated, a fact that offers a tremendous incentive to hold down costs. It is fair to predict that a National Health Insurance program based on the offer of consumer choice would induce insurers to seek better ways of offering medical services and would activate market forces in both a direct and an indirect sense, with the result that better economic order would be brought to this major service activity.

This system presumes that coverage would be extended by mandating that all employers make available—but not necessarily pay for—a range of health plans in the fashion outlined above. Most health-care proposals now under congressional consideration envisage mandated coverage. But the employment mechanism does not reach anyone. Methods of coverage would have to be found for those who do not fit into the employer-employee pattern. Finding such a method is not as formidable as sometimes thought. In fact, a few simple changes in existing laws governing the marketing of health insurance, some imaginative adjustments within the existing system of unemployment insurance, plus minor revisions in Medicare and Medicaid programs would extend coverage to everyone within the framework of a market-force, insurance-oriented program.

The task here is to bring cost-efficient, group rates to the thirty or forty million people who do not have access to group insurance, and to find ways to cover the ten to fifteen million Americans now totally without any protection against medical costs. The first step in this process would simply involve adopting a broader definition of "dependent" for health-insurance purposes. By adopting the IRS definition, for example, a substantial number who today are uninsured—such as students over a certain age and non-family dependents—would automatically become eligible for group coverage through the insurance plan of another family member. This adjustment would be nothing more than a minor acturial inconvenience, scarcely affecting the cost of insurance under group plans.

A second step—equally simple—would be a provision in the proposed National Health Insurance Act abolishing existing prohibitions against formation of groups for the sole purpose of buying group insurance. Such laws, requiring that insurance groups have an acknowledged existence for other purposes, were adopted by most states to assure random selection of the insured population, thereby minimizing the likelihood that a group would be dominated by a high-risk population (adverse risk selection). The prohibition has little relevance to health insurance as it is marketed today. More and more, health insurance is marketed under cost-plus arrangements whereby the carrier can draw from a mutually held reserve to make up any loss resulting from underestimating benefits paid. The carrier, therefore, does not need this kind of protection against adverse risk selection. If groups could form explicitly for health-insurance purposes, economical group rates would become available to those in small businesses, those self-employed, and others now uninsured or reliant on expensive individual insurance. Such a change in the law would also permit small groups to merge into larger ones, resulting in savings in administrative costs and in the broader sharing of risks.

These two basic measures, involving minimum government interference, would all but fill the existing coverage gap with the exception of the transitionally unemployed and the chronically unemployed, or "medically indigent," not covered by Medicaid. Not all the transitionally unemployed are without health insurance. Even in this category, some are covered by plans of employed family members (and this number would be increased if the definition of dependent were expanded). Others are covered by their health plans for a certain period after lay-off, often until new employment can be found. The same is true, to a lesser extent, of those just above the Medicaid eligibility limits.

Bringing the uncovered members of these two groups under insurance programs would not be without cost to the national budget. It is difficult to estimate the extent of the additional budget cost since many of these uncovered individuals could be included in existing family plans if dependent status were expanded. In years of high unemployment, perhaps the cost could reach twenty billion dollars annually. This is a large sum, but hardly bankrupting in a federal budget that may exceed three-quarters of a trillion dollars this year.

An administratively feasible program to provide coverage to the unemployed would consist of two parts. First, for the transitionally unemployed, the federal government would supplement unemployment compensation in the form of a premium payment voucher which could be used to continue his premium payments to the health-insurance group plan in which he was enrolled at his most recent place of employment. The exact value of the voucher would have to be related to the average cost of insurance plans, preferably at mid-level basic deductible and with the stipulation that it could, in no case, exceed the premimum paid by the employee while he was employed. These conditions would act as a disincentive to thoughtless acceptance of the health-insurance voucher when the furloughed employee might otherwise be covered by another family member.

Second, to provide coverage to unemployed individuals who are neither recipients of unemployment compensation, eligible for Medicaid, nor dependents of anyone already enrolled in a health plan, each state would be offered the incentive of additional federal support for its Medicaid program if it would expand coverage to the so-called medically indigent. "Medically indigent," in turn, could be redefined to include all unemployed persons not eligible for membership in some other group health plan. Slightly more than half of the states already provide some coverage to the medically indigent under a more restricted definition.

At the same time, Medicaid and Medicare coverage should be made consistent with the proposed standard NHI coverage described earlier. Obviously, it would be senseless to offer the variable deductible option to Medicaid eligibles since, by definition, these individuals require complete coverage. The market-oriented technique could, however, be applied with good effect to Medicare, replacing the complex series of deductibles, co-payments, limitations, and exclusions now part of the Medicare program. Essential to reforming Medicare in this context would be amalgamation of Medicare's Parts A (hospital insurance) and B (ambulatory care) into one health plan with the deductibles applying to the total medical expenditures. The current separation of these two forms of coverage was a political accident which serves only to complicate the management of the program. Just as in the private sector, under the plan proposed here, any part of the government's contribution toward the premium not used because the insured opted for less costly, high deductible coverage, would accrue to his monthly annuity.

Bringing the relatively few remaining uninsured persons into an insurance program that would provide basic coverage with the option of choosing a level of self-insurance appropriate to one's personal needs would add little to demand for medical services. In the long run, it should curtail medical inflation by inducing increasing numbers to self-insure against minor medical expenses. Moreover, this program would encourage experimentation with health-care delivery systems and induce the development of more effective instruments to achieve the best possible distribution of medical services.

In spite of arguments to the contrary, market forces can play the central role in the financing of medical costs without penalizing the poor or jeopardizing anyone's access to medical care. Countries which long ago adopted monolithic national health-insurance systems under government management find themselves plagued by cost, supply, and distribution problems, with long waiting lists for elective surgery, and with periodic disputes over physicians' wages or fee levels. The arbitrary methods for controlling costs and allocating resources inherent in those systems have not worked well. The fact is that in medicine, as in all life's activities, resources are limited, and it is not possible to provide everyone with all the medical services they may like without sacrificing resources devoted to some other activity. Priorities must be assigned, and individuals acting in their own behalf are still most likely to bring about an allocation of resources acceptable to the largest number.

FURTHER READINGS SUGGESTED BY THE AUTHOR

"The Ills of Man" by John H. Dingle in *Scientific American*, September 1973.

The Hospital That Ate Chicago by George Fisher (New York: Holt, Rinehart, & Winston, 1979).

Who Shall Live by Victor Fuchs (New York: Basic Books, 1974).

The Patient as Consumer by John Krizay and Andrew A. Wilson (Lexington, Mass.: Lexington Books, 1974).

Part II
Mainstream Medicine and Americans Marginal to It

Medical Ghettos

ANSELM L. STRAUSS

In President Johnson's budget message to Congress this year he proposed a quadrupling of federal spending on health care and medical assistance for the poor to $4.2 billion in fiscal 1968:

> The 1968 budget maintains the forward thrust of federal programs designed to improve health care in the nation, to combat poverty, and assist the needy. . . . The rise reflects the federal government's role in bringing quality medical care, particularly to aged and indigent persons.

Three years earlier in a special message to Congress the President had prefaced reintroduction of the medicare bill by saying:

> We can—and we must—strive now to assure the availability of and accessibility to the best health care for all Americans, regardless of age or geography or economic status. . . . Nowhere are the needs greater than for the

15 million children of families who live in poverty.

Then, after decades of debate and massive professional and political opposition, the medicare program was passed. It promised to lift the poorest of our aged out of the medical ghetto of charity and into private and voluntary hospital care. In addition, legislation for heart disease and cancer centers was quickly enacted. It was said that such facilities would increase life expectancy by five years and bring a 20 percent reduction in heart disease and cancer by 1975.

Is the medical millenium, then, on its way? The President, on the day before sending the 1968 budget to Congress, said: "Medicare is an unqualified success."

"Nevertheless," he added, "there are improvements which can be made and shortcomings which need prompt attention." The message also noted that there might be some obstacles on the highroad to health. The rising cost of medical care, President Johnson stated, "requires an expanded and better organized effort by the federal government in research and studies of the organization and delivery of health care." If the President's proposals are adopted, the states will spend $1.9 billion and the federal government $1 billion in a "Partnership for Health" under the Medicaid program.

Considering the costs to the poor—and to the taxpayers —why don't the disadvantaged get better care? In all the lively debate on that matter, it is striking how little attention is paid to the mismatch between the current organization of American medicine and the life styles of the lower class. The major emphasis is always on how the *present* systems can be a little better supported or a trifle altered to produce better results.

I contend that the poor will never have anything approaching equal care until our present medical organization undergoes profound reform. Nothing in current legislation or planning will accomplish this. My arguments, in brief, are these:

■ The emphasis in all current legislation is on extending and improving a basically sound system of medical organization.

■ This assumes that all those without adequate medical services—especially the poor—can be reached with minor reforms, without radical transformation of the systems of care.

■ This assumption is false. The reason the medical systems have not reached the poor is because they were never designed to do so. The way the poor think and respond, the way they live and operate, has hardly ever (if ever) been considered in the scheduling, paperwork, organization, and mores of clinics, hospitals, and doctors' offices. The life styles of the poor are different; they must be specifically taken into account. Professionals have not been trained and are not now being trained in the special skills and procedures necessary to do this.

■ These faults result in a vicious cycle which drives the poor away from the medical care they need.

■ Major reforms in medical organizations must come, or the current great inequities will continue, and perhaps grow.

I have some recommendations designed specifically to break up that vicious cycle at various points. These recommendations are built directly upon aspects of the life styles of the poor. They do not necessarily require new money or resources, but they do require rearrangement, reorganization, reallocation—the kind of change and reform which are often much harder to attain than new funds or facilities.

In elaborating these arguments, one point must be nailed down first: *The poor definitely get second-rate medical care.* This is self-evident to anyone who has worked either with them or in public medical facilities; but there is a good deal of folklore to the effect that the very poor share with the very rich the best doctors and services—the poor getting free in the clinics what only the rich can afford to buy.

The documented statistics of the Department of Health, Education, and Welfare tell a very different story. As of 1964, those families with annual incomes under $2,000 average 2.8 visits per person to a physician each year, compared to 3.8 for those above $7,000. (For children during the crucial years under 15, the ratio is 1.6 to 5.7. The poor tend to have larger families; needless to add, their child mortality rate is also higher.) People with higher incomes (and $7,000 per year can hardly be considered wealthy) have a tremendous advantage in the use of medical specialists—27.5 percent see at least one of them annually, compared to about 13 percent of the poor.

Health insurance is supposed to equalize the burden; but here, too, money purchases better care. Hospital or surgical insurance coverage is closely related to family income, ranging from 34 percent among those with family income of less than $2,000 to almost 90 percent for persons in families of $7,000 or more annual income. At the same time, the poor, when hospitalized, are much more apt to have more than one disorder—and more apt to exhaust their coverage before discharge.

Among persons who were hospitalized, insurance paid for some part of the bill for about 40 percent of patients with less than $2,000 family income, for 60 percent of patients with $2,000-$3,999 family income, and for 80 percent of patients with higher incomes. Insurance paid three-fourths or more of the bill for approximately 27 percent, 44 percent, and 61 percent of these respective income groups. Preliminary data from the 1964 survey year showed, for surgery or delivery bills paid by insurance, an even more marked association of insurance with income.

Similar figures can be marshaled for chronic illness, dental care, and days of work lost.

Strangely enough, however, *cash* difference (money actually spent for care) is not nearly so great. The under $2,000 per year group spent $112 per person per year, those families earning about three times as much ($4,000-$7,000) paid $119 per person, and those above $7,000, $153. Clearly, the poor not only get poorer health services but less for their money.

As a result, the poor suffer much more chronic illness and many more working days lost—troubles they are peculiarly ill-equipped to endure. Almost 60 percent of the poor have more than one disabling condition compared to about 24 percent of other Americans. Poor men lose 10.2 days of work annually compared to 4.9 for the others. Even medical research seems to favor the affluent—its major triumphs have been over acute, not chronic, disorders.

Medical care, as we know it now, is closely linked with the advancing organization, complexity, and maturity of our society and the increasing education, urbanization, and need for care of our people. Among the results: Medicine is increasingly practiced in hospitals in metropolitan areas.

The relatively few dispensaries for the poor of yesteryear have been supplanted by great numbers of outpatient hospital clinics. These clinics and services are still not adequate—which is why the continuing cry for reform is "more and better." But even when medical services *are* readily available to the poor, they are not used as much as they could and should be. The reasons fall into two categories:

—factors in the present organization of medical care that act as a brake on giving quality care to everyone;

—the life styles of the poor that present obstacles even

when the brakes are released.

The very massiveness of modern medical organization is itself a hindrance to health care for the poor. Large buildings and departments, specialization, division of labor, complexity, and bureaucracy lead to an impersonality and an overpowering and often grim atmosphere of hugeness. The poor, with their meager experience in organizational life, their insecurity in the middle class world, and their dependence on personal contacts, are especially vulnerable to this impersonalization.

Hospitals and clinics are organized for "getting work done" from the staff point of view; only infrequently are they set up to minimize the patient's confusion. He fends for himself and sometimes may even get lost when sent "just down the corridor." Patients are often sent for diagnostic tests from one service to another with no explanations, with inadequate directions, with brusque tones. This may make them exceedingly anxious and affect their symptoms and diagnosis. After sitting for hours in waiting rooms, they become angry to find themselves passed over for latecomers—but nobody explains about emergencies or priorities. They complain they cannot find doctors they really like or trust.

When middle class patients find themselves in similar situations, they can usually work out some methods of "beating the system" or gaining understanding that may raise staff tempers but will lower their own anxieties. The poor do not know how to beat the system. And only very seldom do they have that special agent, the private doctor, to smooth their paths.

Another organizational barrier is the increasing professionalism of health workers. The more training and experience it takes to make the various kinds of doctors, nurses, technicians, and social workers, the more they become oriented around professional standards and approaches, and the more the patient must take their knowledge and abilities on trust. The gaps of communications, understanding, and status grow. To the poor, professional procedures may seem senseless or even dangerous—especially when not explained—and professional manners impersonal or brutal, even when professionals are genuinely anxious to help.

Many patients complain about not getting enough information; but the poor are especially helpless. They don't know the ropes. Fred Davis quotes from a typical poor parent, the mother of a polio-stricken child:

Well they don't tell you anything hardly. They don't seem to want to. I mean you start asking questions and they say, "Well, I only have about three minutes to talk to you." And then the things that you ask, they don't seem to want to answer you. So I don't ask them anything any more. . . .

For contrast, we witnessed an instance of a highly educated woman who found her physician evasive. Suddenly she shot a question: "Come now, Doctor, don't I have the same cancerous condition that killed my sister?" His astonished reaction confirmed her suspicion.

Discrimination also expresses itself in subtle ways. As Frank Riessman and Sylvia Scribner note (for psychiatric care), "Middle class patients are preferred by most treatment agents, and are seen as more treatable. . . . Diagnoses are more hopeful. . . ." Those who understand, follow, respond to, and are grateful for treatment are good patients; and that describes the middle class.

Professional health workers are themselves middle class, represent and defend its values, and show its biases. They assume that the poor (like themselves) have regular meals, lead regular lives, try to support families, keep healthy, plan for the future. They prescribe the same treatment for the same diseases to all, not realizing that their words do not mean the same things to all. (What does "take with each meal" mean to a family that eats irregularly, seldom together, and usually less than three times a day?)

And there is, of course, some open bias. A welfare case worker in a large Midwestern city, trying to discover why her clients did not use a large, nearby municipal clinic more, described what she found:

> Aside from the long waits (8 a.m. to about 1 p.m. just to make the appointment), which perhaps are unavoidable, there is the treatment of patients by hospital personnel. This is at the clinic level. People are shouted at, ridiculed, abused, pushed around, called "Niggers," told to stand "with the rest of the herd," and in many instances made to feel terribly inferior if not inadequate. . . . This . . . was indulged in by personnel other than doctors and nurses. . . .

Even when no bias is intended, the hustle, impersonality, and abstraction of the mostly white staff tend to create this feeling among sensitive and insecure people: "And I do think the treatment would have been different if Albert had been white."

The poor especially suffer in that vague area we call "care," which includes nursing, instructions about regimens, and post-hospital treatment generally. What happens to the lower class patient once released? Middle class patients report regularly to their doctors who check on progress and exert some control. But the poor are far more likely to go to the great, busy clinics where they seldom see the same doctor twice. Once out they are usually on their own.

Will the poor get better care if "more and better" facilities are made available? I doubt it. The fact is that they underutilize those available now. For instance, some 1963 figures from the Director of the Division of Health Services, Children's Bureau:

In Atlanta, 23 percent of women delivered at the Grady Hospital had had no prenatal care; in Dallas, approximately one-third of low-income patients receive no prenatal care; at the Los Angeles County Hospital in 1958, it was 20 percent; at the D.C. General Hospital in Washington, it is 45 percent; and in the Bedford Stuyvesant section of Brooklyn, New York, it is 41 percent with no or little prenatal care.

Distances are also important. Hospitals and clinics are usually far away. The poor tend to organize their lives around their immediate neighborhoods, to shut out the rest of the city. Some can hardly afford bus fare (much less cab fare for emergencies). Other obstacles include unrealistic eligibility rules and the requirement by some hospitals that clinic patients arrange a blood donation to the blood bank as a prerequisite for prenatal care.

Medical organization tends to assume a patient who is educated and well-motivated, who is interested in ensuring a reasonable level of bodily functioning and generally in preserving his own health. But health professionals themselves complain that the poor come to the clinic or hospital with advanced symptoms, that parents don't pay attention to children's symptoms early enough, that they don't follow up treatments or regimens, and delay too long in returning. But is it really the fault of whole sections of the American population if they don't follow what professionals expect of them?

What are the poor really like? In our country they are distinctive. They live strictly, and wholeheartedly, in the present; their lives are uncertain, dominated by recurring crises (as S. M. Miller puts it, theirs "is a crisis-life constantly trying to make do with string where rope is needed"). To them a careful concern about health is unreal—they face more pressing troubles daily, just getting by. Bad health is just one more condition they must try to cope—or live—with.

Their households are understaffed. There are no servants, few reliable adults. There is little time or energy to care for the sick. If the mother is ill, who will care for her or take her to the clinic—or care for the children if she goes? It is easier to live with illness than use up your few resources doing something about it.

As Daniel Rosenblatt and Edward Suchman have noted:

The body can be seen as simply another class of objects to be worked out but not repaired. Thus, teeth are left without dental care. . . . Corrective eye examinations, even for those who wear glasses, are often neglected. . . . It is as though . . . blue-collar groups think of the body as having a limited span of utility; to be enjoyed in youth and then to suffer with and to endure stoically with age and decrepitude.

They are characterized by low self-esteem. Lee Rainwater remarks that low-income people develop "a sense of being unworthy; they do not uphold the sacredness of their persons in the same way that middle-class people do. Their tendency to think of themselves as of little account is . . . readily generalized to their bodies." And this attitude is transferred to their children.

They seek medical treatment only when practically forced to it. As Rosenblatt and Suchman put it: "Symptoms that do not incapacitate are often ignored." In clinics and hospitals they are shy, frustrated, passively submissive, prey to brooding, depressed anxiety. They reply with guarded hostility, evasiveness, and withdrawal. They believe, of their treatment, that "what is free is not much good." As a result, the professionals tend to turn away. Julius Roth describes how the staff in a rehabilitation ward gets discouraged with its apparently unrehabilitatable patients and gives up and concentrates on the few who seem hopeful. The staffs who must deal with the poor in such wards either have rapid turnover or retreat into "enclaves of research, administration, and teaching."

The situation must get worse. More of the poor will come to the hospitals and clinics. Also, with the increasing use of health insurance and programs by unions and employers, more will come as paying patients into the private hospitals, mixing with middle class patients and staff, upsetting routines, perhaps lowering quality—a frightening prospect as many administrators see it. As things are going now, relations between lower-income patients and hospital staff must become more frequent, intense, and exacerbated.

It is evident that the vicious cycle that characterizes medical care for the poor must be broken before anything can be accomplished.

In the first part of this cycle, the poor come into the hospitals later than they should, often delaying until their disorders are difficult to relieve, until they are actual emergency cases. The experiences they have there encourage them to try to stay out even longer the next time—and to cut the visits necessary for treatment to a minimum.

Second, they require, if anything, even more effective communication and understanding with the professionals than the middle class patient. They don't get it; and the treatment is often undone once they leave.

What to do? The conventional remedies do help some. More money and insurance will tend to bring the poor to medical help sooner; increased staff and facilities can cut down the waits, the rush, the tenseness, and allow for more individual and efficient treatment and diagnosis.

But much more is required. If the cycle is to be *broken,*

the following set of recommendations must be adopted:

- Speed up the initial visit. Get them there sooner.
- Improve patient experiences.
- Improve communication, given and received, about regimens and treatment to be followed.
- Work to make it more likely that the patient or his family will follow through at home.
- Make it more likely that the patient will return when necessary.
- Decrease the time between necessary visits.

This general list is not meant to be the whole formula. Any experienced doctor or nurse, once he recognizes the need, can add to or modify it. An experience of mine illustrates this well. A physician in charge of an adolescent clinic for lower-income patients, finding that my ideas fitted into his own daily experience, invited me to address his staff. In discussion afterward good ideas quickly emerged:

- Since teen-age acne and late teen-age menstrual pain were frequent complaints and the diagnoses and medications not very complicated, why not let nurses make them? Menstruating girls would be more willing to talk to a woman than a man.
- Patients spend many hours sitting around waiting. Why not have nursing assistants, trained by the social worker and doctor and drawn from the patients' social class, interview and visit with them during this period, collecting relevant information?

Note two things about these suggestions: Though they do involve some new duties and some shifting around, they do not call for any appreciable increase of money, personnel, or resources; and such recommendations, once the need is pointed out, can arise from the initiative and experience of the staff themselves.

Here in greater detail are my recommendations:

Increased efforts are needed for early detection of disease among the poor. Existing methods should be increased and improved, and others should be added—for instance, mobile detection units of all kinds, public drives with large-scale educational campaigns against common specific disorders, and so on. The poor themselves should help in planning, and their ideas should be welcomed.

The schools could and should become major detection units with large-scale programs of health inspection. The school nurse, left to her own initiative, is not enough. The poor have more children and are less efficient at noting illness; those children do go to school, where they could be examined. Teachers should also be given elementary training and used more effectively in detection.

Train more sub-professionals, drawn from the poor themselves. They can easily learn to recognize the symptoms of the more common disorders and be especially useful in large concentrations, such as housing projects. They can teach the poor to look for health problems in their own families.

The large central facilities make for greater administrative and medical efficiency. But fewer people will come to them than to smaller neighborhood dispensaries. Imperfect treatment may be better than little or no treatment; and the total effectiveness for the poor may actually be better with many small facilities than the big ones.

Neighborhood centers can not only treat routine cases and act to follow up hospital outpatients, but they can also discover those needing the more difficult procedures and refer them to the large centers—for example, prenatal diagnosis and treatment in the neighborhoods, with high-risk pregnancies sent to the central facilities. (The Children's Bureau has experimented with this type of organization.)

There must be better methods to get the sick to the

clinics. As noted, the poor tend to stick to their own neighborhoods and be fearful outside them, to lack bus fare and domestic help. Even when dental or eye defects *are* discovered in schools, often children still do not get treatment. Sub-professionals and volunteers could follow up, provide transportation, bus fare, information, or baby-sitting and housecare. Block or church organizations could help. The special drives for particular illnesses could also include transportation. (Recent studies show that different ethnic groups respond differently to different pressures and appeals; sub-professionals from the same groups could, therefore, be especially effective.)

Hours should be made more flexible; there should be more evening and night clinics. Working people work, when they have jobs, and cannot afford to lose jobs in order to sit around waiting to be called at a clinic. In short, clinics should adapt to people, not expect the opposite. (A related benefit: Evening clinics should lift the load on emergency services in municipal hospitals, since the poor often use them just that way.)

Neighborhood pharmacists should be explicitly recognized as part of the medical team, and every effort be made to bring them in. The poor are much more apt to consult their neighborhood pharmacist first—and he could play a real role in minor treatment and in referral. He should be rewarded, and given such training as necessary—perhaps by schools of pharmacy. Other "health healers" might also be encouraged to help get the seriously ill to the clinics and hospitals, instead of being considered rivals or quacks.

Lower-income patients who enter treatment early can be *rewarded* for it. This may sound strange, rewarding people for benefiting themselves—but it might bring patients in earlier as well as bring them back, and actually save money for insurance companies and government and public agencies.

Hospital emergency services must be radically reorganized. Such services are now being used by the poor as clinics and as substitutes for general practitioners. Such use upsets routine and arouses mutual frustrations and resentments. There are good reasons why the poor use emergency services this way, and the services should be reorganized to face the realities of the situation.

Clinics and hospitals could assign *agents* to their lower-income patients, who can orient them, allay anxiety, listen to complaints, help them cooperate, and help them negotiate with the staff.

Better accountability and communication should be built into the organization of care. Much important information gets to doctors and nurses only fortuitously, if at all. For instance, nurses' aides often have information about cardiac or terminal patients that doctors and nurses could use; but they do not always volunteer the information nor are they often asked, since they are not considered medically qualified. This is another place where the *agent* might be useful.

It is absolutely necessary that medical personnel lessen their class and professional biases. Anti-bias training is virtually nonexistent in medical schools or associations. It must be started, especially in the professional schools.

Medical facilities must carefully consider how to allow and improve the lodging of complaints by the poor against medical services. They have few means and little chance now to make their complaints known, and this adds to their resentment, depression, and helplessness. Perhaps the agent can act as a kind of medical *ombudsman:* perhaps unions, or the other health insurance groups, can lodge the complaints; perhaps neighborhood groups can do it. But it must be done.

Treatment and regimens are supposed to continue in the home. Poor patients seldom do them adequately. Hospitals and clinics usually concentrate on diagnosis and treatment and tend to neglect what occurs after. Sometimes there is even confusion about who is supposed to tell the patient about such things as his diet at home, and there is little attempt to see that he does it. Here again, follow-up by sub-professionals might be useful.

Special training given to professionals will enable them to give better instructions to the poor on regimens. They are seldom trained in interviewing or listening—and the poor are usually deficient in pressing their opinions.

Clinics and hospitals could organize their services to include checking on ex-patients who have no private physicians. We recommend that hospitals and clinics try to bring physicians in poor neighborhoods into some sort of association. Many of these physicians do not have hospital connections, practice old-fashioned or sub-standard medicine—yet they are in most immediate contact with the poor, especially before hospitalization.

Medical establishments should make special efforts to discover and understand the prevalent life styles of their patients. Since this affects efficiency of treatment, it is an important medical concern.

I strongly recommend greater emphasis on research in medical devices or techniques that are simple to operate and depend as little as possible on patients' judgment and motivation. Present good examples include long-term tranquilizers and the intrauterine birth-control device which requires little of the woman other than her consent. Such developments fit lower class life style much better than those requiring repeated actions, timing, and persistence.

As noted, these recommendations are not basically different from many others—except that they all relate to the idea of the vicious cycle. *A major point of this paper is that equal health care will not come unless all portions of that cycle are attacked simultaneously.*

To assure action sufficiently broad and strong to demolish this cycle, *responsibility must also be broad and strong.*

■ Medical and professional schools must take vigorous steps to counteract the class bias of their students, to teach them to relate, communicate, and adapt techniques and regimens to the poor, and to learn how to train and instruct sub-professionals.

■ Specific medical institutions must, in addition to the recommendations above, consider how best to attack *all* segments of the cycle. Partial attacks will not do—medicine has responsibility for the total patient and the total treatment.

■ Lower class people must themselves be enlisted in the campaign to give them better care. Not to do this would be absolutely foolhardy. The sub-professionals we mention are themselves valuable in large part because they come from the poor, and understand them. Where indigenous organizations exist, they should be used. Where they do not exist, organizations that somehow meet their needs should be aided and encouraged to form.

■ Finally, governments, at all levels, have an immense responsibility for persuading, inducing, or pressuring medical institutions and personnel toward reforming our system of medical care. If they understand the vicious cycle, their influence will be much greater. This governmental role need not at all interfere with the patient's freedom. Medical influence is shifting rapidly to the elite medical centers; federal and local governments have a responsibility to see that medical influence and care, so much of it financed by public money, accomplishes what it is supposed to.

What of the frequently heard argument that increasing affluence will soon eliminate the need for special programs for the poor?

■ Most sociologists agree that general affluence may never "trickle down" to the hard-core poverty groups; that only sustained and specialized effort over a long period of time may relieve their poverty.

■ Increased income does not necessarily change life styles. Some groups deliberately stand outside our mainstream. And there is usually a lag at least of one generation, often more, before life styles respond to changed incomes.

In the long run, no doubt, prosperity for all will minimize the inferiority of medical care for the poor. But in the long run, as the saying goes, we will all be dead. And the disadvantaged sick will probably go first, with much unnecessary suffering.

The Health of Haight-Ashbury

DAVID E. SMITH, JOHN LUCE, and ERNEST DERNBERG

Conventional middle-class populations receive the best care our present conventional medical institutions can supply. Middle-class people pay their bills on time or have health insurance, which does it for them. They trust the doctor to do what is best for them. They have diseases that go with respectability, and the doctor who treats them need not feel tainted by associating with people whose medical problems arise from activities that are illegal or immoral.

People who do not measure up to middle-class standards pose a problem for organized medicine. They require medical care no less than others, but the profession does not do well in providing it. People who have no money or insurance, who mistrust doctors, who seem to the physician to be immoral criminals, find it difficult to get care. Doctors don't like them; they don't like the doctors. The profession, used to providing medical care in a style that suits it, and supplied with plenty of middle-class patients who like that style, has never bothered to figure out how to deliver medical care in a way that suits other populations who live differently.

San Francisco's hippie invasion of 1967 created an acute problem of this kind. The city's officialdom made no adequate response to the medical and public health problems it produced, but a number of volunteers founded the Haight-Ashbury Free Medical Clinic, a unique experiment in providing medical care to a deviant population on terms it would accept. The story of the clinic—the problems of staffing, supplies, finances and the changing population needs it encountered—suggests some of the difficulties and some of the possibilities involved in such an innovation.

Three years ago *Time* magazine called San Francisco's Haight-Ashbury "the vibrant epicenter of America's hippie movement." Today the Haight-Ashbury District looks like a disaster area. Some of the frame Victorian houses, flats and apartment buildings lying between the Panhandle of Golden Gate Park and the slope of Mount Sutro have deteriorated beyond repair, and many property owners have boarded over their windows or blocked their doorways with heavy iron bars. Hiding in their self imposed internment, the original residents of the area seem emotionally exhausted and too terrified to leave their homes. "We're all frightened," says one 60-year-old member of the Haight-Ashbury Neighborhood Council. "The Haight has become a drug ghetto, a teen-age slum. The streets aren't safe; rats romp in the Panhandle; the neighborhood gets more run down every day. The only thing that'll save this place now is a massive dose of federal aid."

Nowhere is the aid more needed than on Haight Street, the strip of stores that runs east to west through the Flatlands. Once a prosperous shopping area, Haight Street has so degenerated by this time that the storefronts are covered with steel grates and sheets of plywood, while the sidewalks are littered with dog droppings, cigarette butts, garbage and broken glass. According to Henry Sands, the owner of a small realty agency on the corner of Haight and Stanyan streets, over 50 grocers, florists, druggists, haberdashers and other merchants have moved off the street since the 1967 Summer of Love; property values have fallen 20 percent in the same period, but none of the remaining businessmen can find buyers for their stores. The Safeway Supermarket at Haight and Schrader streets has closed, Sands reports, after being shoplifted out of $10,000 worth of merchandise in three months. The one shopowner to open since, stocks padlocks and shatterproof window glass. "The only people making money on Haight Street now sell dope or cheap wine," the realtor claims. "Our former customers are all gone. There's nothing left of the old community anymore."

Nothing is left of the Haight-Ashbury's new hippie community today either. There are no paisley-painted buses on Haight Street, no "flower children" parading the sidewalks, no tribal gatherings, no HIP (Haight Independent Proprietor) stores. Almost all the long-haired proprietors have followed the original merchants out of the district; the Psychedelic Shop at Haight and Clayton stands vacant; the Print Mint across the street and the Straight Theatre down the block are both closed. Allen Ginsberg, Timothy Leary, Ken Kesey and their contemporaries no longer visit the communal mecca they helped establish here in the mid-1960s. Nor do the rock musicians, poster artists and spiritual gurus who brought it international fame. And although a few young people calling themselves Diggers still operate a free bakery and housing office out of the basement of All Saints Episcopal Church on Waller Street, Father Leon

Harris there considers them a small and insignificant minority. "For all intents and purposes," he says, "the peaceful hippies we once knew have disappeared."

They started disappearing almost three years ago, when worldwide publicity brought a different and more disturbed population to the Haight and the city escalated its undeclared war on the new community. Today, most of the long-haired adolescents the public considers hip have left Haight Street to hang out on Telegraph Avenue in Berkeley or on Grant Avenue in San Francisco's North Beach District. Some of the "active" or "summer" hippies who once played in the Haight-Ashbury have either returned home or reenrolled in school. Others have moved to the Mission District and other parts of the city, to Sausalito and Mill Valley in Marin County, to Berkeley and Big Sur or to the rural communes operating throughout northern California.

A few are still trapped in the Haight, but they take mescaline, LSD and other hallucinogenic drugs indoors and stay as far away from Haight Street as possible. When they must go there, to cash welfare checks or to shop at the one remaining supermarket, they never go at night or walk alone. "It's too dangerous for me," says one 19-year-old unwed mother who ran away from a middle-class home in Detroit during the summer of 1967. "Haight Street used to be so groovy I could get high just being there. But I don't know anybody on the street today. Since I've been here, it's become the roughest part of town."

A new population has moved into the district and taken over Haight Street like an occupying army. Transient and diverse, its members now number several thousand persons. Included are a few tourists, weekend visitors and young runaways who still regard the Haight-Ashbury as a refuge for the alienated. There are also older white, Negro and Indian alcoholics from the city's Skid Row; black delinquents who live in the Flatlands or the Fillmore ghetto; Hell's Angels and other "bikers" who roar through the area on their Harley Davidsons. Finally there are the overtly psychotic young people who abuse any and all kinds of drugs, and psychopathic white adolescents with criminal records in San Francisco and other cities who come from lower-class homes or no homes at all.

Uneducated and lacking any mystical or spiritual interest, many of these young people have traveled from across the country to find money, stimulation and easy sex in the Haight and to exploit the flower children they assume are still living here. Some have grown long hair and assimilated the hip jargon in the process, but they resemble true hippies in no real way. "Street wise" and relatively aggressive in spite of the passive longings which prompt their drug abuse, they have little love for one another and no respect for the law or for themselves. Instead of beads and bright costumes they wear leather jackets and coarse, heavy clothes. Instead of ornate buses they drive beat-up motorcycles and hot rods. Although they smoke marijuana incessantly and drop acid on occasion, they generally dismiss these chemicals as child's play and prefer to intoxicate themselves with opiates, barbiturates and amphetamines.

Their individual tastes may vary, but most of the adolescents share a dreary, drug-based life-style. Few have any legal means of support, and since many are addicted.to heroin, they must peddle chemicals, steal groceries and hustle spare change to stay alive. Even this is difficult, for there is very little money on Haight Street and a great deal of fear. Indeed, the possibility of being "burned," raped or "ripped off" is so omnipresent that most of the young people stay by themselves and try to numb their anxiety and depression under a toxic fog. By day they sit and slouch separately against the boarded-up storefronts in a drug-induced somnolescence. At night they lock themselves indoors, inject heroin and plan what houses in the district they will subsequently rob.

Altough the results of this living pattern are amply reflected in the statistics available from Park Police Station at Stanyan and Waller streets, the 106 patrolmen there are apparently unable to curb the Haight-Ashbury's crime. Their job has been made easier by the relative decrease in amphetamine consumption and the disappearance of many speed freaks from the district over the past few months, but the rate of robbery and other acts associated with heroin continues to rise. Making regular sweeps of Haight Street in patrol cars and paddy wagons, the police also threaten to plant drugs on known dealers if they will not voluntarily leave town. Yet these and other extreme measures seem only to act like a negative filter in the Haight, screening out the more cunning abusers and leaving their inept counterparts behind.

Furthermore, the narcotics agents responsible for the Haight-Ashbury cannot begin to regulate its drug flow. According to one agent of the State Narcotics Bureau, "The Haight is still the national spawning ground for multiple drug abuse. The adolescents there have caused one of the toughest law enforcement problems we've ever known."

They have also created one of the most serious health problems in all of San Francisco. Many of the young people who hang out on Haight Street are not only overtly or potentially psychotic, but also physically ravaged by one another as well. Although murder is not particularly popular with the new population, some of its members seem to spend their lives in plaster casts. Others frequently exhibit suppurating abrasions, knife and razor slashes, damaged genitalia and other types of traumatic injuries—injuries all caused by violence.

Even more visible is the violence they do to themselves. Continually stoned on drugs, the adolescents often over-exert and fail to notice as they infect and mangle their feet by wading through the droppings and broken glass. Furthermore, although some of the heroin addicts lead a comparatively stabilized existence, others overlook the physiological deterioration which results from their self-destructive lives. The eating habits of these young people are so poor that they are often malnourished and inordinately susceptible to infectious disease. In fact, a few of them suffer from protein and vitamin deficiencies that are usually found only in chronic alcoholics three times their age.

With gums bleeding from pyorrhea and rotting teeth, some also have abscesses and a diffuse tissue infection called cellulitis, both caused by using dirty needles. Others miss their veins while shooting up or rupture them by injecting impure and undissolvable chemicals. And since most sleep, take drugs and have sex in unsanitary environments, they constantly expose themselves to upper respiratory tract infections, skin rashes, bronchitis, tonsillitis, influenza, dysentery, urinary and genital tract infections, hepatitis and venereal disease.

In addition to these and other chronic illnesses, the young people also suffer from a wide range of drug problems. Some have acute difficulties, such as those individuals who oversedate themselves with barbiturates or "overamp" with amphetamines. Others have chronic complaints, long-term "speed"-precipitated psychoses and paranoid, schizophrenic reactions. Many require physiological and psychological withdrawal from barbiturates and heroin. In fact, heroin addiction and its attendant symptoms have reached

epidemic proportions in the Haight-Ashbury, and the few
doctors at Park Emergency Hospital cannot check the spread
of disease and drug abuse through the district any better
than the police can control its crime.

To make matters worse, these physicians appear unwilling to attempt to solve the local health problems. Like
many policemen, the public health representatives seem to
look on young drug-abusers as subhuman. When adolescents come to Park Emergency for help the doctors frequently assault them with sermons, report them to the
police or submit them to complicated and drawn-out referral procedures that only intensify their agony. The
nurses sometimes tell prospective patients to take their
problems elsewhere. The ambulance drivers simply "forget"
calls for emergency assistance. They and the other staff
members apparently believe that the best way to stamp out
sickness in the Haight is to let its younger residents destroy themselveas.

Given this attitude, it is hardly surprising that the
adolescents are as frightened of public health officials as
they are of policemen. Some would sooner risk death than
seek aid at Park Emergency and are equally unwilling to go
to San Francisco General Hospital, the city's central receiving unit, two miles away. Many merely live with their
symptoms, doctor themselves with home remedies or nar-
cotize themselves to relieve their pain. These young people
do not trust "straight" private physicians, who they assume
will overcharge them and hand them over to the law. Uneducated about medical matters, they too often listen only
to the "witch doctors" and drug-dealers who prowl the
Haight-Ashbury, prescribing their own products for practically every physiological and psychological ill.

A few are receptive to responsible opinion and anxious
to be properly treated, particularly those individuals who

want to kick heroin and those younger adolescents who have just made the Haight their home. Unfortunately, however, they have nowhere to go for help. Huckleberry's for Runaways and almost all the other service agencies created to assist the hippies in 1967 have suspended operations in the area. Although Father Harris and several other neighborhood ministers offer free advice at their respective churches, they can hardly deal with all the young people who come their way. Indeed, the only major organization that can reach the new population is the Haight-Ashbury Free Medical Clinic. But today, the first privately operated facility in America to employ community volunteers in providing free and nonpunitive treatment of adolescent drug and health difficulties has serious problems of its own.

This is ironic, for although it is still somewhat at odds with the local medical establishment, the clinic is better staffed and funded than at any point in its 2½-year history. It is also more decentralized, with several facilities in and outside of the Haight-Ashbury. Its oldest operation, a Medical Section located on the second floor of a faded yellow building at the corner of Haight and Clayton streets, is now open from 6 p.m. until 10 p.m. five evenings a week. Over 40 dedicated volunteers are on hand in the 14-room former dentist's office, so that 558 Clayton Street can accommodate more than 50 patients a day.

Of the young people who use the facility, only half live in the immediate area. The rest are hippies, beats and older people who come with their children from as far away as southern California. Accepting the clinic because it accepts them, the patients are treated by a staff of over 20 volunteer nurses and physicians in an atmosphere brightened by poster art and psychedelic paraphernalia. Some of these health professionals are general practitioners committed to community medicine. Others are specialists hoping to broaden their medical understanding. Many are interns and residents looking for experience or studying the Medical Section as a philosophic alternative to the practices of the Public Health Department and the American Medical Association.

Whatever their motivation, the doctors' primary objectives are diagnosis and detoxification. After examining their patients, they attempt to treat some with donated drugs which are kept under lock and key in the clinic pharmacy. Others require blood, urine and vaginal smear tests that can be performed in the laboratory on equipment furnished by the Medical Logistics Company of San Francisco and its 35-year-old president, Donald Reddick, who serves as the clinic's administrative director. Most of the patients have chronic problems, however, and cannot be treated adequately on the premises. They must therefore be referred and/or physically transported to other facilities, such as Planned Parenthood, the Society for Humane Abortions, the Pediatrics Clinic at the University of California Medical Center on Parnassus Street six blocks south, Children's Hospital, San Francisco General Hospital and the Public Health Department Clinic for VD. The Medical Section maintains a close working relationship with these institutions and can therefore act as a buffer between its hip patients and the straight world.

Although the physicians and nurses contribute to this mediating process, much of the referring, chauffeuring and patient-contacting at 558 Clayton Street is carried out by its staff of clerks, administrative aides and paramedical volunteers. Twenty such young people donate their time and energy to the Medical Section at present, most of them student activists, conscientious objectors fulfilling alternative service requirements and former members of the Haight-Ashbury's new community. Emotionally equipped to handle the demands and the depressing climate of ghetto medicine, several core members of the paramedical staff live together in the Haight as a communal family.

Supervising the volunteers is Dr. Alan Matzger, a 37-year-old general surgeon from San Francisco who developed an interest in community medicine after working at 558 Clayton Street for over a year. The clinic's first full-time resident physician, Dr. Matzger is actually employed by the United States Public Health Service, which has asked him to conduct a long-range investigation of health needs in the Haight-Ashbury. He is now nearing completion of this study and will soon develop an objective and comprehensive plan for community medical care.

Since heroin addiction is such a pressing current problem, Dr. Matzger and an anesthesiologist named Dr. George Gay have recently launched a heroin withdrawal program at the Medical Section. Working there five afternoons a week for the past four months, the two physicians have treated over 200 patients, less than 50 percent of whom consider the Haight their home. "The remainder are adolescents from so-called good families," Dr. Matzger reports, "most of them students at local colleges and high schools. Significantly, they follow the same evolutionary pattern as young people have in this district, progressing from hallucinogenic drug abuse to abuse of amphetamines and then to abuse of barbiturates and opiates. The 'Year of the Middle-Class Junkie' in San Francisco may well be 1970. If it is, we hope to expand our program as addiction problems mount throughout the entire Bay area."

Another expansion being considered at the clinic is a dentistry service. Organized by Dr. Ira Handelsman, a dentist from the University of the Pacific who is paid by a Public Health Service grant to study periodontal disease, this would be the first free program of dentistry in the city outside of the oral surgery unit at San Francisco General Hospital. As such, the service is under fire from the local dental society, which is opposed to this form of free dental care. Nevertheless, Dr. Handelsman is committed to his effort and has recently secured three donated dental chairs.

Although this and other programs at 558 Clayton Street are intended to operate somewhat autonomously, they are closely coordinated with those operated out of the clinic's second center in the Haight-Ashbury. Known as "409 House," it is located in a pale blue Victorian residence at the corner of Clayton and Oak Streets, across from the Panhandle. On the first floor of this building is a reading and meditation room supervised by Reverend Lyle Grosjean of the Episcopal Peace Fellowship who counsels some adolescents about spiritual, marital, draft and welfare problems and offers shelter for others coming in from the cold.

On the third floor at 409 Clayton Street is the clinic publications office, staffed by volunteers who oversee the preparation of the *Journal of Psychedelic Drugs,* a semi-annual compilation of articles and papers presented at the drug symposia sponsored by the clinic and the University of California Medical Center Psychopharmacology Study Group. Aided by several health professionals, the volunteers also answer requests for medical information and administer the affairs of the National Free Clinics Council, an organization created in 1968 for the dozens of free facilities in Berkeley, Boston and other cities that modeled their efforts after those of the Haight-Ashbury Free Medical Clinic programs.

Sandwiched in between the Publications Office and Reverend Grosjean's sanctuary is the Psychiatric Section. This service, which is supervised by Stuart Loomis, a 47-year-old associate professor of education at San Francisco State College, provides free counseling and psychiatric aid for over

150 individuals. Roughly one-half of these patients are hippies and "active hippies" who either live in the district or commute from rural and urban communes where physicians from the Medical Section make house calls. The remaining 50 percent is made up of young people who suffer from the chronic anxiety and depression common in heroin addicts.

Loomis and the other 30 staff psychologists, psychiatrists and psychiatric social workers at 409 Clayton Street are able to counsel some of these patients in the Psychiatric Section. They usually refer the more disturbed multiple drug-abusers and ambulatory schizophrenics now common to the Haight either to such facilities as the drug program at Mendocino State Hospital or to the Immediate Psychiatric Aid and Referral Service at San Francisco General, whose director, Dr. Arthur Carfagni, is on the clinic's executive committee. When intensive psychiatric intervention is not called for, however, they frequently send the patients to the clinic's own Drug Treatment Program in the basement downstairs.

This project, nicknamed the Free Fuse, is led by a Lutheran minister in his mid-thirties named John Frykman. Financed by personal gifts and by grants from such private foundations as the Merrill Trust, its goal is to wean drug-abusers away from their destructive life-style. Using methods developed by Synanon and the Esalen Institute, Frykman and the other Free Fuse counselors have attempted to create a close and productive social unit out of alienated adolescents living together as the clinic's second communal family. They have also provided educational and employment opportunities for more than 500 young people in the past $1\frac{1}{2}$ years.

Since many Free Fuse graduates are still involved in his project, Frykman has also found it possible to expand. Having recently opened an annex in the drug-ridden North Beach District under the supervision of a psychiatric nurse, he has allowed the Drug Treatment Program to geographically qualify for inclusion in the Northeast Mental Health Center, a cachement area encompassing one-quarter of San Francisco. Because of this, the Free Fuse will participate in a substantial grant from the National Institute of Mental Health being administered by Dr. Carfagni. Frykman's Drug Treatment Program has already received some of these funds, and he is therefore making arrangements with the downtown YMCA to open a similar center in the city's Tenderloin area. "We've never gotten a penny from any public agency before," he says, "but the future looks bright from here."

This optimism certainly seems justified, and Frykman is not the only staff member who insists that the clinic is in better shape than at any other point in its history. Yet, as indicated earlier, the facility has problems all the same. In the first place, although the volunteers working at 409 and 558 Clayton Street can point to their share of therapeutic successes, they cannot really help most of the individuals who now live in the Haight-Ashbury. Many of the volunteers are actually .former patients; some of them can keep off drugs only if they are kept on the staff.

Second, and most important, is the fact that the Haight continues to deteriorate in spite of the clinic's efforts. Thus, the relatively healthy adolescents tend to abandon the district, leaving behind their more disturbed counterparts, as well as the older individuals who preceded them in the area. Because of this, some staff members at the Medical and Psychological Sections believe that the clinic has outlived its usefulness in its present form. Others argue that the facility should address itself to the problems not only of the new population but of the old community as well. Dr. Matzger will probably have an important voice in this matter, and although his study might prompt the United States Public Health Service to support the work at 409 and 558 Clayton Street, it may mean a radical transformation in these centers as they now stand. This is a distinct possibility, for the clinic's future, like its past, is intimately connected with the district it serves.

To fully appreciate this it is necessary to visualize the Haight in 1960, before its present population arrived. In that year, rising rents, police harassment and the throngs of tourists and thrill-seekers on Grant Avenue squeezed many beatniks out of the North Beach District three miles away. They started looking for space in the Haight-Ashbury, and landlords here saw they could make more money renting their property to young people willing to put up with poor conditions than to black families. For this reason, a small, beat subculture took root in the Flatlands and spread slowly up the slope of Mount Sutro. By 1962 the Haight was the center of a significant but relatively unpublicized bohemian colony.

Although fed by beats and students from San Francisco State, this colony remained unnoticed for several years. One reason was its members' preference for sedating themselves with alcohol and marijuana instead of using drugs that attract more attention. Another was their preoccupation with art and their habit of living as couples or alone. This living pattern was drastically altered in 1964, however, with the popular acceptance of mescaline, LSD and other hallucinogens and the advent of the Ginsberg-Leary-Kesey nomadic, passive, communal electric and acid-oriented life-style. The beats were particularly vulnerable to psychoactive chemicals that they thought enhanced their aesthetic powers and alleviated their isolation. Because of this, hallucinogenic drugs swept the Haight-Ashbury, as rock groups began preparing in the Flatlands what would soon be known as the "San Francisco Sound." On January 1, 1966 the world's first Psychedelic Shop was opened on Haight Street. Two weeks later, Ken Kesey hosted a Trips Festival at Longshoreman's Hall. Fifteen thousand individuals attended, and the word "hippie" was born. A year later, after Diggers and HIP had come to the Haight, the new community held a tribal gathering for 20,000 white Indians on the polo fields of Golden Gate Park. At this first Human Be-In, it showed its collective strength to the world.

The community grew immeasurably in size and stature as a result of this venture, but the ensuing publicity brought it problems for which its founders were ill prepared. In particular, the immigration of more young people to the Haight-Ashbury after the Be-In caused a shortage in sleeping space and precipitated the emergence of a new living unit, the crash pad. Adolescents forced to reside in these temporary and overcrowded structures started to experience adverse hallucinogenic drug reactions and psychological problems. The new community began to resemble a gypsy encampment, whose members were exposing themselves to an extreme amount of infectious disease.

Theoretically, the San Francisco Public Health Department should have responded positively to the situation. But instead of trying to educate and treat the hippies, it attempted to isolate and thereby destroy their community. Still convinced that theirs was a therapeutic alternative, the young people packed together in the Haight grew suicidally self-reliant, bought their medications on the black market and stocked cases of the antipsychotic agent Thorazine in their crash pads. Meanwhile, the Diggers announced that 100,000 adolescents dropping acid in Des Moines and Sioux Falls would flock to the Haight-Ashbury when school was out. They then tried to blackmail the city into giving them food, shelter and medical supplies necessary to care for the summer invasion.

Although the Public Health Department remained unmoved by the Diggers' forecast, a number of physicians and other persons associated with the University of California Psychopharmacology Study Group did react to the grisly promise of the Summer of Love. Among them were Robert Conrich, a former private investigator-turned-bohemian; Charles Fischer, a dental student; Dr. Frederick Meyers, internationally respected professor of pharmacology at the Medical Center; and Dr. David Smith, a toxicologist who was then serving as chief of the Alcohol and Drug Abuse Screening Unit at General Hospital. Several of these men lived in or were loyal to the Haight-Ashbury. Many had experience in treating bad LSD trips and felt that a rash of them would soon occur in the district. All had contacts among the new community and were impressed by the hippies' dreams of new social forms. But they also knew that the hippies did not number health among their primary concerns, although they might if they were afforded a free and accepting facility. In April they decided to organize a volunteer-staffed crisis center which might answer the growing medical emergency in the area.

As they expected, the organizers had little difficulty in gathering a number of hip and straight persons for their staff. However, they did face several problems in implementing their plans. First, they were unable to find space in the Haight until Robert Conrich located an abandoned dentist's office and obtained a lease for half of its 14 rooms. Paying the rent then became problematical, but Stuart Loomis and an English professor from State College, Leonard Wolf, offered funds if they could use half the facility for an educational project called Happening House. Finally, the organizers learned that local zoning regulations prohibited the charity operation they envisioned. This obstacle was overcome only after a sympathetic city supervisor, Jack Morrison, suggested that Dr. Smith establish the clinic as his private office so that his personal malpractice insurance could cover its volunteers.

Once this was accomplished, the organizers dredged up an odd assortment of medical equipment from the basements of several local hospitals. Utilizing the University of California Pharmacology Department, they also contacted the "detail men" representing most of America's large pharmaceutical houses and came up with a storeroom full of donated medications, including some vitally needed Thorazine. They then furnished a calm center for treating adverse LSD reactions at the facility.

Next, the organizers told the Public Health Department of their efforts. Its director, Dr. Ellis Sox, indicated that he might reimburse the organizers or open his own medical center if it was required in the Haight-Ashbury. Encouraged by this, the organizers alerted the new community that they would soon be in business. On the morning of June 7, 1967 the door to 558 Clayton Street was painted with the clinic's logo, a blue dove of peace over a white cross. Underneath this was written its slogan, Love Needs Care. The need itself was demonstrated that afternoon when the door was opened and 200 patients pushed their way inside.

Although the organizers anticipated the need for a regional health center in the Haight, they never dreamed that so many adolescents would seek help at the Medical Section. Nor did they suspect that the Diggers would be so close in their estimate of the number of individuals coming to the district that summer. Not all 100,000 showed up at once, but at least that many visitors did pass through the Haight-Ashbury during the next three months, over 20,000 of them stopping off at 558 Clayton Street along the way. A quarter of these persons were found to be beats, hippies and other early residents of the area. A half were "active" or "summer" hippies, comparatively healthy young people who experimented with drugs and might have done so at Fort Lauderdale and other locations had not the media told them to go West. The final quarter were bikers, psychotics and psychopaths of all ages who came to exploit the psychedelic scene.

Most of these individuals differed psychologically, but sickness and drugs were two things they all had in common. Some picked up measles, influenza, streptococcal pharyngitis, hepatitis, urinary and genital tract infections and venereal disease over the summer. Uncontrolled drug experimentation was rampant, so others had bad trips from the black-market acid flooding the area. Many also suffered adverse reactions from other drugs, for the presence of psychopaths and multiple abusers brought changes in psychoactive chemical consumption on the street. This first became obvious at the Summer Solstice Festival, where 5,000 tablets were distributed containing the psychomimetic amphetamine STP. Over 150 adolescents were treated for STP intoxication at the clinic, and after an educational program was launched, the substance waned in popularity in the district. But many of its younger residents had sampled intensive central nervous system stimulation for the first time during the STP episode. As a result, many were tempted to experiment next with "speed."

Such experimentation increased over the summer, until the Haight became the home of two separate subcultures, the first made up of "acid heads" who preferred hallucinogens, the second consisting of "speed freaks" partial to amphetamines. At the same time, the district saw the emergence of two different life-styles, the first character-ized by milder adolescent illnesses, the second marked by malnutrition, cellulitis, tachycardia, overstimulation and the paranoid-schizophrenic reactions associated with "speed." This naturally affected the calm center, where student volunteers were treating more than 50 adverse drug reac-tions every 24 hours. It also made extreme demands on the doctors in the Medical Section, who were dealing with more than 250 patients a day. Discouraged and exhausted by their efforts, the physicians pleaded with the Public Health Department for assistance. Yet the department refused to help the facility and never attempted to open a crisis center of its own.

Fortunately, this refusal did not pass unnoticed by the local press, and 558 Clayton Street received a great deal of community aid. Shortly after the clinic's plight was reported, the facility was flooded with doctors disappointed by the Public Health Department and with medical stu-dents who came from as far as Indiana to volunteer. Sev-eral Neighborhood Council members dropped by with food for the workers, while contributions began arriving through the mail. One of us (Dernburg) and more than 30 other psychiatrists arrived at 558 Clayton Street and established a temporary Psychiatric Section on the premises. They were followed by Donald Reddick and his partners in Medical Logistics, who donated over $20,000 worth of equipment and organized the staff procedures along more efficient lines. The second set of seven rooms was leased; a labora-tory, pharmacy and expanded calm center were installed. Then, Dr. William Nesbitt, a general practitioner, invited the organizers to join Youth Projects, an agency he headed, and to use its nonprofit status to accept donations. When

all was completed, the clinic was the best-equipped neighborhood center in town.

It was also the most chaotic, of course, a fact that was
causing increased friction with the psychiatric staff. Once
a Psychiatric Section was furnished at 409 Clayton Street,
however, the doctors were able to counsel young people in
relative privacy, to segregate the more violent amphetamine-
abusers and to reduce the traffic in the Medical Section to a
more manageable flow.

While this was going on, the clinic was also involving
itself in the crumbling new community. *Time* and other
publications somehow assumed that the Haight was still
full of hippies at this point, but the physicians at 558 Clayton Street knew otherwise. Realizing that the district was
becoming even more disorganized, they created an informal council with Huckleberry's for Runaways, All Saints',
the Haight-Ashbury Switchboard and other groups trying
to prevent its total collapse. They then launched the *Journal
of Psychedelic Drugs* to disseminate pharmacological information and started to participate more actively in community town hall meetings at the Straight Theatre. These
several activities greatly enhanced the clinic's reputation
in and outside of the Haight-Ashbury.

Although this publicity proved helpful to the facility
in certain respects, it also caused several new crises. The
first occurred two days after the publication of a *Look*
magazine article on the clinic, when Dr. Smith was notified that his malpractice insurance was to be cancelled
because he was "working with those weirdos in the Haight."
This crisis was resolved when Dr. Robert Morris, a patholo-
gist who was then chairman of the executive committee,
suggested that he apply for group coverage under the
auspices of the San Francisco Medical Society. Dr. Smith

doubted that this organization would ever support his advocacy of free medical care. He was therefore delighted
when the Medical Society not only granted him membership
but also endorsed the programs at 558 and 409 Clayton
Street.

His delight did not last long, however, for shortly after
the endorsement the clinic had to contend with a number
of persons who tried to capitalize on its good name. First
were a number of bogus doctors, most of whom worked under stolen or forged medical licenses in the Haight-Ashbury. Then came the Diggers who resented the facility's
influence in the community. Finally, the Medical Section
was besieged by several older psychopaths, one of whom,
a drug-dealer named Al Graham, hoped to turn it into his
base of operations in the Haight. "Papa Al" was ultimately
exposed and run out of the clinic, but shortly after he left,
Robert Conrich, who was close to collapse after serving for
two months as administrator, retired.

Although a severe blow in itself, Conrich's departure
was also an ill omen. In fact, less than a week after he
tendered his resignation, the Medical Section ran out of
funds. The volunteers rallied to meet this new crisis;
phone calls were made to potential contributors; and several paramedical staff members begged for money on Haight
Street. Two dance-concert benefits with local rock groups
that used the facility were also held, but only one was successful. In desperation, Peter Schubart called Joan Baez,
who helped take patient histories and sang to entertain the
lonely youngsters as they sat quietly in the waiting room.
Yet even she could not save the clinic. On September 22
the door was locked at 558 Clayton Street. Two weeks
later, what was left of the new community held a "Death
of Hip" ceremony to bury the term "hippie" and remove
the media from its back. "Haight used to be love," a par-

ticipant wrote on the steps of the Medical Section after the event. "Now, where has all the love gone?"

This question could be easily answered, for by the end of the Summer of Love almost all of the original hippies had moved to urban and rural communes outside of the Haight. Many summer hippies had also left the district, and those who remained either fended for themselves or were assimilated into the new population. Staying in the Haight-Ashbury, they quickly changed from experimental drug-users into multiple abusers and needed even more help. For this reason, the clinic organizers were determined to open the Medical Section again.

At the same time, they had another good reason to renew their efforts in the Haight. With the hippie movement spread across the United Statets by this point, other cities—Seattle, Boston, Berkeley, Cambridge, even Honolulu—were being swept by drug problems. New clinics were being created in the face of this onslaught, all of them looking to the Haight-Ashbury for guidance. Although always a confused and crisis-oriented center, the Haight-Ashbury Free Medical Clinic had become the national symbol of a new and successful approach in reaching a deviant population of alienated adolescents. Thus, its organizers had not only their medical practice but also their position of leadership to resume.

However, not all of them could still work in the Haight, a few were turning to other projects, others went back to prior commitments such as teaching.

But in spite of the losses the organizers looked to what was left of the new community for support. Another dance-concert benefit was held, this one under the guidance of Fillmore Auditorium owner Bill Graham, and several thousand dollars was raised. Smaller events were hosted at the Straight Theatre and at the John Bolles Gallery. In addition, a wealthy local artist named Norman Stone stepped forward to finance a substantial part of the Medical Section program. The clinic had still received no private or public grants, but by the end of October it had the funds necessary to open again.

When operations were resumed, however, the staff had a great deal more speed and more violence to contend with. In late February of 1968 a tourist ran over a dog, prompting a large crowd of adolescents to assemble on Haight Street. This in turn allowed Mayor Joseph Alioto to unleash his latest weapon for crime control, the 38-man Tactical Squad. After cleaning the street with tear gas and billies that afternoon, the squad vowed to return and enforce its own type of law and order. It did so four months later, when the district was ripped by three nights of rioting, rock-throwing and fires.

After the flames died down, it became apparent that the disturbance had marked yet another turning point in the history of the clinic. Many of its nurses, doctors and paramedical volunteers interpreted the riot as a sign that the Haight was now hopeless; mail contributions also ceased; and several psychiatrists who felt they could do little with or for the new population resigned from their positions. Low on money at this point, the clinic's business manager decided to host a three-day fund-raising benefit over the Labor Day weekend at the Palace of Fine Arts. The Affair was sabotaged by Mayor Alioto, who denied the cooperation of his Park and Recreation Commission. When the benefit, Festival of Performing Arts, was finally over, the organizers had lost $20,000. Two days later, the Medical Section was once again closed.

But, in spite of these obstacles, some progress was made. First, one of us (Smith) was awarded a grant to study adverse marijuana reactions which could be run in conjunction with the clinic. Stuart Loomis was installed as chief of the Psychiatric Section; Roger Smith raised more money for the Drug Treatment Program. In December the clinic received financial pledges from Norman Stone, the San Francisco Foundation and the Mary Crocker Trust. By January 7, 1969, 558 Clayton Street was in business again.

In contrast to previous years, its business went relatively smoothly in 1969. The amphetamines gradually ran their course in the district, and many of the multiple drug-abusers here switched to opiates, barbiturates and other "downers" after becoming too "strung out" on "speed." This change in chemical consumption naturally affected treatment practices, as heroin addiction increased tenfold and young people suffered even more types of chronic illness as a result of their drug abuse. Yet, in spite of the new population's problems, the year was a productive one for the clinic. Over 20,000 patients were treated at the Medical and Psychiatric Sections; research programs were initiated; efforts were made to reach the hippies in their communes; the volunteers became more experienced, although fewer in number; and several ex-staff members became involved in treatment programs of their own.

This year has also been a period of growth. More grants have been secured, and the inclusion of the Drug Treatment Program in the Northeast Mental Health Center, which provides for 14 new paid staff positions, has meant the facility's first official recognition by a public agency. In sum, the Haight-Ashbury Free Medical Clinic has finally become established—and, some say, part of the Establishment. From its third opening until the present, it has enjoyed a time of expansion, improvement and relative peace.

Whether these conditions continue depends, as always, on the Haight-Ashbury. This is particularly true today because its resident population seems to be changing once again. As some of the drug-abusers drift out of the area, their places are apparently being taken by adventurous college students. More black delinquents from the Fillmore ghetto are also frequenting the district, contributing to its heroin problem, though participating in the Drug Treatment Program for the first time. The Neighborhood Council and Merchants' Association still function, but both are demoralized and at a political impasse. In addition, the area is seeing an increased influx of older Negro families. Because of this, some staff members are urging changes at the Medical and Psychiatric Sections. One faction sees the clinic evolving into a health center for the entire neighborhood and wants to purchase one of the abandoned buildings on Haight Street so that all future programs can be consolidated under one roof. Another argues for more decentralization, de-emphasis of certain activities and/or increased expansion within and without the Haight.

Dr. Matzger, who knows the district intimately, has not yet decided what policy changes will stem from his United States Public Health Service study. However, he does not feel that both 409 and 558 Clayton Street will be different tomorrow from what they are today. "The clinic is at a crossroads," he says. "It may continue as a screening, diagnosis, detoxification and referral unit. It may become an expanded Drug Treatment Program. It may evolve into a large neighborhood health facility, particularly if we get the required dose of federal aid. On the other hand, it may have to cut back on some of the present programs. But whatever happens, it will continue to be an amalgam of individual efforts and an inspiration to people who seek new approaches in community medicine. Furthermore, no matter how the Haight-Ashbury changes, we are certain that the clinic will never close again."

Needed... A Revolution in Caring for the Retarded

GEORGE W. ALBEE

Nearly 6,000,000 Americans are mentally handicapped. By 1970, the number will reach almost
6,500,000. A retarded child is born every four minutes;
126,000 will be born this year.

Largely because of the deep personal interest of
President Kennedy, in recent years there has been considerable activity to help the retarded. Since 1963,
Federal funds for research and training have increased
at an unprecedented rate. Unfortunately, most of these
funds are not being used to help the *majority* of the
retarded—those who are normally slow, not victims
of inherited or acquired diseases. Instead, money is
being poured into costly bio-medical research centers
and "treatment" clinics to help a *minority*—those who
are retarded because of organic reasons, like injuries,
trauma, infections, and biochemical imbalances.

The majority of the retarded need, not medical treat-

99

ment, but rehabilitative training—so they can use their maximum potential. While every promising research lead should be pursued, and every significant effort in the whole field of retardation should be supported, a truly generous part of the new Federal funds ought to be invested in research aimed at helping the retarded lead lives as normal as possible. And more funds should be spent to train people who will, in turn, help train the majority of the retarded.

At the root of this error in priorities is a tragic misconception—namely, that mental retardation is an inherited or acquired disease. Recently, for example, the National Institute of Child Health and Human Development announced that it was allocating new funds for research centers whose purpose will be to (1) discover organic causes of retardation and (2) mount medical efforts to reduce its incidence. The Institute's press release went on: "Inherited diseases are among the leading causes of mental retardation." On May 16, 1967, the U.S. Public Health Service announced a grant for the construction of a $2.2 million center for medical research at a Midwestern university. Its press release stated:

"Several research studies will be aimed at identifying metabolic abnormalities in patients with unknown causes of mental retardation. Through bio-chemical studies of the urine, blood, and tissues of retarded patients, defects or absences of necessary biologic metabolic enzymes may be uncovered, paving the way for new attacks on mental retardation."

Between the lines of both statements is the promise that the incidence of retardation, because of such medically oriented research, may be significantly reduced. This promise is based on ignorance—or on a distortion of reality.

The truth is that most retardation is *not* an inherited disease. Quite correctly, President Kennedy's Panel on Mental Retardation emphasized the fact that

". . . about 75 percent to 85 percent of those now diagnosed as retarded show no demonstrable gross brain abnormality. They are, by and large, persons with relatively mild degrees of retardation. . . . Unfavorable environmental and psychological influences are thought to play an important contributory role among this group. Such influences include interference with normal emotional and intellectual stimulation in early infancy, unfavorable psychological or emotional experiences in early childhood, and lack of normal intellectual and cultural experiences during the entire developmental period."

More basically, brightness and dullness are a reflection of inherited capacities—the result of the interaction of a large number of genes operating in a perfectly normal, nonpathological way. While intelligence is thus genetically determined, so is a person's height—and neither stature *nor* mental retardation is an illness.

People are born retarded simply because intelligence is distributed normally throughout the entire population. A certain percentage of all children—slightly more than 2 percent, as it happens—will be born without defect and yet have I.Q.s below 70. Similarly, a certain percentage—also 2 percent—will be born with an I.Q. as high as that of the average graduate student.

Edward Zigler of Yale put it this way:

"We need simply to accept the generally recognized fact that the gene pool of any population is such that there will always be variations in the behavioral . . . expression of virtually every measurable trait or characteristic of man. From the polygenic model advanced by geneticists, we deduce that the distribution of intelligence is characterized by a bisymmetrical bell-shaped curve. . . .

"Once one adopts the position that the familial mental retardate is not defective or pathological but is essentially a normal individual of low intelligence, then the familial retardate no longer represents a mystery but, rather, is viewed as a particular manifestation of the general developmental process."

This point has crucial implications. It illuminates the inappropriateness of our present priorities, whereby 90 to 95 percent of the Federal construction funds for retardation centers will be used to house research and training on bio-medical approaches. It says the large majority of retarded children and adults are *not* retarded because of an acquired physiological abnormality, or because of a defect in their metabolism, or because of brain injury, or because their mothers had German measles, or because of the effects of any other infectious disease, or because of any other discovered or undiscovered exogenous or bio-medical defects.

Rather, the majority of retarded children and adults are produced from the more or less accidental distribution of polygenic factors present in the entire human race. Each parent transmits—often untouched—a large and varied set of genetic potentials from his myriad ancestors to his descendants. Thus each human is potentially the parent or grandparent or great-grandparent of a retarded child. Because of various forms of gene linkage, "familial" retardation is somewhat less common in bright families than in dull families. It occurs most commonly in "average" families—because there are many more of them.

The cold, but realistic, fact must be faced: It is no more likely that medical research findings will raise the intelligence of most retardates than it is that research will raise the intelligence of college students.

Let me make it very clear that I am not opposing medical research, or deprecating the triumphs of biology and medicine in uncovering the causes of several (albeit rare) forms of retardation in the past decade or so. What I am arguing against is the almost exclusive investment of Federal monies in medically-oriented research. For the plain truth is that, even after all the post-conception organic causes and all the metabolic and chromosomal defects are discovered and prevented or corrected, at least 2 percent of the general population will *still* be born retarded. And this situation will prevail for the indefinite future.

I believe, therefore, that it is not only unfair but unreasonable that almost every new federally funded, university-affiliated center to train people and to engage in research in this field is in a medically-dominated and bio-medically-oriented center. Even in the Mental Retardation Research Centers being funded by the new National Institute of Child Health and Human Development, the major efforts are bio-medical. Instead, at least half of these centers should be designed for research in special educational methods and rehabilitation; others should be designed primarily for research in the social and behavioral-science approaches to helping the retarded.

Why is the emphasis, both in research and in treatment, on organic approaches to retardation? One reason: the academic medical institutions' insatiable need for research money. Because of the enormous Federal funds recently made available for constructing research and training facilities in the area of retardation, medicine—particularly psychiatry and pediatrics—has discovered and promulgated compelling arguments why these research centers should be placed in medical settings. Almost exclusive emphasis has been on all of the external causes of retardation—the metabolic, the infectious, the undiscovered causes of brain damage. In addition, by controlling the advisory committees that rule on applications for construction funds to build the university-affiliated facilities, the doctors have controlled the character of these centers still further.

Another reason: The powerful citizens' committees in the field of retardation are composed largely of well-informed parents of retarded children. But in these families, normal, garden-variety retardation is relatively rare. These parents, from the numerically small but politically advantaged upper-middle classes and upper classes, are more likely to have children who are retarded because of *exogenous* damage than because of normal polygenic inheritance. Their retarded children are more likely to be represented in the below-50 I.Q. group of the seriously-handicapped than among the much more common 50-70 I.Q. group. As a consequence, these citizens' committees militate for bio-medical discoveries that will prevent, or cure, exogenous retardation. Their aspirations coincide with the eagerness of academic medicine to have large, expensive research labs. Both groups push legislation—and the rules implementing legislation—in the direction of an overwhelming emphasis on bio-medical research.

There are still other reasons to explain the overemphasis on biological or injury explanations of retardation.

In child-worshipping American society, and particularly in the great sprawling suburban areas, parents are gravely concerned about the academic success of their children. Their children's scores on intelligence tests are therefore exceedingly important to these parents. And when a parent is told that his child tests at the 135-I.Q. level, his response is a feeling of pride, even elation. It means that Johnny can go far, that a society that rewards intellectual success (not necessarily achievement) will eventually be at his feet.

But consider the parent who is told that his child is functioning at a 65-I.Q. level and must be placed in a special class for slow-learners. After his original shock and panic have subsided somewhat, the parent begins to cast about for an explanation. What could have happened? What accident, injury, or disease could have caused this terrible thing?

Now, two currently popular diagnoses for mentally deficient children are *minimal brain damage* and *maturational lag*. The trouble is that the neurological and psychological tests upon which these diagnoses are based leave much to be desired. Nevertheless, one or the other of these diagnoses is made with increasing frequency, perhaps because they are very useful to give to parents who somehow feel personally responsible for a retarded child and seize upon such a diagnosis as an exculpation.

It is difficult for a pediatrician, a psychiatrist, or a consulting psychologist to tell parents their child is just slow mentally, and not because of illness, disease, or exogenous damage. Similarly, one of the most difficult diagnoses for parents in our society to accept is that their child is normal and has a limited intellectual capacity. No special explanation is required for a child who is bright—he "just comes by that naturally." But when a child is slow intellectually, something must have happened. Thus the diagnosis of *minimal brain damage,* or *maturational lag,* has great psychological appeal. Most parents can recall an illness or accident at some point in the child's life, or in the expectant mother's. This is certainly an easier explanation to accept, in an extremely painful situation, than garden-variety, normal retardation. Nor is it hard to understand that such a parent's desire to "do something" leads to still more support of bio-medical research.

Whatever the reasons for its origin, the imbalance in the field of mental retardation should be remedied swiftly—if our society truly believes that *everyone* should have the opportunity to develop his potential to the maximum. We need social and educational research into retardation as much—or more—than we need biological and medical research. What follows is just one example of a recent significant study involving teachers, children, and intelligence (Robert Rosenthal and Lenore Jacobsen, 1967).

At the beginning of the school year, intelligence tests were given to children in a city school of 18 classrooms (three at each grade level from first to sixth). By pre-arranged plan, the teachers in the school were told that the tests measured potential for "intellectual blooming." One child in five—chosen at random—in each classroom was said to have scored high on the test. This child, the teacher was told, very probably would show marked intellectual improvement within the next several months.

Eight months later, at the end of the school year, another intelligence test was given. The specially-identified children in the first and second grades had made dramatic improvements. In first grade, the average gain was more than 15 points; in the second grade, more than 10 points. In actuality, these children had been randomly chosen for identification. Yet, by some mysterious alchemy, the teachers had behaved in such a way toward these young children, who were designated as special, as to elicit more of their basic potential.

This study illustrates how research can clarify a point that is of crucial importance in planning educational experiences for intellectually handicapped youngsters. The point made in the study is that teachers with the right attitudes and expectations are of critical importance—and can have a significant effect on the development of the child's capacity to its fullest. This is the sort of research we need more of!

Too often we approach the task of teaching retarded children with the expectation that they will not, or cannot, learn. We have not yet begun to tap much of the potential of these children, a potential that might be unlocked not only with new techniques but with new expectations. Such insights and progress, of course, will *not* result from our exclusive reliance on biological research.

But it is not only research efforts that are out of balance. So are efforts at rehabilitation.

For example, the Children's Bureau of the Department of Health, Education, and Welfare has struggled painfully—for 11 years—to develop 134 clinics across the nation for the retarded. These clinics ostensibly are operated to demonstrate the value of bio-medically-oriented treatment that uses a so-called multi-disciplinary approach. As J. William Oberman (technical adviser on Medical Aspects of Mental Retardation for the Children's Bureau) notes somewhat plaintively, these 134 clinics are able to offer only a very small fraction of the amount of care needed by the retarded and their families. He estimates that each year some 30,000 individuals are served by these clinics and that perhaps "other multi-disciplinary clinics under medical direction" provide care for an additional 10,000 retarded children. But this is a trifle compared with the needs of the 6,000,000 retarded children and adults in the United States. Dr. Oberman notes that even 2500 new clinics (as impossible to staff as 2500 new major-league baseball teams!) could barely handle the present demand. And the demand keeps increasing. Unmet needs grow. Of what profit is it to demonstrate that an expensive treatment clinic, expertly staffed with high-priced professionals, can see a handful of children a year with modest effectiveness, when it is impossible ever to duplicate such clinics? How long will Congress stand still for this nonsense?

The justification for these clinics having medical direction and treatment (largely unavailable full-time) rests on two highly emotional arguments. One, as we have seen, stresses the pathological or accidental—and theoretically preventable—causes of a high percentage of the severely retarded. The second stresses the concomitant additional physical handicaps, which are alleged to require continuing diagnostic follow-up and medical care.

The truth is that 85 percent of the retarded, after thorough medical evaluation, ordinarily require no more medical care than many other handicapped groups in society. The associated physical complications that are correctable, in a majority of cases, are visual and auditory—outside the competence of the ordinary psychiatrist or pediatrician. A significant number of retardates also have speech problems, and these demand the special skills of a speech therapist rather than a physician.

The kind of professional manpower required for effective and functional care of the retarded is not more physicians, nurses, and psychologists with highly specialized training in this field. These people do not spend any significant amount of their professional time working with the retarded anyway. *More than anything else, we need teachers and vocational-guidance specialists.*

According to the President's Panel, a very large majority of the retarded "can, with special training and assistance, acquire limited job skills and achieve a high measure of independence; they represent 85 percent of the retarded group." Yet many states even now do not provide any classes for the "trainable" retarded, and no state has enough classes for the "educable" retarded. Only one of every five retarded children is now being reached by any kind of special-education program. The President's Panel found 20,000 special-education teachers across the nation, many of them poorly trained, where 55,000 were needed. The panel predicted that by 1970 the need for special teachers will reach 90,000. And state vocational agencies that provide urgently-needed vocational rehabilitation for the mildly retarded are currently reaching only 3 percent of them.

In one investigation in Massachusetts, Simon Olshansky studied over 1000 children whose families were receiving aid for dependent children. He found that 6.7 percent were retarded. Virtually none were getting any significant help. The mothers were "too immobilized" to recognize the problem, or to seek help. Social agencies, as is frequently the case, had no workers to reach out and seek cases that would add to their excessive caseloads.

To provide adequate help to the 110,000 children born each year with mild but handicapping retardation, and to provide care and rehabilitation for the other 5,500,000 mildly retarded people in our society, we need teachers, teachers, and more teachers—and then taxes to support a massive educational effort. Among teachers in this context I include all those specially trained and devoted professional people willing to spend hours and hours in daily and patient interaction with retarded children, unlocking and strengthening whatever skills and abilities are in them. Also included are the vocational-rehabilitation workers and those in occupational therapy, in recreational therapy, and in nonprofessional but patient and warm interaction therapies that the retarded yearn for.

Needed desperately, in addition to teachers, are skilled caseworkers, sheltered-workshop personnel, vocational-guidance counselors, speech therapists, and all of the range of other people who have chosen careers that make them their handicapped brother's keeper. Many of these people could be trained in bachelor's or even two-year junior-college programs.

But, first and foremost, it is essential to escape the bio-medical orientation that controls our efforts. Fourteen university-affiliated facilities for the retarded, all devoted to research and training, have now been approved for construction with Federal funds. The Federal Government already has allocated the millions of dollars to build these research centers. Every last one of them is in a medical setting where most of the research, the research training, and the education of professionals will be relevant to a small minority of retarded children. What have these huge new research centers to do with training special-education teachers and vocational counselors? The answer: Next to nothing.

There *is* a place where medical care is truly needed to prevent retardation, and where it has not been available—in the prenatal and perinatal care of "medically indigent" expectant mothers in our·large cities. A significant number of their children are born prematurely, and the prematurity rate is two to three times greater in low-income families where prenatal care is haphazard. Almost 500,000 indigent mothers deliver babies each year in our tax-supported city hospitals. At least 100,000 of these need special medical services for complications in pregnancy and birth. Most of them do not get it.

Here is an area for good medical research and action, because mental retardation that may well have an organic base is associated with prematurity and low birth weight. Among infants who weigh below three pounds at birth, nearly three-quarters subsequently develop physical or mental defects. In an average big-city hospital, the baby girl born to a Negro mother on the "staff service" (free service) weighs nearly a pound less than the baby born to a suburban white mother on the private service of the general hospital. A large percentage of urban indigent Negro mothers are "walk-ins" who receive little or no prenatal care, no special instructions on diet, and no medical guidance until labor pains begin. The retardation rate in infants born to these indigent mothers is ten times the white rate.

If American medicine were to turn its massive resources to the solution of these problems—adequate medical care fo₅ the poor—many more cases of retardation could be prevented than will result from the present emphasis on research into esoteric causes. Unfortunately, the growing shortage of physicians, the fee-for-service philosophy of American medicine, and the high prestige of complex research activities in academia all combine to make this significant prevention-effort unlikely.

At the root of our double standard of care and intervention with the retarded is the fact that the nice people—the people who do the planning, the governing, the writing, the reading, and the decision-making in our society—are members of the economically-favored group. Most of them have arranged their lives in such a way as to be sealed off—geographically and socially—from the have-not groups, the disadvantaged, and the dispossessed.

But parents of the retarded—parent-citizen groups in particular—are, for the most part, prosperous, and they at least have the advantage of some special insights into some of the darker social forces in our society. Most of them know from personal experience the hardships and heartaches that are the lot of the child or adult in our society who has limited intellectual capacity. Such citizen groups must take the lead in demanding that at least half of the tax dollars be spent for educational and rehabilitative approaches for all our intellectually-handicapped children and adults.

Our efforts are out of balance and out of joint. It is only an informed citizenry that can study the facts and act on them. The retarded cannot speak for themselves.

FURTHER READING SUGGESTED BY THE AUTHOR:

A Proposed Program for National Action to Combat Mental Retardation (U.S. Public Health Service, 1962). Report of the President's Panel on Mental Retardation. A good overview of the problem and of the recommendations to President Kennedy.

Intelligence and Experience by J. McV. Hunt (New York: The Ronald Press, 1961). While somewhat technical and research-oriented, this is an excellent treatise on factors influencing intelligent behavior.

The Wild Boy of Aveyron by J.M.G. Itard (New York: Appleton-Century-Crofts, 1932). This report of the attempt of a 19th-century physician to teach a mentally retarded boy is a classic.

Psychopathology of Childhood by Jane W. Kessler (Englewood Cliffs, N.J.: Prentice-Hall, 1966). This excellent textbook has chapters summarizing historical and contemporary approaches to mental sub-normality and to learning problems.

Early Education of the Mentally Retarded by S. Kirk (Urbana, Ill.: University of Illinois Press, 1958). All of Dr. Kirk's writings must be on any required-reading list in this field.

Psychological Problems in Mental Deficiency (Third Edition) by S. Sarason (New York: Harper & Row, 1958). Dr. Sarason has pioneered in the development of a psycho-educational clinic at Yale that is a model for a meaningful approach to the problem discussed in this article.

Professionalization and Poverty in a Community Hospital

CHARLES NANRY and JACQUELINE NANRY

"Central" hospital is a 780-bed institution which was founded in the late nineteenth century under the control of the local city administration. Long a focus of controversy in the city where it is located, this hospital became a state medical college in 1968. Before 1968 hospital jobs were viewed as plums in the spoils system of the city's politics, and the hospital was a haven for political appointees. In fact, the administrative head of the hospital at the time of the state medical college take-over was a local photographer who was active in city politics. Hospital employees were regularly given election day off in order to solicit votes for the local political machine.

The city served by Central hospital has a population of more than 300,000. In recent years there have been several serious racial conflicts, which burgeoned into a major insurrection in the late sixties. Area residents, angered by an urban renewal project which cleared vast tracts of land surrounding the hospital for medical school construction, fired at the hospital building during the disturbance. Most of the city's residents are black and Puerto Rican, although large white ethnic neighborhoods lie within and adjoining the city. The community is badly polarized along racial lines.

Traditionally, the Central hospital staff saw as its primary function the treatment of the acutely ill. Under the auspices of the medical college the hospital now has an additional mission of teaching and research. In order to meet these goals the hospital staff attempts to control its patient population to provide appropriate teaching and research cases for the medical students, as well as providing mandated acute-care services.

People in the community, on the other hand, view the hospital as a place to take both major and minor medical problems and general problems in living. In their view the hospital is a general service institution that ought to expand its services and broaden available health care. Slum residents who often cannot afford rudimentary health care and family physicians, use the hospital in order to get medication and treatment for relatively minor maladies. Parents who feel the need to get away from their children for a night on the town may use the hospital as a baby-sitting service, saying, "My baby has diarrhea, please admit him to the hospital." Occasionally, children are simply left in clinic waiting rooms for the weekend. Parents and grandparents are committed to the hospital when the burden of their care is too much to bear.

The conversion of the hospital to a medical school represented a critical sharpening of the divergent lay and professional definitions of the institution's goals. Most of the statements issued by the hospital at that time (and since) have stressed the need for upgrading skills within its own organization. These statements clearly reflect the assumption made by the hospital and medical school staffs that upgrading staff skills and professionalizing areas such as social service would significantly improve the services rendered to the community. Appeals for state, federal and local funds were and still are made on that basis.

In our judgment, without either a change in the hospital's size (i.e., number of beds), the addition of supplementary services in the community or a shift in the allocation of resources (for example, more community control over hospital beds), substantial change is unlikely for those who depend on the hospital. A hospital is limited by institutionalized patterns of use. Some marginal flexibility may be introduced by increasing the number of beds within it. Other small gains may be made by shortening the length of stay per patient, since patient care involves some temporal flexibility. For the most part, however, once a physical plant is designed and built, its ecology, coupled with community concepts of hospital use, limit its expansion. If the supply of hospital beds remains fairly constant, demand for those beds, no matter how obstreperous, will not change things substantially. The major thrust of the hospital's public relations campaign following the medical college takeover has been that things would be much better because of professional upgrading of the hospital's personnel.

It is often assumed that professionalization in institutional settings leads to better service for clients. Our research experience has led us to believe that that assumption ought to be reevaluated. If professionalization involves the notion of an ideal client, then those who do have problems which differ from those of the ideal client may not be served well. Professional social workers ori- ented toward psychoanalytic casework or medical practitioners interested in narrowly defined specialties may reveal a trained incapacity for dealing with the real, if often mundane, problems of poor people. Large sums of state and federal monies channeled into the hospital during the period of our study went to hire more professionals, particularly more black professionals, and into upgrading the medical school facilities. On the whole, this infusion of resources meant very little to the average patient.

At issue here is a triangular conflict of goals for the hospital as an organization. The community wants and needs broad-gauged health-care facilities, including care for the chronically ill. The hospital administration wants and needs to limit the definition of the hospital to an acute-care facility. Medical college staff wants and needs a training facility that provides teaching cases. Because of the magnitude of the health problems in the city served, the hospital is always in grave danger of being overwhelmed by the needs of sick people who have few other resources at their command. A social law of large numbers is at work here: the number of persons needing help approaches infinity, while the hospital, as an organization, attempts to rationalize its limits and satisfy internal demands, especially the professional pursuit of special limited and clearly defined problems. There is some danger of deflating the value of each person seeking services since the fact that a large number of people are taken care of does not mean that the institution reaps a larger profit. Service institutions such as hospitals do not work within the same parameters as commercial institutions.

We gathered data for the report during January and February 1967 and January and February 1969. The method of collection included participant observation, review of patient emergency-room records, and an exami-

nation of charts of patients discharged on one medical and two surgical floors. We have presented our case-study material in narrative form. Employing a technique widely used in industrial sociology, we will discuss the "processing" of patients as a problem of inputs and outputs. What follows, then, is a description of how inputs into the hospital are discouraged and outputs encouraged.

Inputs

The manifestly ill patient brought to the emergency room by ambulance is examined, given urgent services and admitted directly to surgery or to a hospital ward. Medical and paramedical staff respond to such an admission with a humane, professional and patient-centered attitude. The definition of the situation as a crisis is shared by members of the emergency-room staff, and has been generated, at least in part, by external forces, such as ambulance sirens and flashing lights, stretchers wheeled in frantically, patients' shortness of breath or bleeding and so forth. A brochure published by the hospital aptly describes the crisis atmosphere involved in such an admission:

> The white night supervisor taking from the arms of a black grandmother a small boy hemorrhaging from the nose and wrapped in a dirty blanket—the supervisor actually running with her precious bundle to the pediatric treatment room where swift emergency procedures stem the bleeding.
>
> The sight of blood everywhere—routine are the stab wounds, the slashed throat, the ripped belly.

The emergency room of a big city hospital represents a negotiated order where all of the action-packed stereotypes of the medical team snatching life from the jaws of death approach reality. When the pressure for emergency treatment approaches the overload point, however, certain steps have become institutionalized to defuse the situation. David Sudnow (in "Dead on Arrival," pp. 193-212) has brilliantly pointed out some of the defusing mechanisms used to forestall overloading. He points out how ambulance drivers label some cases as "possible DOAs." Cues such as special siren signals and voice tone tell the emergency-room staff to take their time in treating an incoming case. Sudnow also points out how the "social value" of a patient affects the kind of effort that will be made to save him. Older patients and morally stigmatized patients, such as alcoholics, drug addicts, prostitutes, attempted suicides and vagrants, get less extraordinary care than do young children and middle-class patients. Sudnow's insights have been substantiated in our research and extend beyond medical care to hospital entry itself, especially for those persons who walk in seeking help.

Ambulatory persons seeking admission through the emergency room are routinely given a number on arrival and directed to a small, crowded waiting room. One by one they are called into the admissions office, where they must laboriously answer questions relating to their personal, medical and financial history.

A guard is stationed by the entrance to this office. His primary function is to deter any potential patient from entering out of turn and to keep relatives and/or friends from accompanying patients beyond this room into the hospital. This separation has important consequences, since it contributes to the total mystification of the patient and restricts admission eligibility status to the discretion of the physician in charge.

The indigent person seeking admission is removed from

the support of family and friends as well as the advocacy
of a private physician during a health crisis. (Private physicians are retained, in part, to guard their patients' best
interests in the medical maze; poor people often cannot
afford an advocate doctor.) The poor patient is wheeled
into a technically sophisticated environment where medicine man language is spoken and where he is questioned,
poked, X-rayed and probed by a host of white-coated
specialists. Unless he is a very sophisticated consumer of
medical services he is going to be mystified by the whole
emergency-room ritual. Therefore, his admission rests
wholly with the examining physician. Failure to submit
meekly to this ritual through an outburst of anger or a
demand for "rights" may result in the denial of admission.

Theoretically, the decision for admission is based on the
urgency of the medical problem. In practice, however,
there must be some discretionary process to insure that
beds are allocated according to the hospital's predetermined
criteria. Among the many arbitrary reasons for a doctor's
refusal to admit a patient are service quotas (medical
service team A has enough patients) and prognosis (doctors do not like to admit terminally ill patients who will
linger and then die or people who appear to be eventual
placement problems such as elderly stroke patients or
malnourished alcoholics). The overloaded hospital admissions process must discriminate between those who will
and those who will not get in. Here again, "social value"
criteria are used. Sudnow's proscriptions about avoiding
the dead or dying label applies also to the admissible or
nonadmissible label:

> Within a limited temporal perspective at least, but
> one which is not necessarily to be regarded as trivial,
> the likelihood of "dying" and even of being "dead"
> can be said to be partially a function of one's place in

the social structure, and not simply in the sense that the wealthier get better care, or at least not in the usual sense of that fact. If one anticipates having a critical heart attack, he had best keep himself well-dressed and his breath clean if there is a likelihood he will be brought into County [hospital] as a "possible."

In the hospital we studied, contracting a rare disease might increase one's chances for admission. Failing that, the best way to insure admission is to come on a day when the quota for the necessary service has not yet been filled.

Patients judged ineligible for admission are given clinic slips and/or prescriptions and told to go home and rest. Persons who repeatedly make "inappropriate" attempts to be admitted are received less enthusiastically and are gradually denied even superficial treatment or examination. One particular category of nonadmissible patients is most troublesome to the admitting department and receives special attention: the barely ambulatory person.

The barely ambulatory person who is refused admission is referred to the social service department for placement. If the social worker responding to the referral is unable to locate family to come for the patient, or if rooming- or boarding-home placements seem inappropriate, the worker approaches the physician on behalf of the patient's admission. The success of this advocacy depends on the physician's appraisal of the worker's ward service. In 1967 the social work staff did not have professional credentials, and therefore was not "specialized." The social worker called to the emergency room also shared responsibility for hospital wards where he or she was involved in many needed but not necessarily professional social work functions. For example, the worker directed discharge planning, but also secured prosthetic appliances;

he coordinated consultations with other hospitals, but also arranged transportation and acted as a referral agent for other community medical and paramedical services.

In general, the 1967 definition of the role of social worker was that of an organizational jack-of-all-trades. Many departmental members were employed at the hospital as a result of political patronage. Some even held other full-time jobs. For a time the social service office even served as a boutique where one member of the department sold allegedly stolen clothing and fancy contraceptives. In spite of the abuses, however, the social worker was free to adopt an advocate-entrepreneur role in the hospital and to exchange favors with the medical staff in order to get services for patients. And patients did get social services even though some of the social service staff members were primarily interested in quick processing in order to get on with outside activities.

If the individual social worker's competence as an organizational "utility infielder" was recognized by the admitting physician, he was more likely to reclassify the patient as admissible for the social worker's services. In a sense, the social workers had what Amitai Etzioni has called the "power of lower participants."

Throughout the period of the study, proper use of hospital beds for the acutely ill remained the central admission issue. However, because of the addition of medical education as a hospital goal, selectivity of potential patients has become more important. Patients who are interesting may be admitted, even though others who are more critically ill have been denied admission. Quota systems related to types of diagnoses are more closely considered; the question becomes: How many CVAs or ulcerated legs do we have? Many more patients are classified as nonadmissible.

Although outpatient clinic facilities have been enlarged and modernized, the number of nonambulatory persons denied hospital admission has also increased dramatically. This is another result of more stringent admission standards. It is important to note again that the number of hospital beds has not increased, nor have medical services in the community been expanded to any large degree.

Nonadmissible and nonambulatory patients are routinely labeled "social problem" on their admission sheet, and are referred to the social service department. Two interesting developments occurred which dramatically differentiated the transaction between the social worker and the physician in 1969 from that in 1967.

The social service department has been professionalized. Since 1968, there has been an almost complete turnover of staff. The new workers have MSW credentials. The department has divested itself of many of the old tasks which are now labeled clerical or nonprofessional. Furthermore, the new staff laments the fact that they are presently unable to devote all of their time to in-depth casework rather than "merely" to referral services. The social-work staff is now more specialized, and one worker is assigned exclusively to the emergency room.

The visibility of increasingly larger numbers of persons labeled nonambulatory and nonadmissible has distressed the new professional emergency-room manager. His ability is judged on the criterion of rapid processing of patients. His aim is perfectly clear: "The amazing thing is the rapid movement of patients. No more do you see stretchers lining the walls of the corridors while patients await treatment."

To bring about this state of affairs in the emergency room and resolve the crowding problem a holding room has been created. This room is in the hospital but not of it. Patients there have not been admitted and are kept in it until their status is resolved. This anteroom to the hospital is designated for "patient observation." It functions as a limbo where persons wait for the social worker to come to decide their fate. Unfortunately, the social workers have lost their exchange power; physicians in the hospital typically value psychological and psychoanalytic insight much less than resourcefulness. Therefore, the holding room becomes a market where bargaining and bartering takes place over the patients' bodies.

Social Worker (pointing to the first of six patients on stretchers): Dr. Smith, I can try to place Mr. X if you will admit Mr. B.

Medical Doctor: Another ulcer (referring to Mr. B) is the last patient that I want to admit.

S.W.: What about Mrs. R, no one is going to take her . . . she's too much trouble and care.

M.D.: O.K. If you get Mr. X and Mr. B out of here I'll check with Dr. L. . . . Maybe he'll take her on Medicine, but you had better be able to place her this week!

(from field notes)

One category of patients that is particularly troublesome to the hospital staff is the chronic, indigent alcoholic. These men, and there are a large number of them in the city served by the hospital, are beset by a variety of illnesses that stem from gross neglect, malnutrition, infections of various kinds, cirrhosis of the liver, exposure to the elements and so forth. Many of them are on an informal "blacklist" which excludes them even from the various soup kitchens in the area (run mostly by religious organizations). Since they tend to spend any money received (welfare or otherwise) on alcohol, they cannot even afford the cheap flophouses in the downtown area of the city.

But our concern here is with the treatment of alcoholics at the hospital. These unfortunates suffer from what we choose to call the "Johnny comes marching home syndrome." They show up at the hospital needing food and shelter and are referred to social service for help. There are no facilities in the area that will care for them, and they are ineligible for hospital service. They are turned back out on the street. (Care is provided for the acutely ill, not for chronics.) Sooner or later acute illness follows, and then care is provided. The most common acute illness suffered by these men is frostbite. The diagnosis: amputation. The result of treatment: eventually the patient with this kind of career dies of attrition, his body gradually cut away.

Everything seems to work against the victim of the "Johnny syndrome." He does not fit the definition of the proper client until it is too late. Even good medical practice conspires to do him in, a piece at a time. Frostbite is very painful. Along with regular surgery the frostbite victim is often given a sympathectomy; that is, nerves are cut to reduce sensation and therefore pain. When "Johnny" is put back out on the street—which he will be since no one will take him—if it is winter, or when winter comes, he will be frostbitten again. When he is he will not feel it until it is further advanced than before because of the sympathectomy. The cycle is repeated again and again until "Johnny" is gone.

It should be noted that the hospital has added an alcohol treatment unit with a fairly large staff of professionals. But this and other efforts are aimed at motivated alcoholics and employ an anti-alcohol posture. Less glamorous but more useful aid might be provided by a no-questions-asked soup kitchen and flophouse. Admittedly,

the person suffering from the "Johnny syndrome" represents an exteme example of the nonadmissible individual.
But his plight is not unique in the community. Legions of
others suffer from the same type of neglect. There is no
room.

Outputs

Emptying hospital beds is just as critical a problem as
selectivity in admissions for an acute care or teaching
hospital. Understandably, the timing and spacing of discharges is subject to a variety of curative factors within
the limits of medical diagnosis and technology. Several
other variables, however, influence discharge decisions,
and these are coupled with a host of coercive measures to
"remove" patients.

Patients routinely leave Central hospital after receiving
a medical discharge from their physician, together with a
clinic appointment for follow-up. Difficult patients, that
is, those who do not adapt well to the hospitalized patient
role (they challenge orders, make discomforting inquiries
or just ask too many questions), are released as early as is
medically and/or legally possible. Likewise, the terminally
ill patient is encouraged to return home or to allow himself to be placed elsewhere if he threatens to die during
a physician's service on a ward (discharges involve less
paperwork than death) or badgers the hospital staff by
frequently talking about the imminence of his death. In
addition, there is a tendency to discharge patients before
the rotation of doctors in order to avoid the time-consuming task of writing transfer-of-patient medical summaries
which are expected for each patient being transferred to
another doctor.

There are two other common routes of exodus for patients: death and release against medical advice. A patient who is not satisfied with medical or auxiliary services may sign himself out of Central hospital against the advice of his doctor. Difficult patients are often subtly invited to take this measure by medical and paramedical staff. Once the patient makes his intention known, however, the staff rallies together ritualistically to warn the delinquent patient of the potential medical hazards of such a decision; to express their individual sincerity in helping him to health; and to advise him that they will no longer be legally responsible after he signs the patient release form. With the exception of interesting teaching cases and the infrequent patient perceived as having political or charismatic clout, little meaningful effort is expended to keep an "ungrateful patient." In spite of the concerned medical team ritual, staff persons safe from any professional or legal ramifications (aides, ward clerks and others) are not discouraged from supporting the patient's decision to sign himself out. "Mr. R, you're just a mean old man who don't belong here."

There are, however, as in the case of admissions, a group of patients who for physical or psychological reasons are not agreeable to the doctor's expectations about discharge scheduling. Hospital personnel employ four techniques to remove a reluctant patient: social service placement; transfer to another service; psychiatric commitment; and isolation as punishment.

Social Service Placement

Most discharge problems are referred to the ward social worker who tries to convince the patient that he is indeed ready to be discharged and then locates available space for the patient with his family, in boarding- or roominghouses, nursing homes or other suitable places. In a large urban hospital, serving an economically deprived population, "discharge planning" is more of a fiction than a real service to the patient because of the dearth of placement facilities. As a consequence, the actual task of physically moving a patient from his hospital bed to a boarding or nursing home bed is carried out perfunctorily, with or without the patient's complete understanding of or consent to the placement. The critical issue becomes one of space and availability, although there is verbal acknowledgment of the importance of an "appropriate placement"; that is, virtually everyone would agree that a 27-year-old amputee should not be tucked away in a chronic-care nursing home, yet that happened. The elderly patient who has trouble signing his name to the transfer papers is arbitrarily sent to the first opening in a nursing home despite his protests. Central hospital will supply a squiggly "X" and verification. Other patients are deceived into signing by being told that they are signing discharge papers or are signing papers to release them to the "discharge center" which they must visit before going home.

Transfer to Another Service

Another common practice in response to patients who are seen as discharge problems, is transfer to another service. This procedure became far more common after the addition of the medical school, because it served two goals at the same time: it supported the discharging physician's patient-turnover scheduling; and it supplied less populated specialty services such as plastic surgery with teaching cases who had already undergone the necessary routine hospital tests and examinations, such as X-rays and various lab and blood work. The staff on plastic surgery was particularily anxious for patients upon whom they might perform cosmetic surgery. It was often the case, moreover, that they would recruit or accept transfers of discharge problem cases, as would the staffs of other services in Central hospital. We should note, though, that most services were less motivated to receive than to give; physicians would often try to transfer discharge problems for additional hospital services (hemorrhoidectomy, ligation of varicose veins and so forth), but these patients were usually not enthusiastically welcomed by the receiving physician unless he was fulfilling an exchange bargain with another service or needed to demonstrate hemorrhoidectomies to a group of medical students. Let us illustrate with an actual case from our field notes.

A social worker was called to the female surgical floor in order to begin discharge plans for a 40-year-old postoperative appendectomy patient. The patient was lying in bed staring at the ceiling and singing to herself. She appeared to be joyfully disoriented. Dr. P, one of the plastic surgeons, walked into the ward during the social worker's visit. When he became aware of the general surgeon's discharge plan for this patient, he cancelled the discharge immediately. As he explained to the social worker, plastic surgery was desperate for good teaching cases this month, and the patient in question was an ideal candidate for nipple reconstruction.

Psychiatric Commitment

Patients who become placement problems because of a prolonged dearth of beds in a placement facility or because of absolute refusal to accept placement plans (assuming these persons are alert and able to resist "railroading" into a placement) are referred to the hospital psychiatrist. The psychiatrist, in turn, routinely commits them to a mental institution on the basis of "impaired judgement." The reasoning behind such a decision is somewhat circular: if a patient is temporarily or permanently nonambulatory, and he has no family to whom he may be discharged, nursing-home placement is necessary. If this same patient refuses placement or insists that he be returned to an "inadequate home situation" rather than be placed, his judgement is impaired. If his judgment is impaired, commitment is necessary. A neat syllogism! In addition to numerous cases in our field notes concerning nonambulatory patients who wanted to return to a life of living alone, we have the following case:

An elderly woman was admitted to the hospital by ambulance after falling in her apartment building. Mrs. S consented to several X-rays and tests at the time of admission, but soon afterward requested that she be transferred back home. Mrs. S refused medical service and could not be influenced to stay by a medical student, chaplain or social worker. The problem peculiar to this situation was that Mrs. S, although mentally alert and intact, could not walk. The hospital would not take the responsibility of transporting her back to her apartment.

Mrs. S lived alone and without family or close friends in the area. Since in the judgment of the hospital staff Mrs. S could not manage alone in her apartment the psychiatrist was called in to "dispose of" Mrs. S; that is, vacate her bed. He administered the routine battery of commitment questions: Where are you? What is today's date? Who is the President? Mrs. S answered each question correctly, she even could tell the examiner the names of the last four presidents. As she was counting backwards by 7s the psychiatrist drew up the commitment papers. Later, when questioned about his action, he agreed that there were no obvious bases for psychiatric committment, but in order to vacate her bed he had cooperated by sending her off. "After all," he said, "shall we not say that this patient is merely wrapping herself in the cloak of sanity?"

Mrs. S went off to a psychiatric institution under protest and very much alone. But others who are not alone and are a problem to friends and/or family may get the compliance of the psychiatric staff in commitment proceedings. For example, we have in our files the case of a little boy sent off because he played hookey. His mother thought that commitment "would do him some good." Many persons do not understand the full implications of psychiatric commitment for themselves and for their loved ones and the problems that the mental illness label can lead to, as well as the difficulty involved in getting out of mental institutions.

Isolation as Punishment

Two less obvious, but nevertheless frequent responses to patients who have long-range discharge or placement problems (some terminally or chronically ill patients fall into this category) are physical punishment and/or isolation. These patients are either removed to a place where they are physically cut off from contact with others on the ward and/or given less and less support for their patient status role. Doctors stop making daily rounds to their bedsides; nurses spend little time with them; medications and meals are given to them last.

A 49-year-old terminally ill postlaryngotomy patient was slowly abandoned and isolated on the ward as it became apparent that he would be hospitalized indefinitely. Physicians' visits became infrequent. No progress notes were entered into his chart for months, and nurses scurried past his door, avoiding eye contact and paying little attention to his gestures to them. The nurses' aides soon became his only link with the rest of the hospital. His life dragged on for several months and then he died. This man was regarded as a hopeless case, and the additional disability involving loss of voice meant extra time and effort would have to made in order for him to communicate. The staff made the decision that he was not worth the effort. Although this case was extreme it was not atypical.

We have here an ethnography of current hospital practices in one community setting. But, more than that, some serious questions have been raised in two areas. First, there is the question of conflicting goals. Much political corruption was cleaned up by the state medical school take-over, but in our estimation the effect on the poor persons who have long depended on this institution for all forms of health care has been minimal. The goals of medical education meant that scarce resources were divided even more thinly as interesting teaching and research cases were sought out and emphasized. Additional resources. brought to the hospital tended to be poured into the second area of concern, professionalization.

Professionalization may not lead to salvation. A common theme of professionalism is the autonomy of the profession. Many. students, doctors and other professionals (such as the social service staff) spoke often about the joys of private practice and the kind of clients that they preferred. (Some medical students referred to the hospital as "the zoo.") As we see it, most people in the community want to get into the hospital for a variety of services and to be able to stay there until their lot is improved. The hospital staff wants efficiency in controlling the flow of patients in terms of its own internal needs. Both congeries of partisans have legitimate claims on the available resources. But legitimate claims (and illegitimate ones as well) may not be reconcilable under the conditions described above. Conventional wisdom about the necessity of professional upgrading and the clarification and rationalization of organizational goals may not bring those goals and interests into a hierarchy that serves the common good.

Two consequences of the medical college take-over have profoundly affected the stratification system of the hospital. The first is the addition of more American doctors to the medical staff. The second is the addition of more black administrators and other professionals to the paramedical staff.

While the hospital was under the aegis of the city, many foreign doctors were on the medical staff. The state medical school has replaced many of these doctors with their own faculty members and with medical students. One shibboleth that ought to be dispelled is that foreign doctors are less medically competent than American doctors. The problem with foreign doctors centered around language and cultural difference between them and their patients. Since medical diagnosis depends heavily on verbal communication, the dysfunctional consequences of the language barrier are easy to understand. Many doctors from other cultures, especially in the Third World, ascribe to a different value system about the parameters of medical treatment. In their homelands it may be considered frivolous for physicians to deal with social problems and minor maladies. In absolute terms, the conditions in the city served by the hospital we studied can hardly be compared to conditions in Calcutta. The character of medical staff, then, has changed, and there can be little doubt that the quality of medical care has improved. But from the point of view of the local community, the amount and kinds of medical services is a paramount issue.

Decentralization of health-care facilities and the development of satellite centers (especially for chronic care and other services unwanted by the medical college) may meet some of the needs of poor people. The danger here is that a two-class system of health-care delivery may be institutionalized as the teaching hospital gains more prestige and narrows its focus to highly specialized medicine while the satellite centers find themselves flooded out by the legions of the sick poor. The community will hardly be better off with the political pressure points moved but not relieved.

The blacks who have been added to the paramedical staff have been placed in a double bind. As blacks, many of these persons realize that they hold their present jobs because of community pressure following in the wake of extraordinary racial tension. They represent the hospital's black constituency. As professionals, they have an obligation to be professional, to apply some set of universal criteria to their work. One criterion of administration is to protect the organization within its own definition. For many blacks their hospital job represents upward mobility and a chance to assume power, to become the new professional elite. For some it represents an opportunity to cut short the process of adequate professional training.

While some of the new administrators and other medical paraprofessionals have succeeded in their quest to improve the lot of poor people whom the hospital serves, many have not. We have discovered three categories for those who have failed under the new regime: the ineffectual militants, the retreatists and the ritualists.

Ritualists and retreatists follow the patterns of response to organizational demands of just "doing their job." For whatever motives—mobility or lack of social concern— their behavior devolves into routinely stamping forms and staring out of windows or "going downtown" on working days. Immunity from the wrath of bureaucracy and/or the community is sometimes claimed and even achieved on the basis of their self-professed negritude.

Ineffectual militants adopt the rhetoric of revolution and justify their excesses in terms of "ripping off" the system by not taking care of business. This posture is often just an ideological defense for retreatism or withdrawal from effective strategies of social change. Wearing Afro hairdos and clutching copies of *Soul on Ice* under their arms, those who follow this pattern of response expend vast amounts of energy spouting the Crow Jim black racism of the new true believers. When confronted with the suggestion that they offer a paradigm for a better medical system for their brothers and sisters they answer with high-flown and often empty slogans. Meanwhile, people are sick and dying.

The category of black paraprofessionals who are really taking care of business are those who came into the hospital out of the community and worked themselves up through the ranks out of a genuine compassion for and grasp of the real needs of the poor people whom they wish to serve. These extraordinary paraprofessionals tend to continue their education (often at night) and offer themselves as advocates for people whose problems arise not from some textbook case but from real problems of living in an oppressive and racist social situation. They adapt and adjust their strategies to the problem at hand and are loath to "use" sick poor people for any other purpose than to make things better for the sick poor.

Part III
How Medical Institutions
Handle Chronicity

Chronic Illness

ANSELM L. STRAUSS

Smallpox, diphtheria, polio, measles—conquered through immunization. Tuberculosis, leprosy, plague, yellow fever, malaria—defeated or checked by sanitation, improved living conditions and effective treatment.

In the old days, people who died from diseases contracted them quickly, reached crisis shortly thereafter, and either died or pulled through. Modern medical researchers have changed this dramatic pattern by taming many once-devastating ailments. Improved conditions of living, along with effective medical skills and technology, have altered the nature of illness in scientifically advanced societies. While patients suffering from communicable diseases once filled most hospitals, treatment centers now serve mainly those afflicted with chronic ailments.

Many who would have died soon after contracting a disease now live and endure their affliction. Today most illnesses are chronic diseases—slow-acting, long-term killers that can be treated but not cured. A 1964 survey by the Department of Health, Education and Welfare indicates that about 40 percent of all Americans suffer from one or more chronic diseases; one out of every four so afflicted have lost some days at work because of disabling symptoms.

A large and growing body of medical literature presents detailed discussions of etiology, symptomatology, treatments and regimens. This outpouring of information, however, generally ignores a basic aspect of chronic illness—how to deal with such ailments in terms that are *social*—not simply medical. How can patients and professionals cope with health-related problems of family disruption, marital stress, role destruction and adjustment, stigmatization and even loss of body mobility?

Each chronic condition brings with it multiple problems of living. Among the most pressing are preventing and managing medical crises (that go even to death), managing regimens, controlling symptoms, organizing one's time efficiently, preventing or living with social isolation, adjusting to changes in the disease trajectory, and normalizing interaction and life, despite the disease. To handle those problems, people develop basic strategies which call for an organization of effort (including that of kinsmen, neighbors and health professionals). To establish and maintain this organization requires certain resources (financial, medical, familial and so forth), as well as interactional and social skills in order to make the necessary arrangements.

Medicine and the health professionals are very much included in this scheme but are neither at the scheme's focal point nor even constitute its primary elements. What is primary is simply the question of living: the difference between chronic sufferers and "normal people" merely being that the former must live with their diseases, their symptoms and often with their regimens. Medicine may contribute, but it is secondary to "carrying on."

Coping with Crises

Some chronic diseases carry a constant threat of grave medical crises. Diabetics may fall into insulin coma and die; epileptics can go into convulsions (which of themselves are not lethal) and be killed in a fall or a traffic accident. In order to prevent crises, minimize their effects, get the critically ill person into the hands of a physician or a hospital staff—and if need be actually save him—the person himself and possibly his kinsmen must be organized and prepared to handle all contingencies.

Relevant to the question of crises is how far they can go (to, or short of, death), how fast they appear, the clarity of advance warning signals to laymen or even to health professionals, the probability of recurrence, the predictability of their appearance, the complexity of the saving operations, and the speed and completeness of recovery from them.

The ability to read signs that portend a crisis is the first important step in managing chronic illness. Thus, diabetics or the parents of diabetic children learn how to recognize the signs of oncoming sugar shortage or insulin shock and what to do in case of actual crisis. Likewise, epileptics and sickle cell disease sufferers, if they are fortunate enough to have warning signs before their crises, learn to prepare themselves: if they are in public they get themselves to a place of safety and sit or lie down. Diabetics may carry instructions with them and may also carry those materials, like sugar or candy or insulin, which counteract the crisis; and epileptics may stuff handkerchiefs between their teeth just before convulsions.

When signs aren't properly read, are read too slowly or are interpreted as meaning something else, then people die or come close to dying. This may happen the first time a cardiac patient experiences severe chest pains and doesn't yet know their cause or treatment. (After the first sequence the patient may put his doctor's name close to the telephone for emergency use.) Even physicians may misread signs and so precipitate a crisis—even death. If an unconscious sickle cell anemia sufferer is brought bleeding to a hospital he may die if the natural immediate effort is made to stop his bleeding. Patients who carry instructions with them can sometimes avoid difficulties. Whenever an unconscious individual is brought into the emergency room of the nearest hospital, the physicians there understandably may treat him for the wrong disease. Inexperienced patients who are on kidney dialysis machinery may not realize that their machinery is working incorrectly and that their bodies are nearing crisis. The complexity of the human body can cause even experienced persons to misread important signs.

Any breakdown or disruption of the crisis-preventing or crisis-coping organization can be disastrous. Family strain can lead to the abandonment of or lessening control over regimens, and temporary absence of "protective agents" or of "control agents" (such as mothers of diabetic children who are prone to eat too much candy) can also be traumatic. A divorce or separation that leaves an assisting agent (a mother helping her cystic-fibrosis child with absolutely necessary exercises) alone, unrelieved with her task, can gradually or quickly lead to a crisis. (One divorced couple arranged matters so that the father relieved the mother on weekends and some evenings.) Even an agent's illness can lead to the relaxation of regimens or the elimination of activities that might otherwise prevent crisis.

There is also a post-crisis period, in relation to the organization of effort. Some failure of organization right in the hospital can be seen when the staff begins to pull away from a cardiac patient, recently saved from a heart attack, but now judged "less critical" than other patients. Back home, of course, some patients require plenty of family organization to prevent additional attacks. What is not so evident is that the patient and his family may read signs of improvement where few exist, or that contingencies may arise which render faulty the organization for crisis prevention and crisis management. Relevant variables here are the length and rapidity of recovery — since both of these may vary for different disease conditions.

During an extended period of crisis the family may need to make special arrangements about their time (for visiting the hospital, for nursing the patient at home) and their living space (having the bed downstairs rather than upstairs, living near the hospital during the peak of the crisis). They may have to juggle the family's finances or spell each other in nursing the patient during his crisis. Even the patient himself — in trying to get better rather than giving up — may have to contribute to the necessary organization of effort to bring the family through the crisis period.

Unless the physician is absolutely helpless in the face of a given chronic disease, he will suggest or command some kind of regimen. Adhering to regimens, though, is a very complex matter, for regimens can sometimes set problems so difficult that they may present more hardships than the symptoms themselves.

Patients do not adhere to regimens automatically. Those who accept and maintain a regimen must have abiding trust in the physician, evidence that the requirements work without producing distressing or frightening side-effects (or that the side-effects are outweighed by symptom relief or fear of the disease itself), and the guarantee that important daily activities, either of the patient or of people around him, can continue relatively uninterrupted.

In addition to the time it takes and the discomfort it causes, an important property of a given regimen is whether it is visible to other people, and what visibility may mean to the patient. If the regimen means that a stigmatized disease can be suspected or discovered, the person is unlikely to carry it out in public.

(Tuberculosis patients sometimes have this problem.) If the visible regimen is no more than slightly embarrassing or is fully explainable, then its visibility is much less likely to prevent its maintenance in public or private.

Another property is also important: if the regimen appears to work for the patient, then that *may* convince him that he should continue with it. But continuance is problematic, not only because the other properties noted above may counteract his best intentions or his good sense, but because once a regimen has brought symptom relief, the patient may forego the routine — no matter what the physician says. This is exactly what happens when tuberculosis patients see their symptoms disappear, and figure that now they can cut out — partially or totally — their uncomfortable regimen.

The very properties of the regimen, then, constitute contributing conditions for adhering, relaxing or even rejecting the prescribed activities. Thus, if the patient simply denies that he has the disease (as with tuberculosis, where many patients experience no symptoms), he may not carry out his regimen. Instructions for a treatment routine may leave him confused or baffled: cardiac patients told to "rest" or "find their own limits" can be frustrated because they don't really know what "sufficient rest" means.

Patients and kinsmen inevitably enter into negotiations with each other, and sometimes with the physician, over relaxing or otherwise changing (substituting one drug for another, one activity for another) the regimen. They are negotiating not only over such matters as the elimination of discomfort and side-effects, but also the possibility of making the management of ordinary life easier or even possible. Physicians, of course, recognize much of this bargaining, but they may not realize just how high the stakes can be for the patient and his family. If a doctor ignores those factors, his patients may go shopping for another physician or, at the least, he may quietly alter his regimen or substitute part of it with something recommended by an amateur — pharmacist, friend or relative.

Symptom Management

The control of symptoms is obviously linked with adherence to effective regimens. Like adherence to regimen, symptom control is not merely a matter of medical management. Most of the time, the patient is far from medical facilities, so he and his family must rely upon their own judgment, wisdom and ingenuity in controlling symptoms — quite aside from faithfully following the prescribed regimens. Some physicians — probably not many — recognize that need for judgment.

Whatever the sophisticated technical references may be, the person who has symptoms will be concerned primarily with whether he hurts, faints, trembles visibly, has had his mobility or his speech impaired, or is evidencing some kind of disfigurement. How much they interfere with his life and social relationships depends on whether they are permanent or temporary, predictable or unpredictable, publicly visible or invisible; also on their degree (as of pain), their meaning to bystanders (as of disfigurement), the nature of the regimen called for to control the symptom; and of course on the kinds of life-style and social relations which the sufferer has been accustomed to.

Even minor, occasional symptoms may lead to some changing of habits, and major symptoms may call for the redesigning or reshaping of important aspects of a patient's life-style. Thus, someone who begins to suffer from minor back pains is likely to learn to avoid certain kinds of chairs and even discover to his dismay that a favorite sitting position is precisely the one he must forego. Major adjustments could include moving to a one story house, buying clothes that cloak disfigurement, getting the boss to assign jobs that require less strength, using crutches or other aides to mobility. In one case a mailman suffering from colitis lived "on a leash," having arranged never to be very far from that necessary toilet. Emphysema patients learn to have "puffing stations" where they can recoup from lack of breath while looking like they have stopped normally.

Ideas for redesigning activities may come from others, too. A community nurse taught an emphysema patient how to rest while doing household chores; a sister taught a patient afflicted with brittle bones (because of a destructive drug) how to get up from the toilet, minus a back brace, without breaking bones in her back. Another woman figured out how her cardiac-arthritic grandfather could continue his beloved walks on his farm, by placing wooden stumps at short distances so that he could rest as he reached each one. Unfortunately, kinsmen and health professionals can function in just the opposite fashion: for instance, a woman with multiple sclerosis had carefully arranged her one-room apartment so that every object she needed was literally within arm's reach; but the public health nurse who visited her regarded the place as in a terrible shambles and proceeded to tidy things up herself.

Perhaps inventiveness, just as much as finances or material resources, is what makes the difference between reaching and not reaching some relatively satisfying redesign of life. The cancer patient with lessened energy who can ingeniously juggle her friends' visits and telephone calls can maintain a relatively unimpaired social life. Arthritic farm women who can get neighbors to bring in groceries can live on their farms during the summer although they must move to town for the winter months. One multiple sclerosis patient who is a student not only has rearranged her apartment but persuaded various people to help her manage despite her increasingly restricted mobility. A veritable army of people have come to her aid: the university architect redesigned certain of the public toilets for her wheelchair and also put in some ramps; the handy men around the university help her up and down stairs, by appointment; they also have rebuilt her cupboards so that she can reach them from her wheelchair; and so on.

Lack of imagination about useful redesigning makes symptom control harder. This lack of imaginative forethought can be seen in many homes for the elderly where stiff-jointed or low-energy people must struggle to rise from sitting positions on low sofas and chairs, or must painstakingly pick their way along highly polished corridors — minus handrails.

The reshaping of activities pertains also to the crucial issue of "interaction." A variety of judicious or clever maneuvers can keep one's symptoms as inobtrusive as possible. Sometimes the tactics are very simple: a college teacher with bronchitis, whose peak load of coughing up sputum is in the morning, arranges his teaching schedule so that he can stay at home, or at least in his office, until after lunchtime. Another person who tends continually to have a runny allergic nose always carries tissue in her hand when in public. Another with a tendency to cough carries cough drops with him — especially important when he attends concerts. An epileptic may have to persuade acquaintances that his epileptic fits are not communicable! Emphysema sufferers learn to sit down or lean against buildings in such a fashion that they are not mistaken for drunks or loiterers.

Agents of various kinds can also be useful — wives who scout out the terrain at a public meeting to find the least obtrusive spot, and then pass on the information to their husbands in wheelchairs or on crutches. Spouses may have prearranged signals to warn each other when a chronic symptom (for example, runny nose) starts appearing. In a more dramatic instance a couple was attending a party when the husband noticed his wife's temporarily slurred speech — a sign of her tiredness and pain from cancer. Since they did not want to have their friends know of her illness, he acted quickly to divert the others' attention and soon afterward manufactured an excuse so that they could leave the party.

When visible symptoms cannot easily be disguised, misleading explanations may be offered—fainting, for instance, is explained away by someone "in the know" as a temporary weakness due to flu or to some other reasonable cause. When a symptom cannot be minimized, then a wife may attempt to prepare others for the distressing sight or sound of her husband's affliction. The sufferer himself may do this, as when a cancer patient who had lost much weight warned friends, over the phone, that when they visited they would find her not looking like herself at all. Each friend who visits is very likely, in turn, to warn other friends what to expect.

Various chronic diseases lead to such disruption that they call for some temporal re-ordering. One all-too-familiar problem is too much time. It may only be temporary, as with persons who are waiting out a post-crisis period, but, for the disabled elderly or victims of multiple sclerosis, it may be a permanent condition. Among the consequences are boredom, decreased social skills, family strains, negative impact on identity and even physical deterioration.

Just as common is not enough time. Not only is time sopped up by regimens and by symptom control, but those who assist the patient may expend many hours on their particular tasks. Not to be totally engulfed, they in turn may need to get assistants (babysitters, housecleaners, cooks) or redistribute the family workload. Occasionally the regimens require so much time, or crises come so frequently (some sickle cell anemia sufferers have been hospitalized up to 100 times), that life simply gets organized around those events; there is not enough time for much of anything else. Even just handling one's symptoms or the consequences of having symptoms may require so much time that life is taken up mainly with handling them. Thus, a very serious dermatological condition forced one woman to spend hour after hour salving her skin; otherwise she would have suffered unbearably. Unfortunately, the people who suffer cannot leave their bodies. Kinsmen and other assisting agents, however, may abandon their charges out of desperation for what the temporal engulfment is doing to their own lives. Abandonment, here, may mean shifting the burdens to a nursing home or other custodial institution, such as a state mental institution.

The term "dying trajectory" means the course of dying as defined by various participants in it. Analogously, one can also think of the course of the chronic disease (downward in most instances). Like the dying trajectory, that course can be conceived as having two properties. First, it takes place over time: it has duration. Specific trajectories can vary greatly in duration. Some start earlier, some end later. Second, a trajectory has shape. It may plunge straight down; it may move slowly but steadily downward; it may vacillate slowly, moving slightly up and down before diving downward radically; it may move slowly down at first, then hit a long plateau, then plunge abruptly even to death. Neither the duration nor shape of a dying trajectory is a purely objective physiological property. Both are perceived properties; their dimensions depend on when the perceiver initially defines someone as diseased and on his expectations of how the disease course will proceed. (We can add further that dying trajectory consists merely of the last phases of some chronic disease trajectories.) Each type of disease (multiple sclerosis, diabetes and so forth) or subtype (different kinds of arthritis) may have a range of variation in trajectory, but they certainly tend to be patterned in accordance with duration and shape.

It would be much too simplistic to assert that specific trajectories determine what happens to a sense of identity; but certainly they do contribute, and quite possibly in *patterned* ways. Identity responses to a severe heart attack may be varied, but awareness that death can be but a moment away—every day—

probably cannot but have a different impact on identity than trajectories expected to result in slow death, or in leaving one a "vegetable" or perfectly alive but a hopeless cripple.

We have alluded to the loss of social contact, even extending to great social isolation, that may be a consequences of chronic disease and its management. This loss is understandable given the accompanying symptoms, crises, regimens and often difficult phasing of trajectories.

It is not difficult to trace some of the impact on social contact of varying symptoms, in accorance with their chief properties. The disfigurement associated with leprosy leads many to stay in leper colonies; they prefer the social ease and normal relationships that are possible there. Disease which are (or which the sufferer thinks are) stigmatizing are kept as secret as possible. But talking about his illness with friends who may understand can be comforting. Some may find new friends (even spouses) among fellow sufferers, especially through clinic visits or special clubs formed around the illness or disability (such as those formed by kidney failure victims and people who have had ileostomies). Some virtually make careers of doing voluntary work for those clubs or associations. People can also leave circles of friends whom they feel might now be unresponsive, frightened or critical and move to more sympathetic social terrain. An epileptic who has used a warning tactic and has moved to a supportive terrain says:

> I'm lucky, I still have friends. Most people who have epilepsy are put to the side. But I'm lucky that way. I tell them that I have epilepsy and that they shouldn't get scared if I fall out. I go to things at the church—it's the church people that are my friends. I just tell them and then it is okay. They just laugh about it and don't get upset.

Some people may chose to allow their diseases to advance rather than put up with their regiments. One cardiac patient, for instance, simply refused to give up his weekly evening playing cards with "the boys"—replete with smoking, beer drinking and late hours—despite his understanding that this could lead to further hear attacks. Another cardiac patient avoided coffee breaks at work because everyone smoked then. He stayed away from many social functions for the same reasons. He felt that people probably thought him "unsociable," but he was not able to think of any other way to stop himself from smoking. Perhaps the extreme escape from—not minimization or prevention of—social isolation was exhibited by one woman with kidney disease who chose to go off dialysis (she had no possibility of getting a transplant), opting for a speedy death because she saw an endless time ahead, dependence on others, inability to hold down a job, increasing social isolation and a purposeless life. Her physicians accepted her right to make this choice.

Those who cannot face physically altered friends may avoid or even abandon them. One individual who was losing weight because of cancer remarked bitterly that a colleague of his had ducked down the street, across campus, to avoid meeting him. Spouses who have known great intimacy together can draw apart because of an illness: a cardiac husband may fear having sex or may be afraid of dying but cannot tell his wife for fear of increasing *her* anxiety. The awkwardness that others feel about discussing death and fear of it isolates many chronically ill people from their friends—even from their spouses. During the last phases of a disease trajectory, an unbridgable gap may open up between previously intimate spouses.

Even aside from the question of death fears, friends may draw apart because the patient is physically isolated from the mainstream of life. One stroke patient who temporarily lost the ability to speak described what happened between himself and his friends: "I felt unguarded and my colleagues—who pretty soon found their conversation drying up in the lack of anything from me—felt bored, or at any rate I thought they were. My wife, who was usually present, saved the conversation from dying—she was never at loss for a word." A cardiac patient hospitalized away from his home town at first received numerous cards and telephone calls, but once his friends had reached across the distance they chose to leave him alone, doubtless for a variety of reasons. He and his wife began to feel slightly abandoned. Later, when he had returned to part-time work, he found that his fellow executives left him relatively alone at first, knowing that he was far from recuperated. Despite his conscious knowledge that his colleagues were trying to help, he still felt out of things.

Friends and relatives may withdraw from patients who are making excessive demands or who have undergone personality changes caused by a crisis or the progress of a disease. Abandonment may be the final result. Husbands desert, spouses separate and adult children place their elderly parents in nursing homes. In some kinds of chronic diseases, especially stigmatic (leprosy) or terribly demanding (mental illness), friends and relatives and even physicians advise the spouse or kinsmen quite literally to abandon the sick person: "It's time to put her in the hospital." "Think of the children." "Think of yourself—it makes no sense." "It's better for her, and you are only keeping her at home because of your own guilt." These are just some of the abandonment rationales that are offered, or which the person offers himself. Of course, the sick person, aware of having become virtually an intolerable burden, may offer those rationales also—though not necessarily alleviating his own sense of estrangement.

The chief business of a chronically ill person is not just to stay alive or to keep his symptoms under control, but to live as normally as possible despite his symptoms and his disease. In the case of chronically ill children, parents work very hard at creating some semblance of a normal life for their offspring. "Closed awareness" or secrecy is the ruling principle of family life. No one tells the child he is dying. Parents of children with leukemia, for example, have a very difficult time. For much of the time, the child actually may look quite well and live a normal life—but his parents have to work very hard at *acting* normal unless they can keep the impending death well at the back of their minds. The parents with children with longer life expectancies need not work so hard to maintain a normal atmosphere in their homes, except insofar as the child may rebel against aspects of a restrictive regimen which he feels makes *his* life abnormal. Some of the difficulties which chronic sufferers experience in maintaining normal interaction are reflected in the common complaint that blind and physically handicapped people make—that people assume they cannot walk and work like ordinary mortals, but rush up to help them do what they are quite as capable of doing as anyone else. The non-sick, especially strangers, tend to overemphasize the sick person's visible symptoms, so that they come to dominate the interaction. The sick person fights back by using various tactics to disavow his deviant status: he hides the intrusive symptom—covers it with clothes, puts the trembling hand under the table—or if it can't be hidden, then minimizes its impact by taking attention away from it—like a dying woman who has lost a great deal of weight but who forces visitors to ignore her condition by talking cheerfully and normally about their mutual interests.

Artful Striving

In setting guidelines for "acting normal" there is much room for disagreement between the ill person and those near to him about just how ill he is. The sick person may choose more invalidism than his condition really warrants. After a crisis or a peak period of symptoms, the sick person may find himself rushed by others—including his helping agents—who either misjudge his return to better health—or simply forget how sick he might still be since he does not show more obvious signs of his current condition. All patients who have partial-recovery trajectories necessarily run that hazard. ("Act sicker than you look or they will quickly forget you were so ill" was the advice given to one cardiac patient who was about to return to his executive job.)

The more frequent reverse phenomenon is when the sick person believes his condition is more normal than others believe. His friends and relatives tell him, "Take it easy, don't rush things." His physician warns him that he will harm himself, even kill himself, if he doesn't act in accordance with the facts of his case. But it sometimes happens that the person really has a very accurate notion of just how he feels. One man who had had a kidney transplant found himself having to prove to his fellow workers that he was not handicapped—doing extra work to demonstrate his normality. A slightly different case is the ill person who may know just how ill he is but wishes others to regard him as less ill and allow him to act accordingly. One dying man who was trying to live as normally as possible right down through his last days found himself rejecting those friends, however well intentioned, who regarded him as "dying now" rather than as "living fully to the end."

As the trajectory of the ill person's health continues downward, he may have to come to terms with a lessened degree of normality. We can see this very clearly with those who are slowly dying, when both they and their friends or kinsmen are quite willing to settle for "something less" at each phase of the downward trajectory, thankful at least for small things. It is precisely when the chronically ill cannot settle for lower levels of functioning that they opt out of this life. When their friends and relatives cannot settle for less, or have settled for as much as they can stand, then they too opt out of his life: by separation, divorce or abandonment. Those who are chronically ill from diseases like multiple sclerosis or other severe forms of neurological illness (or mental illness, for that matter) are likely to have to face this kind of abandonment by others. The chronically ill themselves, as well as many of their spouses, kinsmen and friends, are remarkably able to accommodate themselves to increasingly lower levels of normal interaction and style; they can do this either because of immense closeness to each other or because they are grateful even for what little life and relationship remains. They strive manfully—and artfully—to "keep things normal" at whatever level that has come to mean.

We must not forget, either, that symptoms and trajectories may stabilize for long periods of time, or in fact not change for the worst at all: then the persons so afflicted simply come to accept, on a long-term basis, whatever restrictions are placed on their lives. Like Franklin D. Roosevelt, they live perfectly normal (even super-normal!) lives in all respects except for whatever handicaps may derive from their symptoms or their medical regimens. To keep interaction normal, they need only develop the requisite skills to make others ignore or de-emphasize their disabilities.

Helping those afflicted with chronic diseases means far more than simply displaying compassion or having medical competence. Only through knowledge of and sensitivity to the *social* aspects of symptom control, regimen management, crisis prevention, handling dying and death itself, can one develop truly beneficial strategies and tactics for dealing with specific diseases and chronic illness in general.

The Public Hospital: Refuge for Damaged Humans

JULIUS A. ROTH

Hospitals are commonly thought of as temporary abodes, to be abandoned as soon as all prescribed diagnostic and treatment procedures have been completed. The hospital patient is expected to go back where he came from, to a life as close to "normal" as his condition allows.

But what if his "home" no longer exists? What if he has no friends or family to welcome his return and provide the aid he still needs? What if his family has lost interest in him or wants to be rid of him? What if his mental, physical, or financial states do not permit him to get along on his own in the kind of housing and social settings commonly available to single people in our cities? The patient may feel ready to leave but have no place to go.

What happens then? One possibility is that he may simply remain in the hospital—indefinitely.

There are many institutions that harbor such "patients." There are thousands of people who become permanent hos-

159

pital residents in this manner every year—even though their immediate mental or physical disabilities have been treated to the fullest extent possible. Thus many hospitals are not so much medical facilities as huge boarding homes for the damaged and derelict of our society.

My colleague, Elizabeth M. Eddy, and I were impressed by the extent of this problem during our two-year study of the rehabilitation program at a chronic care institution we will call Farewell Hospital. The program was, in effect, trying to rehabilitate patients for a life which most of them would never have the opportunity to lead. But this situation became evident only gradually, because it was not part of the stated purpose of the hospital administration nor the rehabilitation staff.

At the time we made our first few visits to the rehabilitation unit, a young patient we will call "Charlene Newcomb" was just going through the final stages of discharge from the hospital to her home. She moved around, pushing her own wheelchair with devices strapped on to aid her in the use of her arms and hands. Despite her serious handicap, she and the therapy staff were convinced that she could be an active mother and housewife, not simply a helpless invalid sitting around all day in her apartment.

Charlene Newcomb had come into the rehabilitation unit with such a badly broken body, including spinal cord damage at a high level, that it did not then seem likely she would ever regain the use of her extremities. The period of treatment and retraining was a long one. But the patient was anxious to cooperate and worked hard. She had something to work for. She had a place to go to, a husband who wanted her back, and a baby whom she had scarcely begun to rear before her accident. The effort was more successful than anyone would have predicted. She left the hospital able to sit up, move around in a wheelchair, and do many tasks for herself, her child, and her family household.

After hearing Charlene Newcomb's success story repeatedly throughout our first few months, we began to realize why this was such a notable event worthy of frequent retelling. A dramatic, clear-cut success is rare in this hospital unit. Patients like Charlene Newcomb are not discharged every month. They are not even discharged every year. The Newcomb case was such a gratifying experience for the dedicated rehabilitation staff members because it is the kind which does not happen very often.

People with any money or insurance usually stay out of the public hospital system, getting private treatment, and conserving their funds by spending much of their time at home while being treated and retrained. The public hospitals generally get poor people with no private physicians. The ones who stay in the public system for long treatment or custodial care are those without any interested family or friends; those whose families no longer want them back; or those whose families live in such cramped quarters, with such poor facilities for caring for a partly or completely dependent person, that the patient's return home would be a great burden. They are mostly elderly people past their working years. Some are dependent on welfare aid even before reaching Farewell Hospital, and almost all are by the time they leave—*if* they leave.

Half of the patients in the rehabilitation program are over 60 years old, despite a deliberate bias in favor of youth in selecting patients for this program. Sixty percent of the patients have an occupational background of semi-skilled or unskilled labor or no occupation at all; another 22 percent have "clerical and sales" background, but usually of a very low level. During our period of study, 51 percent of the males and 83 percent of the females were single, widowed, separated, divorced (to say nothing of the virtual-

ly separated status of some of those still officially married).
Thirty-five percent of all of these patients had no family
or interested friends at all at the time of hospitalization.
Fifteen percent had some family in the area, but the family
showed no interest whatever in their welfare. Another 15
percent initially had an interested family, but the family
lost interest during their period of hospitalization.

For Farewell Hospital as a whole, the picture is even
more drab. Eighty percent of all the patients are above 60
years of age. Many have severe chronic illnesses which are
not likely to improve, especially with the minimal medical
and nursing care which is given. In many cases, the family
and friends of these patients cannot even be traced or when
traced show no interest in offering them a home. Sixty-
three percent of all discharged from this hospital are deaths
—almost two-thirds of those admitted live out their lives
here.

There are a small number of patients who are injured
and disabled in "the prime of life"—the young adult para-
plegics and quadriplegics fall into this category. Here it
would seem that the rehabilitation program has its ideal. The
trouble is that almost all of these patients have been abandoned by their families, if they had one at the time they
were disabled. Therefore, there is nowhere to send them
when they have reached their "maximum" on the rehabilitation program. The rehabilitation process is truncated and
incomplete. The "rehab" unit ends up being a boarding
home for unwanted young men—a severe embarrassment to
a staff which prefers to think of its program as a temporary
stop-over for patients receiving therapy and retraining.

Even the physical disorders which the physicians and
therapists are expected to treat often become secondary.
Take, for example, the case of "Grant Whitfield," a hemiplegic who spent a few months on the rehab unit before be-

ing shunted off to one of the custodial units in the hospital. Whitfield had been in a general hospital for treatment of his condition and then had been placed on a home-care program. After a short time, his wife complained to the home-care service that she could not take care of her husband at home. She induced the home-care people to hospitalize him, which they did at Farewell Hospital. The staff at first had some hope of sending him back to his home when they were through with him. But after the social worker had talked to Whitfield's wife and read the home-care records, it became clear that the wife did not want him back. The wife saw this as a permanent solution to her "problem." At this point the rehabilitation staff threw up their hands, decided that there was no place for him to go in the community, and, after they had also decided that he was not receiving any benefit from their program, transferred him to a custodial unit.

Rather than say Whitfield is in Farewell Hospital because he is a hemiplegic, it might be more correct to say that he is in Farewell Hospital because his wife does not want him at home. Obviously, Farewell Hospital cannot accommodate all the men in the city whose wives do not want them at home. But if the man has a physical disability *and* his wife does not want him, he may very well end up in Farewell Hospital as a permanent resident. Thus the physical disability is often the excuse rather than the reason for hospitalization.

There are clear advantages in having an interested family or friends, especially those who can offer a home when one is ready to leave the hospital. In the cases of 18 patients whose families were continuously interested in their welfare, 11 were discharged from the hospital. In another group of six where the family had never shown any interest in the patient, not a single one was discharged from the hospital. In a group of eight whose families seemed to be initially interested, but then did not want the patient back home again, only two were discharged. (One of these was rescued by a niece after her son and daughter-in-law had abandoned her. The other was placed in a boarding home as a kind of experiment on the part of the staff after they gave up trying to get her back to her original home.) Of 18 patients who had no family connections whatever, only seven were discharged from the hospital and two of these simply went to similar institutional settings. With very few exceptions, in order to get out of Farewell Hospital without going into another institution, a patient must either be in good physical condition and able to fend for himself *or* he must have an interested family or friends who are willing to take him in.

Our society has many homes for unwanted people. In addition to custodial homes and hospitals like Farewell, we have numerous mental hospitals, institutions for the retarded, nursing homes, old-age homes, training schools for delinquents, and so on. The specific kind of institution a person "qualifies for" is often arbitrary. Many Farewell patients have sufficient signs of mental deterioration or behavior disturbance to qualify them for a mental hospital. A few of the patients we observed, in fact, had been dumped by their families in mental hospitals earlier; some of those now in Farewell will eventually end up in nursing homes, old-age homes, or mental hospitals to live out their lives. To the patient who is stuck in such an institution, it often makes little difference in which one he ends up, except that the facilities and personnel at one may be somewhat more tolerable than those of another.

Although institutions for the unwanted all do much the same thing, they have differing "excuses" for existence, and these excuses make *some* difference in how they operate.

The active philosophy of a physical rehabilitation unit is the rehabilitation of patients toward greater self-care and, if possible, return to the community and even to a job. Much emphasis is placed on physical independence—independence in feeding, dressing, grooming, toileting, locomotion. The cooperative and "motivated" patient is the best bet and receives most attention. In many mental hospitals there is also an active philosophy of promoting psychological normality—making the patients' behavior more acceptable to the norms of the larger society. Again, the staff tries to promote a form of independence—independence in handling one's daily affairs and being able to relate to others without unusual strain or repeated overt conflict. Again it is the "motivated" patient who gets the most attention. Nursing homes and old-age homes occasionally have programs designed to keep inmates active and interested in life. Prisons and training schools sometimes have programs designed to shift the prisoner's way of life to greater conformity with the law-abiding society—providing him with occupational and social skills to live in that society.

But these programs are diluted in a number of ways. For one thing, the inmate must be trained to life suited to the limitations of the institutional facilities and the convenience of the staff. Sometimes the institutional needs coincide with those of an active therapy or training program. For example, in increasing the patient's ability to care for himself, the training staff is not only increasing his chances of being discharged from the hospital, but also making him less bother. But often the two aims conflict. In mental hospitals, patients are trained for work to maintain the hospital, not for work outside the institution. At Farewell Hospital, wheelchairs are well adapted to life within a hospital, and the staff may allow patients to remain at this level.

Then, too, if the population is a large one, the active program is likely to involve only a small part of the population. Thus at Farewell, out of almost 2,000 beds, only 100 were devoted to an active rehabilitation program. Even of these patients, about one-third were not on an active program at any given time. Mental hospitals usually have only a few intensive treatment wards; the bulk of the institution is primarily for custodial care. In institutions for the mentally retarded, those defined as "educable" or "trainable" are often only a minority.

Even those selected for an active program spend only a very small part of their time receiving therapy or training. Mental patients on the therapy program commonly get only a few hours of psycho-therapy or group therapy each week and perhaps a few more hours of occupational therapy or recreational therapy. At one point on the Farewell rehabilitation unit we found that of 85 patients, only 50 were on an active physical therapy program, 11 in functional occupational therapy, and 7 in diversional occupational therapy, each averaging about one hour a day in gymnasium or shop.

Rehabilitation programs are also diluted by the long time it takes to accomplish anything. At Farewell, for example, active therapy is carried on only during regular working hours between 9:00 a.m. and 4:00 p.m. (3:00 p.m. during the summer). No program at all is conducted on weekends or on the many holidays. The patients we observed took from three to eight months (median four months) to obtain prosthetic legs after the legs had been ordered. From the time they finished training and the final adjustments on the legs had been made until the time they were discharged from the rehab program took from one to ten months (median four-and-a-half months). If they needed wheelchairs, they waited around for a month just to have the wheelchair ordered and for an average of five months before the wheelchair was delivered. When the staff decided to discharge a patient to the community, it took up to four-and-a-half months to process.

The chronic custodial institution, in comparison with a short-term treatment institution, seems like a study in slow motion. Even the staff of several years experience are often misled about the pace at which their program moves. Their predictions about when a patient will reach a given point in his program almost always fall short. "Transfer in two weeks" becomes three months. "Will get him in a furnished room in one month" turns out to take four months. "Will have information from his consultation next week" means information two months later. It is something the staff becomes accustomed to, and after a while they notice only the extreme cases—the wheelchairs that take eight months to deliver instead of the usual five months. It is something the patients also become accustomed to, but with much more bitterness.

Another characteristic common to such institutions is that they foster social and economic dependence. They strip the patient of all his assets and the possibility of earning any money. They try to make all his decisions for him and tend to block independent action whenever it is out of line with established practice and policy. Of course, individual staff members sometimes encourage independent action on the part of the inmates—for example, suggesting to a patient that he leave the hospital against the advice of the staff. But such efforts must be kept under cover. Social workers, who like to think of institutional inmates as their clients, often find themselves unable to help the inmate without subverting hospital or public agency policies and, thus, risking their own positions.

For a patient to survive with any possibility of independent action in such a situation, he must either be able to aggressively and skillfully coordinate his own program and fight for action on many aspects of that program, or he must have an independent agent working on his behalf—an agent who is independent of the entire institutional system in which he is an inmate. A few patients are able to act fairly effectively as their own agents. A few others have family members or friends who are willing and able to help —especially by offering an escape by providing a place to live. The majority, however, have no such agent and must accept whatever disposition is offered them. They may, for example, accept a foster home placement just to get out of the hospital, even though they consider such an arrangement grossly unsatisfactory and hope later to arrange something better. But in most cases, they are simply stuck in the hospital with no way of getting out.

A question we might raise is—how can an active therapy or rehabilitation program operate in such a setting where the bulk of the population are "poor candidates for rehab" who must be taken on the program because there are no better ones around. By the staff's own working definitions of success and failure, they fail in the majority of cases. Of 60 patients we followed closely through the rehab program at Farewell Hospital, 37 were clearly considered failures and another 9 showed very slight and dubious improvement. For the staff, rehabilitation is, statistically speaking, a program where failure is the norm, significant improvement and discharge from the hospital the exception, and dramatic success a rarity. In an institutional system which selects the deteriorated, the destitute, the unwanted, and then closes off opportunities for initiative on the part of the inmates, the outcome could scarcely be otherwise.

Staff members in other homes for the unwanted also experience failure in active therapy and retraining programs. That is one reason why mental hospitals, institutions for the retarded, homes for the aged, and training schools for the delinquent are often considered the backwaters of the health and welfare field, and the recruitment of competent personnel is difficult. They commonly have a goal of retraining inmates to a "society" which really doesn't want them.

Farewell Hospital has an enormous turnover among its professional staff, many of whom come there right after their formal training program to get a short period of "experience" before moving on to more agreeable and rewarding positions elsewhere. Those staff members who stay around for a number of years come to more or less accept the limited selection of patients, the delays, the institutional assaults upon the patients' initiative, and the fact that their rehabilitation program has little relationship to the larger institution where most patients end up feeling rejected and abandoned. It is not surprising, therefore, that most of the more experienced professional staff members turn their backs on the therapy program and spend as much time as possible building professional enclaves of research, administration, and teaching—activities which, in part, serve as an escape from a treatment program which offers little satisfaction and reward.

If we look at institutions for the unwanted from a traditional medical and administrative viewpoint, we can see certain changes that would be helpful. In Farewell Hospital, for example, there are some patients who can use specialized therapy and assistive appliances; and in a small number of cases, getting these may mean getting out of the hospital. Providing such services and appliances can certainly be made much more efficient; the periods of waiting can certainly be greatly reduced; the chances of overlooking patients who are in need of special services can be reduced; the financial burden on the patients can be lessened; and patients can be provided with much more information about their cases, so that they will have a better basis for participating in decisions about their own treatment and disposition, especially about placement in the community.

But even if such reforms are instituted, they would still not deal with some fundamental issues which face the staff. A central fact to be recognized about an institution such as Farewell Hospital is that it is not so much a hospital as a huge nursing home. Treating the institution as if it were primarily a hospital is an obstacle to thinking about how it may be best used to serve the inmates. The same thing may be said about other chronic and custodial institutions dominated by medically-oriented practices and medical personnel.

We must ask ourselves what we can do to make life most livable from the *inmates'* point of view. Perhaps the first thing the treatment or caretaking staff must do is to become completely aware of the kind of population they have and to consider what kind of "treatment" or "care" is appropriate. For example, is rehabilitation as traditionally conceived really helpful to most of these people, or is it forced on them like an ill-fitting suit? May the pursuit of physical relearning and independence and return to community life frequently lead the dedicated staff members to give the patient something he cannot use and does not want?

The only way to avoid the high rate of failure among rehabilitation programs in institutions such as Farewell Hospital is to develop different criteria of success. We might start by inquiring about the patient: What has this person come to, and what does he want to do with what is left of his life? The second part of this question is not easy to answer. You do not find out simply by asking the inmates —not even those who are verbally fluent (and many are not). But much may be accomplished by careful observation of the inmates. What seems to distress them, and what seems to satisfy them? Over a period of time, patterns of distress and satisfaction can be detected for an individual or even for groups. Such patterns may then point the way to future activity of the staff.

For many patients, the most important staff activities will be those which make them more comfortable and/or give them something enjoyable to do to occupy their time. In terms of professional specialties, this may mean, for example, that occupational therapy might put less emphasis on functional therapy to promote muscle strength and self-care skills and more emphasis on a greater variety of "diversionary activities." Group work, in organizing programs and activities, might make the patient's enjoyment the major criterion in selecting things to do rather than focusing on activities designed to promote social interaction. The ward staff might think less in terms of participating in a medical treatment program and more in terms of providing essential services for the patient's maintenance and comfort. Regarding this last point it is likely that nursing personnel, who are largely trained and committed to medical treatment, are probably not the best suited for such a task—except on units set aside for the treatment of acute illness, post-surgical care, and the like. Untrained persons hired specifically for the job of personal service to patients (including ward housekeeping) would probably satisfy the patients' wants more closely.

Given the choice, the patient might choose to spend most of his time sitting or lying around "doing nothing." Such an outcome would be difficult indeed for the ardent rehabilitation specialist to accept. A patient will never learn to care for himself this way and will have no chance of ever escaping some form of custody. Experts in physical medicine can also point out that lack of use leads to atrophy and, in extreme cases, to regressive changes in body chemistry. But we should keep in mind that smokers are much more subject to a number of fatal diseases than non-smokers and that gluttons have shorter life spans than those who adhere to a more abstemious diet. Yet in our society, we generally allow people a choice as to whether or not they want to take these risks. Can we allow the same choice to the aged and disabled, even when they are destitute public charges?

This is not to say that a hospital or a home for the unwanted should be run with no staff input or initiative. The staff can certainly offer inmates much valuable information and advice, and many kinds of treatment and activity. In fact, the more kinds of things the patients are offered, the more choices they will have in constructing the kinds of lives they want to lead. Thus, variety and diversity of stimuli for the patients might become a goal in itself, with patients being given the choice of whether or not they want to participate. Of course, variety and diversity are difficult to program, and that is precisely the reason they are not usually a feature of "total institutions." But again, this is a relative matter, and greater diversity in inmate living patterns could be deliberately stimulated by a staff willing to accept the chance that an inmate, given the opportunity, may make the "wrong" choice.

Worlds That Fail

DOROTHY H. MILLER

In the bonny halls of Bedlam,
Ere I was one-and-twenty,
I had bracelets strong, sweet whips ding-dong,
And prayer and fasting plenty
Now I do sing, "Any food, any feeding,
Feeding, drink or clothing?
Come dame, or maid, be not afraid,
Poor Tom will injure nothing."

                                    Anonymous Elizabethan poet

What happens to patients inside mental hospitals has changed greatly in the four centuries since Poor Tom sang his song. What happens to them outside has changed too, but not nearly as much—the labelling and stigma, the loss of livelihood, the feelings of isolation, worthlessness, bitterness, and depression. "Once a patient, always a patient," a released state mental patient told us. She was talking about the feelings of disgrace and hopelessness that follow them, like a long haunting shadow, often for the

173

rest of their lives.

During the past decade important and radical changes in the length of hospitalization for the mentally ill have taken place. Seldom is there confinement for life. The majority begin their "careers" as mental patients with a relatively short stay in the hospital followed by outpatient care and treatment. In California today, 85 percent of patients admitted to hospitals are released within six months. Half are discharged; the rest are put on "leave of absence," which means that they are supposed to receive outside care by psychiatrists and psychiatric workers.

The differences between the forms of release are more apparent than real. Both "discharged" and "on leave" patients return to the hospital at a high rate—36 to 40 percent. Releasing patients earlier means that many more are available to come back than before.

We have found, in our study of 1,405 California patients on leave of absence, that what allows a mental patient to stay out is not primarily the severity of his medical diagnosis and prognosis. It depends on whether he has been able to (or has been helped to) construct a social and psychological world that will support him and allow him to function adequately in the outside world.

In this article, therefore, we define a mental patient as Erving Goffman (*Asylums,* Anchor Books, 1961) does— not as a person suffering from the limitations imposed by a specific mental illness, recognized as such by society, but simply as someone who has been confined to a mental hospital. This is a definition that the patients understand well. It, rather than their medical diagnosis, is the dominant feature of how they regard themselves and the world outside regards them. Being a mental patient can become a kind of lifetime career—it gives one a role and a label and determines much of one's future. It starts, not with the psychiatric symptoms, but upon admission to the mental hospital. "Clinical experience supports the impression that many people define mental illness as 'that condition for which a person is treated in a mental hospital.' . . . until they go almost anything they do is normal." (Elaine and John Cumming, *Closed Ranks,* Harvard University Press, 1957.) They believe also, and with some justice, that it was circumstances as much as mental disturbance that put them in the hospital (lack of money, proximity to a mental hospital, a relative who wanted to be rid of them, and so on). And such circumstances—or lack of the support they need—may also bring them back.

We started with some basic assumptions, resulting from long-term observations:

■ Being in a mental hospital apparently results in the destruction or radical alteration of a person's self-definition and the creation of another.

■ This change in the self is real—that is, real consequences flow from it.

When a person is released, how can he re-structure the definition of himself as a mental patient and alter the consequences, in order to adjust successfully to life outside? What does he need to stay out of a mental institution?

Let us examine some of the characteristics of the 1,045 patients.

They were state mental hospital patients, placed on leave of absence with the Oakland Bureau of Social Work from California state hospitals in 1956. (Between 80 and 85 percent of the mentally ill are cared for in state or federal institutions.) In general, they had not come voluntarily—they had been "committed" by the family or the community, and so started out with a legacy of despair and feelings of betrayal. They had not sought nor paid for their care while in the hospital. Most of them, after release, did not consider themselves "free." The "leave of absence" status seemed to them more like a parole, depending on good behavior and obedience to orders, rather than proof of recovery and discharge.

Looking backward, we found that some of the patients had histories of disturbance covering most of their lives. All cases were followed for at least five years (1956-61). Of the total sample, 71 percent had returned to the hospital at least once during those five years, and 24 percent had been rehospitalized an average of 4.4 times. About 85 percent stemmed originally from the poorest class and 65 percent had never finished high school. After release, only 26 percent were able to find any job; and 27 percent had to rely on public welfare for total support. Their chances for social and economic independence were not good.

In our country, man achieves most of his identity, and his apparent place in society, through two functions: family and work. He is a parent, spouse, child, or some combination; worker or merchant, employed or unemployed, laborer, white collar worker or housekeeper. The great majority of these ex-patients were on the fringes of both of these worlds. Few could find jobs available that amounted to anything, or support themselves; few were considered any longer to be important to their families.

In California, 85 percent of all adults are married; only 48 percent of these released patients were. The majority of them had only marginal or casual connections with their families —they were not heads of houses, nor did they have important roles in family affairs, maintenance, or support. In general they were on the fringes, dependent and "extra," often unwelcome guests in other people's homes. Before hospitalization about one-third of them had important family positions but these had been lost or reduced, so that a released patient was likely to dwell, not with a spouse, but with a parent; or not to stay with a relative, but to live alone. Generally, they were important to nobody.

Before admission to the hospital 13 percent were white collar workers; after release, only 4 percent could find white collar jobs at any level. Another 29 percent had been blue collar workers; only 12 percent found any employment after release. Altogether, only 16 percent could find any kind of full-time job, and another 16 percent found part-time or "sheltered" jobs.

Many lived alone. Typically, these stayed in skid row hotels and were on relief. Some, though adult, moved back with parents—who were very frequently aged and infirm, barely able to take care of themselves, subsisting mostly on state welfare and social security. Those who lived with other relatives generally found themselves becoming Cinderellas in other people's chimney corners.

Among those who were married, 69 percent were women. They each had, during the study, on the average, the care of two to three children apiece. Yet 40 percent of them were unable to care adequately for their homes or their families. Among released husbands, over half were unemployed and four out of five were serious drinkers; after release they often became the dependent and passive partners in the marriages. Fifty-five percent of all married ex-patients were having extreme marital troubles and conflict; and 30 percent of all children of ex-patients were in trouble with school or juvenile authorities.

In short, these mental patients lived in, or with, the kinds of families that make up the hard core of social case work—disrupted, problem-ridden, often apparently hopeless. Their mental and domestic troubles were inseparable, being so closely intertwined that cause and effect were seldom clear. Often their return to the mental hospital was just one more result of social and family disruption.

Psychiatrically, 60 percent had been diagnosed schizophrenic; 11 percent suffered from organic damage or had a central brain syndrome; 15 percent were depressive psychotics; 4 percent were retarded; and 6 percent had a variety of personality disorders or neuroses. At release, 18 percent were judged "chronic"—still suffering from mental illness and in continuing need of care. Nearly two-thirds were supposed to remain under some form of drug therapy, though many quit the drugs often against medical advice. After release, while in the community, 29 percent continued to have occasional benign hallucinations and delusions; another 21 percent suffered periods of serious depression; and 25 percent were arrested for drunkenness or other mildly antisocial behavior.

This recital of characteristics is sufficiently depressing to justify pessimism. Yet others managed to make their adjustment, and to live with a measure of success, and even contentment, outside. How did they do it? How did they differ from those who returned?

Everyone carries with him an interpretation of the world, based on his perceptions and interactions. His interpretation covers what the world seems to be telling him about himself, his glories and sins, how others judge him, and the bases on which to judge himself. We construct this world out of the materials we find, or which are supplied to us. Since the status of a mental patient is so derogatory, mental patients are especially vulnerable to the cues, treatment, and regard they receive or seem to receive from others.

What perceptions are necessary to the construction of a world in which a mental patient can feel he belongs and can function adequately?

We can get some insights from the work of Goffman on the creation of another kind of world—the con game. Goffman has pointed out that con men, in the "big con" games for high stakes, make a practice of deliberately and skill-fully supplying the elements for an illusory world. They lead their "marks" (victims) in its construction; when the marks are thoroughly convinced that this con world is the only real one, they can then be fleeced. It is a fake world, based on an interlocking web of carefully induced false impressions (such as fake bookie joints, complete with telegraph reports and phony bettors). But the fact that it is deliberately and analytically planned and constructed—and that it is convincing—indicates that any kind of believable world can be constructed.

Objection might be made that the mark creates much of his own con world because he so desperately wants to believe in it for status and profit that he ignores common caution. But even the induction of such a hopeful state of mind is an important part of world-building; and there is little doubt that ex-patients also desperately want to believe in a world, illogical or not, in which they have place and dignity. It should also be noted that, as Goffman points out, techniques involving deliberately induced perceptions, often false, are used all through a patient's hospital career. State patients are usually brought in by relatives or police-men who mislead them—often with the best intentions—in order to get them to come along peacefully. They are given interviews and examinations which seem casual and in-determinate, but which have been carefully arranged and are binding. Once admitted, procedures and regulations designed primarily for administrative or housekeeping pur-poses are often presented to them as therapy—and staff and equipment function as "shills" and "props" in order to reinforce these perceptions.

In important ways, all the world's a con: our perceptions are built up from the cues we receive from others; we try to affect their impressions by the cues we send out. Both released mental patients and the people who know them are unusually sensitive, defensive, and unsure of their abilities to control interactions between them. The con—the careful accumulation of favorable perceptions—is therefore unusually important to them.

Using Goffman's ideas in terms appropriate for post-hospital mental patients, we deduced that in order to make a successful outside adjustment, each patient would need to a considerable degree, *all* of the following elements:

—An adequate source of material support as well as a professional group to assure him that he is now well and capable of dealing adequately with his life and society (the "shills," and the "set-up").

—Someone close and important to him who supports this notion and helps convince him of its truth (the con man).

—A series of natural opportunities for spontaneous relationships with others.

—The ability to define a new situation as one where he has some control, in which he is "normal" and "ordinary."

By our hypothesis, if any element is missing, the patient will fail in some important dimension of civil life, and may soon return to the hospital.

We analyzed our cases in the light of these criteria.

■ MATERIAL AND PROFESSIONAL SUPPORT. We found that those patients with an adequate source of material and emotional support were more likely, by a significant margin, to remain out than those without. This also depended on the kind of support, and where it came from. Those patients able to remain out were generally self or spouse supported; those who had to depend on parents or welfare were much more likely to return. This was true even when there was marital tension.

Closely allied to financial independence, of course, is the patient's status in his household. To a large extent, husbands had a lower return rate than bachelors or wives; husbands more frequently hospitalized their wives than vice versa; sons had a lower return rate than daughters.

Of those who must, or prefer to, live alone, the employed or financially independent are far less apt to return.

The amount and quality of aftercare services available to the patient and his family did *not*, by themselves, determine likelihood of return. For example, those placed on medication, while on leave were more likely to return (this is probably due largely to the fact that medication is often part of a last ditch effort to keep the patient out).

We found that the 20 percent of the sample who received *no* aftercare services (resisted contacts with the psychiatric staff, left without a forwarding address, or were thought not to need aftercare) were able to stay out much more successfully. They were, we felt, more resistant to identification with the "patient" label than the others, and much better able to convince themselves, and others, that they were "well"—that they more properly fit in with that portion of humanity that does not belong in mental hospitals. In this they had both financial and moral support from their families and those professionals who agreed with them.

Does this mean that aftercare is of no value? Not at all. It means merely that something beyond psychiatric help, something more directly connected with world-building, was equally, or more, important. In that portion of the sample—28 percent—in which patient and spouse both believed in aftercare and cooperated with it, the patients stood a considerably better chance of remaining outside than when there was family disagreement.

In other words, support and consensus were important. If patient, spouse, and professional agreed that the patient needed aftercare—or that he was well enough to do without it—and supported him in this decision, then he was apt to make a successful adjustment. Where they did not, he failed.

■ THE SPOUSE. Patients able to go back into families as wives or husbands—that is, those who had husbands or wives willing to accept them back in those roles—were much more likely to remain in the community than those who came back to live with parents or relatives.

World-building seems to require support from someone close, a partner in life—in other words, usually a spouse. This is especially true if the patient is still so disturbed that he cannot rebuild his own world without help. If he must, like Cinderella, exist on the edge of someone else's family (or even in his own), reduced until he has little power or importance, then he will fail to construct (or reconstruct) his world outside the hospital walls. (At least inside the walls he had *some* sort of place and support.)

To drive the point home, we found a definite significant relationship between the positive feelings the spouse had for the returning patient and his chances of remaining out. The spouse's confidence that he could stay out, while helpful, was actually not as important as regard and support. Affection, apparently, is more therapeutic than optimism.

■ INITIAL DEFINITIONS AND SPONTANEITY. Goffman makes an important, but subtle, psychological point regarding the necessity of the appearance of "spontaneity" in world-building. One judges a world to be "really real" only if it seems spontaneous. Any suggestions of manipulation can be shattering to a carefully constructed world, raising immediately the old terrors, the feelings of persecution, isolation, and betrayal. For the ex-patient spontaneous acceptance as a "normal," "beloved," "respected" person is essential to world-building.

The second half of our study dealt with shattered worlds

—the patients who had returned to the hospital, who had failed to build worlds, or had destroyed them.

As noted, the great majority of our cases returned to the hospital one or more times during the five year follow-up period. Since we know that a sizeable number of those who did not return left the state, died, or returned to other hospitals or nursing homes, the percentage of mental patients who adjusted (or at least somehow escaped rehospitalization altogether) is undoubtedly less than our figures show.

It is, however, a very significant percentage. What are the special social and medical characteristics of these people that allowed them to adjust? Unfortunately, we do not have those data yet. However, these non-returning patients are being located and studied in order to isolate the factors that allowed them to function well enough to escape return.

It should also be noted that, though the majority did return one or more times, most were also re-released one or more times, so that about 77 percent of our sample are likely to be in the community now (though in and out of the hospital periodically).

We do not have enough direct information about what went "right" with the worlds of those who adjusted successfully to the outside; but we can speak with more authority about what went wrong with the worlds of those who returned—with the failures.

Their histories continually emphasized breakdown in communication—and even open rejection—not only between patient and family, but between patient and professionals (social workers). There were few spontaneous welcomes, little respect for the patient and his capabilities for recovery—and not even much simple trust. Breach of faith was common. For example, one-third of the patients did not even know that they were being rehospitalized—frequently the social worker and the spouse had arranged it privately, and "conned" the patient into unwitting co-operation.

We asked 249 consecutive returning patients why they were being rehospitalized. (They and their families were interviewed by William Dawson, psychiatric social worker, who saw them at the crucial point of re-entry.) Forty-two percent said they felt they had to return because of too much stress from families or the outside world. But their families did not agree. The families claimed that the fault lay with the patients themselves, in their mental trouble or antisocial behavior. In only 16 percent of cases did all three respondents (family, social worker, patient) agree on the reason for return. (In this study, the psychiatric social workers had average case loads of more than 78 patients apiece.)

Obviously no "real" world extended a "spontaneously" warm welcome to these homebound patients, or treated them as worthwhile and well. Neither intimates nor professionals gave the patient comfort. No commonly defined world could therefore be developed or maintained for any length of time.

According to Goffman, the initial definition of a situation, laying out the path for future development, is important to building the new world. But we found to a significant degree that the returned patients saw themselves as "well" much more frequently than their families or social workers, who generally considered them "the same," or criticized the hospital for releasing them "too soon." (It is as though the mark, brought into the fake bookie joint, eager to believe that he is important enough to be given secret information to beat the races, is told bluntly by the bookie's manner that all is a fraud, that he is a fool, that he will make no money, and will lose all he has.)

Almost all mental patients are eventually released, most within a fairly short time. Our findings, based on Goffman's model, indicate that what is needed to keep the great majority of them out are things so simple that most of us take them for granted: adequate livelihoods; indications from doctors, employers, and other professionals that they are well, competent, respected; a life partner to extend affection, share burdens, lend support; a consistent, structured, reassuring self-image and world. Yet our findings also show that most released patients do not have these things. Their outside careers are fragmented, marginal, depressing, disillusioning.

The community must offer these patients and their families much more to help them build the new worlds they require.

As Kathleen Jones describes it *(Lunacy, Law and Conscience)*, when the original Toms o' Bedlam were released and sent out into the world, each was given a horn to wear around his neck as a symbol of his need and entitlement to receive help, and as a practical means of attracting attention. His claim was legitimate and recognized; as he approached a farmhouse he would blow the horn, and the householders would often fill the horn with grain, bread, or other food.

We have came a long way. Today we turn the state mental patients back into the community without a horn, crust, or much hope, to forage as best they can in a world that most of them see as a strange and savage land.

A Hiding Place to Die

ELIZABETH MARKSON

Francis Bacon said, "Men fear death as children fear to go in the dark; and as that natural fear in children is increased with tales, so is the other." Much of this fear of death is valuable for survival, but it has also tended to obscure the actual conditions under which people die. Death has either been romanticized, the Victorian solution, or minimized, as in the United States today. The elaborate American funeral rituals described in Evelyn Waugh's *The Loved One* and Jessica Mitford's *The American Way of Death* are not contradictory evidence on this point, for the actual *act of dying* is shunned and much of the ceremony seems designed to deny that death has really occurred.

Few tales of death have been told by anyone, including social scientists, but the recent work of Barney G. Glaser and Anselm L. Strauss in *Awareness of Dying* and *Time for Dying* and other studies marks the opening of this

187

area of inquiry. The study reported on here supports the idea, first suggested by Glaser and Strauss, that the anathema of dying is not only a problem for lay people, but also for health professionals, and describes one way in which professionals attempt to avoid the dying. Their success in doing so, it appears, depends on the relative status of the dying person.

There is a norm, subscribed to by at least some professionals, that old people should be allowed to die at home, but in fact most people die in hospitals or other institutions. It is suggested here that though it is desirable to die at home, for it is more comfortable, such comfortable deaths are a privilege accorded only to higher status people. Put another way, the lower the status of the dying person, the less likely are those around him to want to participate in his death.

It is well known that older patients who enter state mental hospitals have an excessive death rate. It has been suggested that this is because they are already dying when they are sent there, the early signs of impending death having been mistaken for insanity. Data gathered in New York State reveal, moreover, that older people tend to have higher death rates in both the state mental hospitals and county infirmaries than they do in any other kind of psychiatric treatment facility. Even those older people who are being treated in general hospital emergency rooms are less likely to die within six months of treatment than are those entering state and county hospitals.

These findings tend to confirm the idea put forward by a number of students of death that the old are sent to lower status institutions, particularly mental hospitals, to die. The following study of deaths of the aged at a state mental hospital will postulate the processes by which both the laity and professionals make the decision to send patients to mental hospitals when they are not mentally ill, but are simply taking too long to die.

This study of whether those who send geriatric patients to state mental hospitals know of the excessive risk of death is founded on an examination of the medical records of 174 elderly patients who were admitted to Fairview State Hospital during an eight-month period in 1967. The hospital serves two boroughs of New York City and their suburbs and is located near a suburban community. During the period studied, the hospital admitted all patients who applied. The medical and nursing staff supported this open-door policy on the grounds that denial of admission to any geriatric patient would be a disservice to both the patient and the community.

The physical illnesses of the 174 patients detected at the post-admission physical examination (Table 1) make it clear that elderly people with a multiplicity of serious physical illnesses, primarily heart and circulatory diseases, either alone or in combination with other disorders, were being sent to the hospital. Indeed, 44 of the 174 (25 percent) died within 30 days of admission. Those patients with one or more severe physical illnesses included proportionately more of those who died within one month than of those who survived, and this difference is statistically significant.

The old people in this study were not only physically ill, but also grossly impaired. Less than half the group were able to walk without assistance. One quarter were described as "feeble," 11 percent were in wheelchairs and 19 percent were on stretchers, including 6 percent who were comatose. Those patients who were mobile were strikingly less likely to die than those who were feeble or worse on admission. Of the mobile group, only 9.1 percent had died within a month of admission; the figure for the incapacitated group was 38.9 percent.

While it seems evident that moribund patients were

TABLE 1: PHYSICAL DISEASES AND DEATHS

Diseases	All Admitted	All Dying Within Month	Dying of Detected Disease
Cancer, all types	7	4	3
Alone	2	1	0
With heart and/or circulatory diseases	3	3	3
With digestive and/or genitourinary diseases	2	0	0
With respiratory diseases	0	0	0
Heart and circulatory diseases, all types	85	24	17
Alone	58	13	7
With respiratory diseases	8	6	6
With digestive and/or genitourinary diseases	13	2	1
With respiratory and digestive or genitourinary diseases	6	3	3
Respiratory diseases	5	1	1
Alone	4	1	1
With digestive and/or genitourinary diseases	1	0	0
Digestive and/or genitourinary diseases alone	15	6	0
None of the above	62	9	0

The two major causes of death listed on death certificates were heart and circulatory disease and respiratory diseases. There is general agreement that such illnesses are often related.

The totals given for each broad disease type, with the exception of cancer, do not include everyone with that disease, since combinations are given. Thus, the table shows 88 patients with heart disease, 85 in that category plus 3 who also have cancer.

being sent to this hospital for the mentally ill, it is possible that these patients were referred to psychiatric care because their behavior mimicked mental illness, as suggested earlier. It might be expected that the dying would resemble at least a portion of those who have an organic brain syndrome but do not die, for both have symptoms of organic origin. To test this hypothesis, the reasons for referral recorded by Fairview's admitting psychiatrists were examined. Virtually all the complaints made about these patients by their families or others interested in having them committed concerned either senile behavior alone or in combination with such major psychiatric symptoms as delusions, hallucinations or depression, but this was equally true of those who died within a month and those who survived with one exception: the ten comatose patients who could not be examined by the psychiatrist. Six of the eight men and one of the two women in this group died shortly after admission.

In sum, it appears that no premonitory or prodromal

TABLE 2: PHYSICAL IMPAIRMENT AND DEATHS

Impairment	All Admitted	All Dying Within Months	
		N	%
None, walked without help	77	7	9.1
Feeble	43	12	27.9
In wheelchair	19	10	52.6
On stretcher	33	15	45.5
Not ascertained	2	0	—
All patients	174	44	25.3

The difference in death rates between patients on stretchers and those in wheelchairs is not statistically significant. It is possible that some patients who might otherwise have been on stretchers were propped up in wheelchairs for convenience in moving them.

TABLE 3: PRESSURE FOR ADMISSIONS AND DEATHS

Agents Referring Patients for Admission	All Admitted	All Dying Within Month	
		N	%
Male	69	24	34.8
Formal agents only	19	5	26.3
Informal agents	34	16	47.1
Family only	28	13	46.4
Family and/or community agents	6	3	50.0
Formal and informal agents	11	2	18.2
Agents unknown	5	1	20.0
Female	105	20	19.1
Formal agents only	18	4	22.2
Informal agents	70	13	18.6
Family only	58	10	17.2
Family and/or community agents	12	3	25.0
Formal and informal agents	17	3	17.7
Agents unknown	0	0	—
All patients	174	44	25.3

signs of death that could be distinguished from psychiatric symptoms were detected among this group of old people, even in psychiatric examination. This is particularly interesting in view of Morton Lieberman's findings that specific personality changes occur among old people several months prior to death. Lieberman was studying a nursing home population, however, which may have differed considerably from the group of elderly mental hospital patients studied here. Further, since our data are drawn from case reports, personality differences associated with either dying or psychosis may have been obscured by inadequate descriptions.

Psychiatric diagnosis at the hospital was apparently routine and cursory. Organic brain syndrome with psychosis was the designation given 114 patients in our study. In more than 88 percent of the cases, this diagnosis differed in either degree or kind from that made by the referring hospital. Follow-up data on patients who survived more than a month showed that more than one-third of those diagnosed at admission as suffering organic brain syndrome with psychosis were found to have had no symptoms whatsoever, or to have been only apathetic, with no impairment of memory or confusion. Thus, it might be said that prodromal signs of death were missed in these cursory examinations, perhaps because the examining psychiatrists were aware that psychiatric treatment for the aged was less important than providing a place to die. Granting these reservations, however, the present data suggest that most patients were known or thought to be dying when referred to Fairview.

What seems crucial is that little effort was made to distinguish between symptoms reflecting an acute physical condition as opposed to chronic disorders of aging.

Some psychiatric hospitals have geriatric treatment programs aimed at helping patients get the most out of life, but Fairview's programs were marked by a fatalism that suggests that old people are expected to do nothing more than die. No physical examinations prior to admission were required, although elsewhere in the state such examinations have been shown to reduce inappropriate admissions. In fact, at the time of the study, deaths of those admitted *as well as those refused admission* at a sister hospital with a stringent screening program were only half as great as those at Fairview. This suggests that those responsible for referring the elderly for psychiatric care had learned where to send their dying patients.

The Fairview program structured the patient's career as one of dying rather than of active physical or psychiatric treatment. While the post-admission physical examination is routinely performed, almost all geriatric patients are classified as being of "failing status because of age and general debility." This designation seems to be applied almost automatically. It certainly is not associated with the presence of physical illness, ability to walk or chronological age. The role of the physician on Fairview's geriatric wards appeared to be to regularize the patients' deaths by tacitly legitimating the actions of the referring hospital. Thus, the high death rate among old people admitted to the hospital is made to seem part of the "natural" process of dying.

The physical disabilities of those who died within a month of admission are so similar to those of the survivors that the mental disability of *most* of the old people admitted may reflect physical problems. In other words, the admission of *most* of the elderly people to Fairview was probably inappropriate; instead they should have been receiving medical treatment or terminal care for their physical disorders in a general hospital ward.

As for the argument that a sick, confused person is easily mistaken for a mentally ill person, it is significant that young patients are never sent to state hospitals in the moribund condition described above. Patients aged 35, on stretchers, in comas or with intravenous tubes running are unlikely to be found applying for admission to Fairview. Yet such patients exist and often display toxic confusions similar to those of the older patients. The older patient is selected for transfer to the state mental hospital because he is considered in hopeless condition by family and physicians, because of the extreme pressure for hospital beds and because he has compounded the low status of old age with illness, and often poverty. The evidence for these conclusions is reported below.

The pressure that ends with an elderly person being sent

to a state mental hospital seems to be begun by the family. Old people coming to Fairview were usually first defined as physically or mentally ill by their families or other community members, usually after a specific health crisis. The patient was either sent directly to the state hospital, or taken first to a medical hospital or nursing home for treatment, depending on available facilities and the attitudes of those in close contact with him.

Among the elderly sent to Fairview, the dying men are somewhat younger than women. The median age for men at death was 74.5; for women it was 78.7. This was not particularly surprising, given the greater life expectancy of women in general. What is surprising, however, is that men whose families have pressed for their admission are more likely to die within a month than men referred only by formal agents such as a nursing home or those referred both by their families and such formal agents. For elderly women, however, this does not seem to be true. There are two factors which may explain this difference. First, there is some reason to believe, from other work I've been doing, that elderly men consistently overrate their health and independence, while elderly women tend to underrate themselves—perhaps a last holding on to the remnants of an instrumental "fit," able-bodied role by the men; women, having greater expressive latitude, can legitimately complain more. Following this line of reasoning, elderly men would perhaps try to compensate and conceal their illness until it became very serious; women, on the other hand, would complain earlier. As soon as complaints become frequent, the family responds by sending the patient to a hospital; men, complaining later, would be in more risk of dying than the female early complainers.

A second factor is differences in family structure. Only

36 percent of the men in the study were still married, but 54 percent of the men who died were married. Women in the study were most likely to be widowed (61.9 percent) and of those who died, 55 percent were widows. Put differently, dying men are most likely to be admitted to Fairview when they become ill and are a burden to their wives who have themselves limited physical (or emotional) strength to deal with an old sick husband who requires nursing care or constant attention. Women, on the other hand, generally outlive their husbands and are most likely to be sent to mental hospitals when they present any kind of management problem, not just terminal illness, to children, other relatives or to an institution.

It has been observed that having one or more children tends to insulate old people against illness and relatively early death. It might also be expected that parenthood might protect the aged from commitment to a mental hospital for terminal care. This did not prove to be the case at Fairview. While 40 percent of the men and 30 percent of the women admitted had no living children, the likelihood of death within one month was the same for this group as for the group having one or more living children. Nor did the number of children living change the odds. This may mean that once a family has decided to send the patient to the hospital, their contact with him is reduced by distance. Or, the decision to send him to the hospital may result from previous difficulty in getting along with the patient, unusual family relationships or other situations reducing the basis for close ties with the old person. At any rate, in such situations the power the children might have had to postpone their aging parent's death is dissipated. The patient is already socially dead. Only his physical death is lacking.

Most patients did not arrive at Fairview from their own

homes, however. Five of six came there from other institutions, most often hospitals. A hospital that is being fully utilized is always in the process of an informal review of patients, seeking out those who can be sent home or referred elsewhere. Combined with this pressure is a feeling, shared by the general public, that general hospital beds are expensive while mental hospitals beds are cheap. Whatever the source of this reasoning, it does not apply to these patients. They are suffering serious, often terminal, illnesses; the care they need will cost the same in any setting that shares the same labor market.

Of the patients sent to Fairview from other hospitals, about half were referred by receiving hospitals, that is, general hospitals with psychiatric service designated as reception centers for the mentally ill. Receiving hospitals in New York City have been the traditional route into state mental hospitals. They are overcrowded and there is considerable pressure to make a quick disposition of patients without concern for the refinements of the individual patient's situation. This may be particularly true for the elderly, whose physical condition is often ignored when a disposition is made. For example, one elderly male patient in the study had been taken to a receiving hospital in the city by his daughter, who stated that he urinated in the hallway and that she "could no longer care for his needs." He was sent to Fairview on a stretcher from the receiving hospital, which had neither admitted nor even examined him. According to the admitting psychiatrist's report, the patient had bedsores, indicating that his problems were long-standing. The psychiatrist observed:

He did not indulge in any spontaneous acts. . . . The eyes were open and vision was intact as he blinked when fingers were brought close to his eyes. He showed fixed gazing and his eyes did not follow any moving object. . . . Patient showed no response to demands and showed no withdrawal from pain. . . . He retained food in his mouth and wet and soiled. He was mute and only made sounds in his throat.

Seventeen days after admission to Fairview, this patient died of bronchopneumonia. This not atypical case illustrates that many old people are sent away without adequate social and medical histories from receiving hospitals and in such impaired physical condition that it is difficult to determine whether or not they are mentally ill.

The remainder of the patients admitted to Fairview from hospitals have been in the medical wards of general hospitals. Like those from receiving hospitals, they often appear to have been sent to Fairview because they failed to respond to treatment or failed to die within a short period after being put on terminal care. For example, a 74-year-old man with an indwelling catheter was transferred from a medical ward to Fairview on a stretcher. The admitting psychiatrist reported:

He was transferred from . . . General Hospital on a health officer's certificate because of increasing obtundation (dullness). The patient was noted to be . . . breathing heavily and in some distress. . . . He was able to respond only to pain and contact with the patient was impossible.

This patient's physical examination after admission indicated merely that he was dehydrated. Five days after admission, he died of congestive heart failure and bronchopneumonia.

Geriatric patients with their numerous medical complaints and limited future are not the favored patients of general hospital personnel, as has been shown by Glaser and Strauss and others. There are, however, institutions like nursing homes specializing in the care of terminal patients. Only five women and five men in the group studied had been sent to Fairview from nursing homes. The cause, ordinarily, was some kind of disruptive behavior. One elderly man who died within a month of arriving at Fairview was admitted from a nursing home with lung cancer and malignant lesions of the brain and bones. While the nursing home had had no difficulty in giving him minimal physical care and controlling his pain, they became upset and turned to Fairview when he threatened to commit suicide. (Upon checking with an internal medical specialist, I was assured that his patient was *under-* medicated for pain—dosage limited to prevent addiction in a dying patient! Motive for suicide?)

Unlike the general hospital, the nursing home does not seem to be concerned with freeing beds occupied by old people. Nor does the threat of death seem to concern them, but rather deviance. They do not like any threat to orderly and routine dying. For example, nursing home patients who survived more than a month of Fairview often had been sent for similar reasons. One female paraplegic cancer patient had been referred because she had tried to set her bed on fire.

It seems obvious that this state hospital functions as a geriatric house of death to which the elderly are relegated because of the despair of their families and the pressure on general hospital beds. There seem to be three elements that establish the pattern of withdrawal of interest and abandonment of the aged to a state mental hospital. One of these is old age itself. The old are already socially dying through relinquishment of roles; as they have little future before them, their lives are considered to have little social worth. But being old in itself is not enough; most old people do not die in state mental hospitals.

The second element is the high probability of dying,

though this alone does not automatically lead to Fairview. Young patients who have terminal illnesses are more likely to be sent home for short periods of time and to return to die in the hospital.

The third element is low social status and lack of power. It has often been shown that the poor and powerless of any age are generally considered to have less moral worth than those with more money or those with access to the ear of those with money. The patients in this study were not only seriously ill and old, they were also from mostly working-class and lower-class backgrounds. Only five had had professional occupations and only 29 had a tenth grade or better education. When old age and relatively low socio-economic status are merged, the person is doubly worthless for he is neither productive nor does he have the reputation for past productivity. A combination of great age, powerlessness *and* terminal illness makes one despised by medical and lay people alike and, unless death comes on schedule, suggests transfer to a state mental hospital. Here the old are hidden away, or taken away, from all that is familiar to them and left to await death. Death here, as Rilke observed, is "factory-like, of course. Where production is so enormous, an individual death is not so nicely carried out, but then that doesn't matter. It is quantity that counts."

The general lack of concern for the way old, sick people die is clearly a disavowal of any right to a death in stable and comfortable surroundings where opportunities for physical, psychological and spiritual comfort are protected. To some extent this is changing. All mental hospitals in New York State, for instance, have recently introduced geriatric screening programs designed specifically to exclude those patients who are dying or whose physical condition is the prime reason for their referral. These screening programs have already enabled some geriatric services to become active psychiatric treatment centers rather than houses of death. But where the old, sick, powerless people who might have died at Fairview will die now remains unresolved.

FURTHER READING SUGGESTED BY THE AUTHOR:

The Dying Patient by Orville Brim, et al. (New York: Russell Sage Foundation, 1970) is a collection of articles on death in its social context, including when, why and where people die, how medical personnel and hospitals cope with death, and ethical, social, legal and economic questions relating to dying.

Awareness of Dying by Barney Glaser and Anselm Strauss (Chicago: Aldine, 1966) is a sensitive study of the process of dying and the ways in which information about impending death is controlled (and acquired) by hospital staff, family and the patient himself.

Pathology, Adversity, and Nursing

IRMA G. ZUCKERMANN

Discrepancies exist between contemporary definitions of social need and prescribed social service solutions. Public health nurses at work act neither completely on the basis of conformity to external organizational restraints, nor wholly on the basis of internalized professional constraints, but on the basis of selected aspects of their environment which take into account their own situational interests.

The Chronic Illness Program

Compared with other program categories, chronic illness is by far the largest area of service—and the least defined. Program goals and standards for the evaluation of nurses have not yet been developed. Combined with aging, chronic illness serves as a "dumping ground" for a miscellany of unspecified conditions which fail to fit under other program headings. Without legitimacy as a specialty in its own right, chronic illness receives scanty and peripheral attention.

The major dilemma for nursing in chronic illness is the matter of patient compliance. For the majority of public health nurses, satisfaction in work is experienced in relation to client progress or improvement. When illness trajectories take a decided downhill turn, and return to mainstream society through rehabilitation is no longer possible, public health nurses feel the need for substitute rewards. These rewards take the form of patient compliance or conformity to plan—token exchange for "wasted" professional effort.

Official policy emphasizes retention of patients within the community. This end is to be accomplished by disbursement of adequate financial and household help and professional monitoring for regular medical supervision; physical safety, and compliance with regimen (diet and medication). The out-of-focus character of these expectations serves to maximize individual discretion and voluntarism as guiding principles of practice.

Care: Barriers and Climate

Conditions prevalent within the health care system as a whole reinforce public health nurses' avoidance behavior in relation to the chronically ill. Nurses do relatively little case finding in chronic illness. Referrals through the usual channels are generally extreme cases—multiproblem, complex, and too advanced for professional intervention to make a difference. Patients, for example, who have successfully eluded the medical world all their lives suddenly find themselves trapped within because of serious illness. Arriving "too late," their lifelong dreads turn into self-fulfilling prophecies.

As "dirty-work" and low-yield investments, chronic illness cases are deployed somewhat selectively by supervising public health nurses. Older, more fragile, and marginal public health nurses seem to acquire an inordinate share. A heavier-than-usual load also serves as an initiation rite for new nurses expected to "prove their stuff." Nurses who, for any reason, volunteer to work with the aged and chronically ill become known as involuntary specialists, and are soon overloaded.

Perceptions, Time, Roles

While the prevailing values of the culture and the principle of triage inform public health nurses' selectivity in relation to client care, actual willingness to work with a client depends primarily on liking him or her. The collusive building of patient reputations through stigma and stereotyping operates among public health nurses as an informal screening mechanism which weeds out undesirables and writes off failures. It is not uncommon to blame the chronically ill victim for his or her circumstances. On the other hand, clients who are perceived as resenting or resisting public health nurse visits, accepting them only out of obligation, are also resented and covertly punished.

When asked directly about time pressures in relation to chronic illness, public health nurses formally deny any external constraints. Informal conversation, however, reveals enormous preoccupation with temporality and abbreviated time frames. Following the precedent set by the medical establishment, care is characteristically episodic and limited to crisis. When longer periods of time become necessary, patients are treated as though on probation. Foreshortened time perspectives and insistence on immediate results blinds public health nurses and renders them insensitive to slow, subtle change and to the ineffable and less perceptible aspects of their patients' lives.

The vulnerability and impotence which public health nurses experience in other aspects of work make it imperative to achieve restitution of power in the domain of nurse-client relations. The authority of medical expertise is often invoked for this purpose, sugar-coated though it is seductive friendliness. Defining the psychosocial aspects as out of bounds safeguards public health nurses' composure and control when these are seriously threatened.

The Quality of "Quality Care"

Professionally defined success in meeting medical objectives involves managing the patient in his environment in order to manage the disease process (through diet, doctors, and pills) within a reasonable period of time. Underlying this requirement is the widespread assumption that patients act as instruments toward goals, rather than acting on the meaning and salience of those goals. "Quality care," therefore, is defined in relation to nursing "inputs" and their eventual outcomes, rather than in terms relative to the patient's system of understanding. In this way the compelling realities of the lay world are easily brushed aside, and professional perspectives are imposed and maintained instead. The problems, experiences, and feelings of anguish which finally culminate in desperate daily refusals of service are as a consequence seldom heeded and never fathomed. Unlike the nurse's autonomy, the patient's is regarded as fearsome.

Ivan Illich has noted in *Tools for Conviviality* (1973) that "the imperialist ideology built into the perspective of professional training and practice cannot be overcome by ethical dedication to the public interest, because it is sincerely believed in as the only way to serve the public interest. Outsiders can no longer evaluate the work. The only legitimate spokesmen are the officially certified . . . . The professional knows the reality to which the patient ought to conform" and need not, as a consequence, help the patient discover or endow that reality with his own meanings and values.

Limits of Expertise

The gaps in public health nurses' knowledge of chronic illness nursing are equaled only by their relative disinterest, and the unavailability of educational resources and sanctioned learning time within their agencies. Patient assessments are flimsily superficial or focused on technical detail. Preoccupation with compliance obscures the understanding of particular illnesses, their overall course, and their phase specificity. Institutionalized short-sightedness precludes anticipatory guidance and the working through of impending crisis and loss in connection with inevitable downside trajectories. Nurses' noted preference for the dramatic serves to shift professional attention away from potential areas of intervention of most significance to the chronically ill themselves (including the prosaics of day-to-day functioning, the setting of realistic goals, the acquisition of new self-images, and the reconstruction of abandoned social worlds).

As Charlotte Bambino has noted in a 1969 dissertation, levels of interpersonal competence in nurse-client relations hold more in common with lay culture than professional expertise. "Support" is based less on empathy or understanding of behavioral dynamics than on technique or primitive, homespun response. A nurse who genuinely likes her patients (although this situation is less common with the chronically ill than with pregnant teenagers or young mothers) can more easily tune into feelings of low self-worth and motivate through her own behaviors.

The Careless Community

While official health department policy proclaims the value of community care, achieving it demands maximal interdisciplinary and interagency integration and cooperation. The loosely organized health and welfare systems can, however, barely provide for even the most rudimentary needs of the chronically ill at home.

Local physicians (who are notably poor) are indifferent to the follow-up of chronically ill patients and send neither for them nor for their records. After one or two visits, patients cease going and become lost in the shuffle. Public health nurses fear crossing the doctors and infrequently challenge their authority. Aligning themselves with that authority instead, they effectively decrease their own liability while, at the same time, increasing their accountability to, and dependence upon the physician, unwittingly bolstering his omnipotence.

Procuring equipment and financial and household help for patients proves to be time consuming and futile. Long intervals intervene between the filing and processing claims; workers quit or are transferred. Agencies keep no lists of homemakers or attendants, and by offering a minimum wage encourage substandard helpers who provide both minimum work and minimal caring. Territorial claims by domineering workers who have authority usurp the nurse's role in the decision making. For those patients who became demoralized in the process psychiatry offers little but tranquilizers.

Trained to pathology, but not to adversity, public health nurses show less tolerance than clients for lonely and squalid living and the risks which it entails. Cleanliness, physical safety, and the goodwill of complaining relatives or neighbors are held in greater esteem than the wishes of the client. Many public health nurses are inclined to see institutional placement as the only and "final" solution. Ironically, no obstacles to community cooperation are encountered in regard to this particular course of action. Psychiatry, medicine, the law, and significant others provide the necessary means. Statements like "the doctor wants her to go" expedite the transfer. Declarations that the patients are not of sound mind open the door, and the intentional cutting off of clients' access to sources of food, neighborly assistance, and money assuredly closes it.

For the nurse with informal knowledge of the community, other options are possible. Rather than save the community from the patient, or the patient from the community, she helps the patient discover the community and build new support instead.

Personal Imperatives

The disidentification of nurses with their chronically ill patients and/or their suffering has consequences for nurses as well as for clients. Gradual blunting and desensitization often occurs. For some public health nurses the need to turn personal tragedy into a joke may have cultural overtones. For others it becomes an everyday defense against helplessness, pain, and existential despair.

The compartmentalization of personal and professional life has other consequences as well. It increases nurses' reliance on instrumental, or "objective," knowledge, and deprives them of the rich resource potential inherent in their own "personal" knowledge (i.e., the distilled essence of their own experience) which, in the case of chronic illness, proves to be considerable.

Strategies and Benefits

Chronic illness public health nursing may be aptly described as a contest or game; its name is "Medical Care." The aim of the game is to move the patient along toward the goal (the doctor). It is a win-or-lose, all-or-nothing situation; the stakes for both players are high. The game must be played, however, according to the nurse's rules. Unbeknownst to the patient, the game is rigged. Most of the moves belong to the nurse. As a group, many (though not all) nurses are experienced players with well-developed strategies.

The immediate outcome of these strategies benefits public health nurses in many ways. Conflict within the system is avoided and job security is maintained. Alignment of perspectives with the institutionalized rationality of the day facilitates professional recognition and interprofessional communication and enhances the public image of nursing. The privatization and individualization of care, the reduction of liability and risk by unknowingly deferring major decision making to others, and the close monitoring of nurse-client interactions combine to give the impression of increased control over work. Finally, partial commitment to work protects nurses from occupational exploitation and safeguards their energies for personal, discretionary use.

Losses and Questions

What is not apparent are the losses experienced by nurses. A residual guilt and anger plagues those who trade client welfare for professional belonging. The belonging itself is achieved at the expense of independent and critical thought. The concepts and terms on which professional understandings are based are, in effect, dictated by others. Even in the matter of referrals, where the public health nurse herself is expert, she caters — often without knowing it — to the problem definitions of others. Unable to step beyond the accepted framework she surrenders symbolic control, and remains a veritable follower in situations she prefers to lead.

Meanwhile, her unworded questions remain. What is health? Whose health? Is "health care" health? What is health for? Does its value supersede all others? What is its real price? And must it be subordinate to professional control?

Group Dieting Rituals

NATALIE ALLON

"Lose those extra pounds!" "Get rid of unsightly flab!" "Remove those unwanted inches in just seven days!" Messages like these bombard us daily from newspapers, magazines, radio and television. Thin is in, fat is out. The ideal of thinness is commonly regarded as a good in itself, while overweight—any deviation from the "norm"—is considered a sin. Americans are obsessed with slimming down to the point that dieting is rapidly becoming the national pastime. And group dieting is one of the most popular of all methods.

Group dieting on a large-scale national basis is a relatively new phenomenon, only about ten years old. I studied one weight-losing organization in the northeast which sponsored about 100 weekly group meetings and reached over 3,000 "patients" a week. There were about 125 "healers" working for this organization, consisting of executives, group leaders, clerks and secretaries.

My basic role was that of participant observer—after experi-

211

menting with a variety of diets for 14 years I have somewhat of an inside viewpoint. I sat in on 90 group-diet meetings sponsored by an organization under the pseudonym of Trim-Down. Altogether I saw over 1,400 healers and patients—about 95 percent were women and 5 percent were men. In many meetings there were 20 to 40 members; many were wives and mothers between 25 and 55 years old. Most members were middle-class women of various ethnic and religious backgrounds. Many had between 20 and 45 pounds to lose—quite a few had lost at least 5 to 10 pounds on the Trim-Down diet and intended to lose more.

It has been estimated that at least 52 million Americans are calorie conscious. They express their devotion to the Ideal of Thinness in various ways, ranging from restriction of food intake, specialized foods and drugs and exercise to prayer, hypnosis, psychotherapy and health spas. Weight-losing groups offer an attractive alternative healing system for the "disease" or "sin" of overweight. Many dieters find comfort in submission to the external authority of the group. The group pressure in this case emphasizes not the final thinness-cure, but the process of healing-thinner. The morally good Trim-Downer is one who attempts to perfect a better and better body. To be such a supreme good, the final cure of a thin body must evolve from a fat body. The holiness is in the act of cleansing. To be a saint, one must start as a sinner.

Not coincidentally, these saints-in-the-making were good paying customers of this profit-making organization. Having arrived at thinness is not such a noble fait accompli, for the cured thin need no longer pay to be healed. Indeed, I noted a constant tension between the missionary fervor of commitment and conversion to group weight-losing and the profit-prestige orientation of recruiting more members.

Almost 75 percent of all Trim-Downers studied were involved in continual dieting cycling and recycling patterns throughout much of their lives. They were on a perpetual merry-go-round of reducing diets, and the Trim-Down cure was just another one of these reducing methods:

So this month it is Trim-Down. Last month I tried one of those exercise spas, and last year I went on a kick of magazine diets. I guess I am just hooked on dieting for life and I am always looking for the magical cure—the final end to my dieting mania when I will be thin forever. I am willing to give everyone a fair chance to cure me and make some money off me. I am very egalitarian. Some of the diets work for a while, and then they peter out. On some of them, like here, you get to meet a lot of interesting people. You just keep looking for the right medicine.

This sentiment is common to many Trim-Downers—many came to the groups at least in part to engage in sociability for its own sake. These dieters look for mutual support from others in the group, who understand them and know dieting doldrums from an inside viewpoint.

Many dieters tried Trim-Down because it was one of the cheapest cures they could find. Other methods, such as spas, were too costly in terms of money, time and energy. Some Trim-Downers had tried medical doctors and were sorely disappointed. Some alternated between the group and medical doctors. As they lost faith in one route, they recaptured faith in the other. Still others went to both simultaneously, feeling that everything and anything helps. Medical doctors presented physiological and nutritional know-how while group leader-healers provided emotional support.

Many Trim-Downers acknowledged their dependence upon individual healers, whether they were in the persons of medical doctors or Trim-Down leaders. Many said that they needed an authority figure to watch over them—they could not trust their own will power to heal themselves. "Depending on your own conscience never pays off—you need a policeman."

Other members stated that they enjoyed the Trim-Down route to thinness because the group was a close-knit, familial gemeinschaft. Trim-Downers did not have cold and aloof secondary relationships with each other, as did traditional medical healers with their patients. Many appeared to transpose their gossipy morning coffee sessions with the girls to the different time and place setting of the Trim-Down group.

Trim-Down healers were self-styled experts whose basic qualifications to lead weight-losing groups was the fact that they had been healed from their own fatness by the Trim-Down diet plan. Most Trim-Down healers offered one uniform diet plan to be followed by their patients, which was based upon an obesity clinic diet. Beside this diet, the quasi-religious service of group dieting was the primary method of operation of the Trim-Down healing system.

Trim-Downers made territorial processions inside the doors of the meetings as rites of entrance. This initiation rite might be viewed as a rite of separation from the healees' previous world, in which they were unclean and unhealed. Once a member had one foot in the door, she became "sacred" because she was on the road to becoming healed from her fatness. The group participation and weight loss which occurred inside the door can be seen as an initiation rite into the culturally-preferred thin American way of life. Participants sought out entrance-partners in this initial walk. Such entrance-partners exchanged pro-fessions of their goodness and con-fessions of their badness in regard to their healing progress.

The second processional march of the meeting took place as the Trim-Downers waited in line to offer their standardized and required alms to lecturers or clerks. As continuing members, they paid $2.00. The initial registration fee was $5.00. Those who missed meetings paid one dollar for each meeting missed, never to exceed the initial $5.00 fee. Trim-Downers thus made a monetary payment for their healing, but there was a noncontractual element to their healing contract.

The dieters appeared to speak with their bodies in pay-in lines. Some were embarrassed by their bodies and snuggled in their coats to hide. Others announced their mixed feelings about their bodies by throwing open their coats and exhibiting tightly fitting clothing. Many engaged in double conversations—eyes sizing up one another while chattering about the diet and social activities.

The third processional march occurred in weigh-in lines. The scale became the totemic representation of the Ideal of Thinness. Some seemed to pray in the presence of the scale. They cried out in joy or sorrow about their weight-losing progress; they stared straight in front of them in devout silence. In their moment of judgment some felt cleansed from their sins of cheating, while others felt exalted in their holiness of good eating. Indeed, Trim-Downers labelled themselves good or bad according to the scale's decree of a two and three digit number.

The Devil

Trim-Downers anthropomorphized the scale, calling it a "kind friend" or a "mean white monster." Many asked the scale to be "fair," "have a heart" or not be a "devil." As they begged the scale to be good to them, some disrobed toward a naked innocence. Shoes and heavy jewelry were taken off; sometimes woolen skirts and pants, slips and girdles were removed.

In a very concrete, quantitative manner, the scale made the final judgment of the degree to which each Trim-Downer was healed each week. The leader-healer read this absolute sentence to each patient. Pounds shed indicated that healing was taking place.

In the social chatter-time that followed, healees "responsively read" each other, verbally and visually. Ego and alter questioned and answered each other about their dieting efforts; they offered each other pep talks. Some seemed to pray with each other at this time as they asked the Ideal of Thinness to bestow Its omnipotent blessings on them. Many believed that thinness did mean beauty, happiness and health.

Believers discussed their faith in the Trim-Down diet creed. Some offered testimonies to the Ideal of Thinness as they lauded its miraculous healing powers. They asserted that since their conversion to the Trim-Down diet they were "born again," or were "really living" for the first time in their lives. Others offered choral refrains in agreement with the marvels of thinness and the Trim-Down diet.

In contrast, others challenged the Trim-Down creed—they did not like the food on the diet, or there was too much or too little food on the diet. Some devil's advocates even questioned the need to be healed from their fatness plight at all—perhaps the Thin Power advocates required healing from their "warped fetish." Nevertheless, all such Atheists, Agnostics and Believers often forgot their differences and indulged in sociable gossip for its own sake.

Next, lecturer-healers were on center stage for the "lecture-sermon." These healers exalted the Ideal of Thinness and the Trim-Down diet plan as the best means to reach the Ideal. Many lecturers told humorous and sad anecdotes about their own weight-losing careers. Some revealed how their lives had been saved by the Trim-Down healing method.

The Straight and Narrow

Other prophetic healers told of the horrors of fatness and the evil fortunes which befell those who resisted Trim-Down healing. They warned that members must not be tempted to stray from the straight and narrow of the diet and eat taboo foods. Some lecturers gave elaborate rationales for parts of the Trim-Down creed. They emphasized how and why the Trim-Down healing system was the best of all healing systems for over-weight, including pills, doctors, diets, exercising and other group methods. Lecturers got their points across through jest-ing, story telling and solemn admonitions.

The detailed and technical question-and-answer period fol-lowed the lecture-sermon. Member-healees and lecturer-healers seemed to engage in responsive readings with each other, with members doing most of the asking, and lecturers doing most of the answering. The ideology of thinness was stressed in the lecture; the question-and-answer period concentrated upon tactics — the "how to do it." There was an elaborate exchange of information about the kinds and amounts of food on the diet. Some clarified and elaborated upon the creed for others. Some affirmed and lauded the Trim-Down creed; others challenged it.

One specific healing procedure was articulated in each weekly meeting as the lecturer read the "recipe-scripture" passage. This presentation was similar to the reading of a sacred text — many listened devoutly to each and every word, carefully writing down and memorizing every last detail. Healees responded to the healer's prescriptions of the recipe-medicine as they became involved in an exigesis of the text. The dieters spent much time and energy on the particulars of ingredients of recipes which were seductive in their mouth-watering names. For example, there were Trim-Down recipes for lasagna, eggplant kebab, pink cloud chiffon pie and lemon custard. But healers and healees did not worship the recipe-scriptures as perfect. Wor-ship of the recipes per se would be idolatry — it was the Ideal of Thinness which was revered. The diet recipes were a significant medium through which this Ideal spoke to Trim-Downers by calling them to respond in faith and obedience.

Again, healees and healers responsively read each other verbally and visually as the healers announced their individual patient's weight losses and gains. With these public announcements of individual and group weight-loss averages, the worthiness of the Trim-Down healing method was confirmed. Most lecturers mumbled weight gains quickly — if they did not completely ignore them. They preferred to minimize the fact that the Trim-Down cure was not working for all. In terms of pounds shed in a total group, the Trim-Down healing method seemed quite effective.

As leader-healers read off weight losses and gains, they offered "individualized benedictions" to members as they wished them well on the diet. That is, they blessed them in their dieting efforts and wished that the members would approach nearer and nearer to the Ideal of Thinness in their bodies. Cheating sins were errors of the past, and holy dieting was the order of the day.

Physical Worship

In some meetings, Trim-Downers seemed to worship the Ideal of Thinness in a direct physical way when they exercised. The exercises seemed to show parallels with religious genuflections and more vigorous body movements, as well as with the recitation of Pater Nosters with rosary beads. During this period, Trim-Downers revered thinness with their bodies as well as with their words.

The meeting was finished. Trim-Downers then partook of their last processional march from inside to outside the door in their rite of exit. Lecturer-healers appeared to be coaches who offered short pep-talk farewell phrases, like "Bye, I'll see you back here next week with a good weight loss," or "You can do it — take it meal by meal."

"Exit-partner" healees wished each other good luck and

happy eating. They did not look over each other's bodies in bidding each other farewell as much as they did at other times during the meeting. Verbal good-byes seemed to symbolize the end of body-readings. Jackets or coats defended or protected many from further body perusals. These actions signified the end of the meeting, just as their verbal farewells did. Many looked each other straight in the eye when they said good-bye. They seemed to have arrived at a certain quality of honesty in tackling a common problem by the end of the meeting. There was a sense of unified sisterhood.

Some remained after the end of the meeting. Healers asked first timers to stay so that they could explain the diet in detail to them. Others lingered to seek out more verbal and visual encouragement from lecturer-healers and sister-healees. Some stayed to challenge the Trim-Down healing method or to question whether the cure from fatness was necessary or even legitimate.

For some, the end of the meeting meant that the time had come to practice the preachings of the Trim-Down healers. Others chose to reject the Religion of Thinness outside the context of the Trim-Down healing sessions—they were purely "Sunday worshippers."

"I have seen the way"

Many of the healees were profoundly affected by the Trim-Down experience. Some Believers had such strong faith that they would proselytize to any and all who would listen (and even some who would not). Sometimes these Believers interrupted others' conversations just to declare the goodness of the Ideal of Thinness and the Trim-Down healing system:

Excuse me, but what you are gossiping about can't be as important as what I must say. This diet has changed me into a different person—I don't hide in my shifts, and I have come out of my shell. I have got energy to do everything, and my husband is proud to show me off to his friends. The Trim-Down desserts are delicious. I must rant and rave as much as I can—I thank the heavenly stars that led me here. Just stick with it, and you will be 100 feet above the ground like I am.

Others were not as fanatical about airing their views but asked to speak. Still others seemed to believe in the Ideal of Thinness in spirit, but the flesh would just not follow.

The healers of the organization attempted to perpetuate a self-fulfilling prophecy—that the Trim-Down healee who lost weight was a better and happier person. Many Believers seemed to buy this party line. The major themes of the confessional, the testimonial and redemption for one's "sins of cheating" were integral parts of Believers routes to the Cure of Thinness. In confessing to others throughout the meeting, these Believers made known to others their past and present errors of their ways in terms of eating patterns. In the Believers' testimonials, they solemnly declared their belief in the goodness of thinness; they offered personal evidence in support of the Ideal of Thinness and the Trim-Down diet plan.

In their redemption, they sought out salvation from their eating sins through the atonement of the earthly representatives of the Ideal of Thinness, the group leader and the scale. In redeeming themselves they sought to compensate for their fatness and gain possession of thinness by paying money which acknowledged their state of sin. Believers evidenced such major themes throughout each Trim-Down meeting; my data have suggested that such orientations were also a microcosm of their attitudes toward eating and dieting shown outside of the group as well.

Healers are also proselytizers—but for a very different reason. Whatever else it may be, Trim-Down is a business; it is concerned with making a profit. Trim-Down healers here attempted to legitimize their brand of cure to the general public at large, beyond the healees reached in Trim-Down meetings. Executives and lecturers havs written articles and advertisements in newspapers and magazines which praise the benefits of thinness and the Trim-Down diet. Common slogans which open such advertisements include: "Tired of being loads of fun? Perhaps you are not at home with your large jolly self;" and "Inside every fat man is a thin man trying to get out."

The Trim-Down organization itself has also printed an abundance of fliers and leaflets which are full of autobiographical details of healers and healees and of the specifics of the Trim-Down cure. Such advertisements were distributed to food and dress stores by healers and healees, these latter being effective "walking advertisements."

Faith, Hope and Charity

Newspaper and magazine reporters wrote short articles about annual luncheons which were held for Trim-Downers. These luncheons stressed the philanthropic aspects of the Trim-Down organization; they were advertised in part as charity benefits, with much of the proceeds going to service organizations such as the Army Emergency Relief Fund and the Heart Association. The organization was advertised as extending itself beyond its own vested interests in order to help the needy—what more legitimate mission could it accomplish! It was a business concerned for the human welfare of the fat as well as of the poor and sick.

The organization has also tried to legitimize itself to the potential and actual dieting population at large. Italian, Chinese and American restaurants had menus which stamped certain dishes as "Trim-Down approved." Breads and low-calorie canned fruits in supermarkets were also labelled "Trim-Down approved." When there were public demonstrations of cooking and women's interests, Trim-Down staff

members operated a booth. The organization was always reaching out to sell its healing system.

One significant salespitch was the appearance of Trim-Down
healers and healees on a television talk show. Participants discussed their overweight problems and the diet. They received
telephone calls on the air from distraught overweight people.
Some demonstrated Trim-Down exercises; others ate Trim-
Down recipes. On the basis of this single television appearance
there were over 7,000 written communications to the Trim-
Down organization. Extra clerical staff was hired to deal with
the onslaught of mail. One healer remarked, "This was the
single most successful piece of publicity that we ever had."

Indeed, Trim-Down healers viewed their mass-media appearance as a legitimation of the Trim-Down cure. Some hoped
for an interview on a late night nation-wide television talk
show. Executive-healers asked nutritional experts to write
books with them. They advertised the Trim-Down cure at some
national group psychotherapy conferences. They were thrilled
to secure the services of a famous nutritional specialist as a
permanent medical consultant to the Trim-Down organization.

Blessed Be the Dieter

Healers tried to convince medical doctors and religious leaders to publicly endorse the Trim-Down cure. Often clergymen
made the best sponsors — they wanted to help people as well as
make money. These sponsors could make a few hundred dollars
a month with little effort by offering time and space for the
group dieting meetings. One priest even went so far as to bless
the Trim-Downers before their meeting in his church. This
priest also announced individuals' weight losses at masses.

Many healers agreed that one of the most important ways to
legitimize the Trim-Down diet plan was to prove that it was
the best of all reducing methods. This proof came in the form

of verbal arguments to Trim-Down healees and outsiders as well. The Trim-Down cure was superior. Intensive exercising only increased your appetite, and you needed to do a lot of exercising to burn up a few calories. Fad diets could be tolerated for only a short time; the Trim-Down diet was a lifetime way of eating. Health spas were expensive, and most people gained back the weight which they lost at such places. Shots and medications had harmful physiological and psychological effects. Intensive psychiatric therapy only frustrated you and permitted you to wallow in your overeating.

When a healer affirmed the superiority of the Trim-Down diet method over other group methods, she needed to do more rationalizing and elaborating. The Pound-Shedders' brand was cheaper than the Trim-Down brand, and allowed for individual preferences in dieting—there was not one standardized diet. Some Trim-Down meetings were dull and boring, compared with the lively zest and fun which pervaded many Pound-Shedders' meetings. Nevertheless, Trim-Down healers did find ways to criticize Pound-Shedders:

We stress the positive approach. We offer help to you who are having a hard time. Pound-Shedders' lecturers use a negative approach; they scold their bad little girls who gain. The bad dieters are teased. It is a humiliating experience to be ridiculed. Pound-Shedders who gain a little weight are really degraded when they wear pig and hippopotamus signs. We don't whip you like little babies. Our diet is a plan for mature adults. The negative approach is demoralizing—it does not put you in a positive frame of mind to lose your weight.

Trim-Down healers had more difficulty in proving the greater legitimacy of the Trim-Down diet plan over the Anti-Fat Vigilantes' plan. The basic diet plans and group methods were much the same in the Anti-Fat Vigilantes' and the Trim-Down programs. And, the Anti-Fat Vigilantes' brand had some hard-to-beat legitimizing credentials—it was the original, oldest and largest international group-dieting program. This organization published a cookbook and monthly magazines. It had its own brands of frozen foods, ran its own restaurants and sponsored summer camps for overweight teenagers.

Impious Language

One Trim-Down healer criticized the Anti-Fat Vigilantes' healers for resorting to the language of drug and alcoholic addiction. They talked about "getting your weekly fix" at meetings and "getting high on diet foods." This Trim-Down healer insisted that overeating was not necessarily a compulsive addiction for everybody. And members who did have drug and alcoholic problems resented the use of such language in relation to their weight, since overweight people were not always "carboholics."

Another way to deflate the Anti-Fat Vigilantes' organization was to call it too impersonal and too commercialized because of its large size. "Our groups are smaller in size, and we have a more personal touch. We offer more individual attention than do Anti-Fat Vigilantes' lecturers." Another Trim-Down healer criticized the Anti-Fat Vigilantes' lecturers:

They treat their members like robots. They say "snap to" and expect their members to become automatic dieters at once. We allow for human error. We are more understanding of the complexities of the overweight problem than those Anti-Fat Vigilantes' promoters who have the simple-minded idea that everybody just sticks to a diet and loses weight. And we are more optimistic than they are. We talk about the pleasures of greater beauty, happiness and health as an inducement for weight reduction. Their lecturers frighten their members when they emphasize the dire consequences of a future of fatness.

Executive Trim-Down healers seemed convinced that Trim-Down healers would feel less threatened by Anti-Fat Vigilante power once the Trim-Down cure became more nationally known and respected. The sale of an increasing number of Trim-Down franchises throughout the country indicated that the Trim-Down cure was taking hold. The organization was beginning to legitimize itself more by publishing articles and books. The Trim-Down cure did have a long way to go before it became as commonly used a household word as was the Anti-Fat Vigilantes' organization. Yet the Trim-Down enterprise was still in the running for top legitimacy each day that it expanded itself and opened more groups and attracted more customer-patients.

Saintly Approval

Many Trim-Down healers felt that the true key to the legitimacy of the Trim-Down cure was its approval and endorsement by medical doctors. "The medical stamp of approval means a triple-A rating for us. If the doctors like us, we must be doing something right." In the contemporary American society, medical doctors often seem to be viewed as gods or saints—doctors are deified cultural heroes. Some Trim-Down healers were no different from others in believing that "a doctor's OK was one of the highest forms of praise available."

Many Trim-Down healers were proud to use the basic diet plan of many state obesity clinics as their fundamental "medicine." They felt safe about having a medical doctor as the nutritional consultant to the organization. They believed firmly in the first formal rule of the Trim-Down cure—that the doctor's advice must always take precedence.

It appears that Trim-Down as well as other group dieting healers are taking some curing business away from traditional Western medical doctors. Some doctors have enthusiastically supported the group healing systems and have urged family members and friends to go the groups: "It is a good way to get a lot of lonely, hysterical, chubby women off my back." Other doctors have not been so certain about the physiological and psychological benefits of the group dieting cure—they are "waiting for more evidence to come in." Other medical men seem cynical: "The groups don't do much good or harm—they are just gossip sessions for frustrated women. It is a sad fact that 80 percent or more of the people who lose weight gain it back fairly quickly." Some doctors appear hostile and defensive about Trim-Down types of healers. "They really don't know what they are doing or why they are doing it—they simply do not have the medical know-how."

Many Trim-Downers desired to achieve the goal which is so revered by doctors—"Doctors know best, and they say you are healthiest if you are thin." But many Trim-Downers also felt that it took a fatty or at the least an ex-fatty to know a fatty—the empathic understanding of overweight in the groups was more significant then all the doctors' pills for weight reduction. For some Trim-Downers, the significantly smaller fee for group dieting treatment than for doctors' prescriptions also made a difference.

That many medical doctors are personally and professionally dedicated to dieting and thinness is clear. It also seems certain that these self-help groups of dieters led by "lay" healers are here to stay as long as medical doctors continue to exalt the Ideal of Thinness.

There is however a Fat Power movement rebelling against this Ideal. Curiously, the movement seems to be recruiting a growing number of ex- as well as continuing group dieters. Some seem to want the best of both worlds. Perhaps they defensively feel that if they cannot make it in the world of the thins, the fats will welcome them with open arms. However, many Fat Power advocates have grown disillusioned with their desperate dieting attempts and have begun to question why fat people are denied their civil rights. The President's Council on Physical Fitness has declared war on fatness. Fat people habitually are subjected to ridicule, negative self-image, guilt feelings, discrimination in education and employment and exploitation by commercial interests. The Fat Power advocates do not want to get fat people to reduce, but want to change social values and institutions which persecute the fat. They do not say that all people must be fat, but that "Fat Can Be Beautiful."

Plump Power

A few doctors, especially psychiatrists, have begun to question whether thinness was such supreme goodness even before the Fat Power movement became as manifest as it is now. Hilde Bruch found that some overweight people were much more competent and creative in their daily tasks when they ate in their preferred patterns than when they forced themselves to diet. There seem to be an increasing number of doctors who are in sympathy with Plump Power, if not out-and-out Fat Power. Some have suggested that plumpness may be a help and not a hindrance to sexual activity. Dieting, rather than excess pounds, makes some people unhappy and neurotic. Fat victims of heart attacks who live tend to survive longer than thin heart attack victims. Fat people rarely get tuberculosis and rarely commit suicide. And on-again and off-again dieting may be more harmful to the body than staying at a somewhat elevated weight.

The Fat Power option seems to ask all people, including thins, fats and traditional medical doctors of whatever size, to be themselves and interact with each other as human beings, not based upon what the absolutistic scale decrees. "Lay" Fat Power sympathizers as well as some medical doctors are becoming increasingly aware that body style is intrinsically bound up with life style, and that weight reduction requires a total actor-environmental change which some people resist. Eating patterns are intrinsically bound up with styles of living; many people do not want to change their way of life.

It is important, however, not to substitute one arbitrary and autocratic ideal for another. The Ideal of Fatness should not wipe out and replace the Ideal of Thinness. Fat Power must open people's eyes to the legitimacy of multiple body styles in the society. Some might find satisfaction in group dieting. Others, however, might choose to reject weight reduction attempts and may resist Trim-Down healers or medical doctors trying to browbeat them down to a certain arbitrary body image.

You Are What You Eat

It seems appropriate here to include a quote from Llewellyn Louderback, the author of the recently published book titled *Fat Power: Whatever You Weigh is Right*.

We have been brainwashed into accepting the notion that obesity is esthetically displeasing and emotionally disreputable.

This does not mean that everyone should eat like gluttons and become as fat as possible . . . . There are some people . . . whose health demands a reduction in weight. There are others who, for various non-health reasons (jobs, social prestige, emotional well-being) are willing to accept a life-time of sacrifice in exchange for a socially acceptable figure. In cases where such diets are successful, it would be point-less—perhaps even dangerous—to end them . . . . The great majority of overweight adults who have dieted and failed—sometimes repeatedly, year after year—are doing themselves a distinct disservice by persevering. If these people are otherwise healthy, with normal blood pressure, low cholesterol readings, and no diabetic symptoms, they should stop making themselves miserable trying to attain some mythical weight ideal that is completely wrong for their body build.

Instead, they should maintain the weight at which they feel and function best—and the insurance companies' height-weight tables be damned. So long as they get a certain amount of daily exercise and continue to have regular medical checkups, there is no reason on earth (aside from blind prejudice) why these people should not be forty, sixty, or even more pounds over what our society considers ideal. The fat person's major problem is not his obesity but the view that society takes of it.

It is important that medical men and laymen alike not condemn people simply because of body style. Perhaps medical doctors and group-dieting healers should support such an acceptance of different body shapes and sizes. Perhaps more people would recognize the legitimacy of various sizes of body styles. The Fat Power option may restore balance and sanity to a thinness-crazed society.

Discharge Planning:
No Deposit, No Return

MARTIN HOCHBAUM AND FLORENCE GALKIN

In the last half dozen years, the operations of nursing homes have been examined thoroughly by legislative committees, investigative bodies, newspapers, university public policy centers, and others. In spite of all this activity, one aspect of the operations of nursing homes, their implementation of government-mandated discharge-planning policies, has received relatively little attention. This is so even though both the federal and state governments, in theory at least, have committed themselves to a discharge-planning program for nursing-home patients. On the national level, federal law requires that patient-care policies "effect awareness of, and provision for, meeting the total medical and psychological needs of patients including . . . discharge planning." Under New York law, operators are required to "maintain a discharge planning program" and "develop and document in the resident's medical record a multidisciplinary discharge plan for all residents; and review . . . the plan as indicated by change in the patient's . . . medical condition." What actually occurs is a compliance which fails to consider adequately the individual patient's potential for discharge. Once admitted to a nursing home, the patient has lost his options; he has arrived at his last residence.

Discharge planning is based on the assumption that each patient has needs and potentials which will be most effectively met by evaluating "the total person and not just his immediate medical needs," in the words of a report published by the Commission on Professional and Hospital Activities. Ideally, the process should begin at admission with an assessment of medical, nursing, social, and emotional needs. This should be followed by evaluation of the patient's rehabilitative potential and review of alternative care plans to meet his needs. Once this is completed, the patient's potential for discharge can be ascertained. Discharge planning is not, however, a one-time process. A patient's potential for discharge must be reevaluated periodically to reflect his current state, needs, and resources. For example, a newly admitted patient may have multiple medical and nursing needs which could be compounded by disorientation. This patient may only be eligible for discharge after months of rehabilitation. Recognizing this, the New York law mandates that the patient's discharge plan be reviewed and revised every 90 days "as indicated by change in" medical conditions or needs. This is obviously a time-consuming process. The discharge planner must gather information from a variety of sources to compile "a total picture of the patient's needs and his discharge potential," again in the words of the Commission on Professional and Hospital Activities report. For example, the discharge planner must be familiar with the availability and effectiveness of such community-based programs as visiting nurses, homemakers, home delivery of meals, public welfare, housing, and home visitation. He must also be able to overcome the pervasive fragmentation of services in these areas.

We concentrate here on discharges from health-related facilities (hrf) because patients in these institutions are better off physically and mentally than those in skilled nursing facilities (snf) and, therefore, stand a better chance of being discharged to their homes. Hrf patients, for Medicaid reimbursement purposes, must have scored between 60 and 180 on a New York State patient assessment scale; snf patients must have scored at least 180. In 1977, out of 17,126 patients discharged from hrfs in New York State, only 1,483 were discharged to their homes. When one discounts the 732 patients "discharged" by death, out of the 16,394 people discharged, only 1,483 (nine percent) were discharged to their homes. The others were discharged to hospitals and facilities offering other levels of care. The figures for 1978 are not very different. Out of 15,908 patients discharged from hrfs in New York, 1,296 were discharged to their homes. Again, discounting deaths, in this case 822, out of the 14,612 patients discharged, only 1,296 or nine percent were discharged home. Most of the others were discharged to hospitals and locations affording other levels of care.

In many cases, the problem begins with the admissions process itself. Most patients are admitted to nursing homes following discharge from a hospital. With hospitals under pressure to empty their beds to satisfy utilization review requirements, there is little opportunity to consider community-based, long-term care options. Moreover, even if there is interest in such alternatives, the chronic nature of the patient's condition often requires multidimensional treatment which the home-care system cannot adequately deliver. The patient is usually confronted with a host of fragmented services with diverse eligibility requirements, rather than a one-stop supermarket mechanism, to meet his varied needs. It frequently becomes simpler to arrange long-term care in a nursing home than in the community. Nursing homes therefore admit patients who lack the ability to live independently or to piece together, from an unorganized and fragmented home health-care system, a solution to their needs. Thus, even for patients who do not require institutionalization, the nursing home may represent the best solution for the individual with chronic conditions. Moreover, it frequently is, or appears to be, the only solution. Once the patient is institutionalized, there is a failure to implement an effective discharge-planning program. This results from a number of interrelated factors:

- Government financial benefits are greater for nursing-home care than for home health care.
- Nursing-home services are not rehabilitative, but aimed at maintaining the patient in the institution.
- Institutionalization is not viewed as part of a continuum of care, but as the end of care.
- Care, including pre-admission assessment, is based on a medical model which ignores alternative long-term care possibilities.

Obstacles to Discharge Planning

Under the present system of Medicaid supplemented by Medicare, the government covers most medical expenses incurred by an elderly indigent person. If the patient lives at home, government payments meet the greatest part of the cost of doctors, nurses, drugs, and certain other medical services. If the patient is placed in a nursing home, Medicaid covers not only all of these expenses but also the cost of lodging, meals, and custodial care normally borne by the patient or his family. This creates a powerful incentive to keep an aged or infirm person in an institution even though better care might be available elsewhere. This situation is compounded by the overwhelming percentage of patients who give up their homes or apartments upon admission to a nursing home. Those on Medicaid no longer possess the financial ability to move from a nursing home to a new apartment because this requires a substantial financial outlay. As Amitai Etzioni has noted, patients become "de facto prisoners of these institutions and of the state since they no longer have . . . the option of returning to the community, even if their health permits it."

Moreover, the Medicare program, which provides little nursing-home coverage, does not provide comprehensive home health-care benefits. Medicare concentrates on skilled services for the acutely ill, rather than on health-related or basic services for the chronically disabled. Personal care services are not covered. Thus, the limited home health care available under Medicare and the payment of all nursing-home costs for eligible patients through Medicaid create a powerful incentive for institutionalization. Once a person is institutionalized, the system of limited home health-care benefits plus the patient's poverty work to prevent his return to the community.

Many nursing-home patients require specialized rehabilitative services to restore them to their highest physical, psychological, and social functioning and thus bring them to a level of maximum independence. These services should enable them to function effectively within their limitations, prevent deformities, and retard deterioration. A wide variety of services can be provided to meet these goals. They include testing, motivating, and keeping patients physically, mentally, and socially active, as well as improving such functions as toileting, walking, and the use of prosthetic devices.

Three of the principal rehabilitative services for which some data are available are physical, occuptional, and speech therapy. According to a national HEW study—based on a review of patients' diagnoses, observed functional status, medical records, and discussion with staff, patients, and others—relatively few patients in skilled nursing facilities receive such services (many respondents in a survey of California's facilities suggested that they "did not have the professional staff to carry out active rehabilitation efforts"). The HEW study demonstrates that, in relation to need, only 11 percent of those requiring occupational and speech therapy and 31 percent of those requiring physical therapy actually receive it. Viewed from another perspective, 89 percent of those requiring occupational and speech therapy and close to 69 percent of those requiring physical therapy were in skilled nursing facilities where they did not receive these services. The HEW study also shows that few of those receiving physical therapy had written plans which were coordinated with rehabilitation programs and that accurate baseline data with which to judge progress is nonexistent.

Where rehabilitative services are available, they are frequently little more than efforts to comply with government regulations aimed at enabling the patient to function in the institution, not in the community. One witness before a congressional committee observed that while the New York State Hospital Code requires nursing homes to provide such services as occupational therapy, this frequently consists of nothing more than "a weekly visit by the occupational therapist, with little or no follow-up between visits." Further indications of this lack of interest are the New York State Moreland Act Commission's making only passing reference to this subject and Ronald Toseland's conclusion, in "Rehabilitation and Discharge: The Nursing Home Dilemma," that the process of rehabilitation in nursing homes is not focused. Even if a patient is potentially capable of discharge, the unavailability of effective rehabilitative services, which could facilitate return to the community, will lead to continued institutionalization. Without such programs aimed at restoring patients to their maximum potential, it is easy to understand why so few are discharged.

The placement of a patient in a nursing home is not viewed as part of a continuum of care which allows for, and encourages, movement back into less restrictive environments. Rather, it is viewed as an individual's final residence or movement into a more restrictive setting. His freedom of choice and right to service in the least restrictive setting are virtually ignored. This is not surprising, given the fact that perhaps as many as fifty percent of nursing-home patients are admitted from hospitals following acute episodes of a chronic condition. Nevertheless, this view makes it virtually impossible for any effective discharge planning to take place. Almost by definition, a patient can only be discharged by death or transfer to a hospital. The fact that so few patients return to the community reinforces this view and makes it a self-fulfilling prophecy.

Further reinforcement of the view of the facility as the last residence arises from the patient's inability to maintain a domicile in the community. This, plus the Medicaid poverty requirement, makes it difficult to find an acceptable community residence. Moreover, Title III of the Older Americans Act and Title XX of the Social Security Act have not yet achieved what the Federal Council on the Aging termed a "focus on long-term care which might make such services a major element in" its delivery.

According to the General Accounting Office (GAO), it is important to prepare an assessment which "identities the chronically impaired elderly's long-term care needs, and to match those needs to the most appropriate level of services." Such assessment must include an evaluation of the individual's potential to perform activities of daily living, his family preferences and lifestyles, his financial status and psychosocial factors. The study goes on to note that what usually occurs is a medical examination which "often cannot distinguish the impaired elderly who require nursing home placement from those who have the potential to remain in the community."

Nursing-home care is based on a medical model which is delivered in a scaled-down hospital. This is often the case in spite of the fact that nursing homes contain patients whose problems are chronic rather than acute, long-term rather than transient. Moreover, nursing homes lack the hospital manpower and technical machinery; their business is treatment, not diagnosis. Nevertheless, it is the medical model with its emphasis, according to Robert and Rosalie Kane, on "staffing standards, care plans, and audits of results" which prevails.

Quality care is jeopardized when the whole person is not considered. More significant for our purpose is that concentration on medical needs virtually ignores the possibility for effective discharge planning and precludes a return to the community. This is especially poignant since patients are often placed in long-term care facilities not because of medical problems but because alternative arrangements could not be worked out. Once institutionalized, the possibility of alternative arrangements that consider the patient's total needs are ignored and medical needs receive the most attention. Hence, it is precisely those factors which often precipitate institutionalization which receive the least attention.

Potentials for Discharge Planning

Many more nursing-home patients could be discharged to live in the community, in part because many patients are placed in institutions who do not belong there in the first place. One government analysis of studies concerned with appropriate placement of nursing-home patients concluded that two-fifths of residents of Intermediate Care Facilities (ICF) were receiving more care than their conditions warranted. Another analysis stated that up to one-fifth of the institutionalized could remain in the community if they received adequate services. As the GAO observed, "assessment mechanisms have not enabled Medicaid adequately to control avoidable institutionalization."

The failure to consider, and the limited nature of, community-based alternatives results in a nursing-home population which is similar to the population resident in the community. This has been documented in a number of studies. One author notes that individuals with the same characteristics as nursing-home patients continue to reside in the community. Another concludes that both nursing homes and community populations contained people whose impairments ranged from moderate to total. A third suggests that the medical conditions of elderly nursing-home patients are shared by many of the elderly in the community. Another estimates that with adequate community services, one-fifth of nursing-home patients could get by in the community.

The unnecessary institutionalization of people able to function in the community, and their retention in these institutions, ignores the many familiar reasons for their remaining in their own residences. These include their preference for doing so, avoiding the institutionalization syndrome, and, in some cases, financial savings. Older people, when confronted with the need for institutional versus home-based care, usually choose the latter. They do so to preserve their independence, dignity, and identity and because institutionalization is often viewed as a prelude to death.

People who are kept in institutions in spite of the fact that they could function in the community are deprived of an opportunity to obtain care in a setting which offers maximum reliance on individual potential and resources. They lack privacy and are insulated from the general society. Months of unnecessary institutionalization will frequently lead to the loss of the mental and physical will to handle one's own affairs. For some patients, the unnecessary reliance on others to care for them, unless caught in time, will lead to their premature dependence.

The unnecessary retention of some patients in nursing homes also leads to a waste of public funds. We are not discussing patients who will require twenty-four hours a day of paid supervision in the community. For them, home-based programs of care would probably not produce financial savings. However, for patients requiring more moderate attention—i.e., those for whom discharge is most likely—there would be financial savings. The potential savings are of two types. The first are those produced by avoiding the high cost of institutional care. According to the survey by the GAO, "in terms of public dollars, the cost of home-based long-term care is less than or comparable to the cost of the equivalent level of nursing home care." Another savings derives from the fact that hospitalized patients are often required to undergo long waiting periods of expensive hospital care before a nursing-home bed is available. By discharging increased numbers of patients from nursing homes, this waiting period would decrease and produce shorter stays and concomitant savings in public funds.

To those who are uncomfortable with increasing the discharge of patients to the community because of the fear of an increase in mortality, we would point out that the results of numerous studies on this subject appear to be contradictory. Relocated patients have been found to have mortality rates higher than, lower than, and the same as those who are not moved. Moreover, it is important to understand that we are not talking about a move from one institution to another, but from an institution back to the community. Such relocation is not proposed where there is a lack of community programs, including both formal and informal supports, to follow up with and serve the patients.

In numerous cases, because of massive, unalterable physical and psychological infirmities, the nursing home is the final resting place before the hospital and/or grave. In other cases, however, elderly residents who can function independently outside the nursing home are denied exit from the institutional setting. But because nursing homes see placement as permanent, their services are skewed toward continued institutionalization. In addition, government and institutional policies often hinder the discharge of elderly persons from long-term care facilities. This situation is incompatible with the implementation of meaningful state and national discharge-planning requirements.

Part IV
Chronic Illness and the
Technological Imperative

The Price of Medical Heroics

JEANNE GUILLEMIN

The middle ground between an analysis of hospital services based on the ethics of preserving human life and one based on cost-benefit analysis is seldom achieved. But as hospital care continues to make its contribution to the accelerated national rate of inflation, questions on the distribution of medical resources, especially on high-priced procedures for rare and critical conditions, become imperative. Can all the options for medical procedures now available be sustained by the American third-party payment system? Are some patients more deserving of treatment or more interesting for research than others? What should be the principles for the allocation of services that, by cost alone, account for a large proportion of medical expenditures but reach only a small percent of the population?

Newborn intensive care (n.i.c.) offers a rewarding case for analysis. Its mandate is to rescue critically ill newborns with rapid intervention and a heavy concentration of specialized therapies. Hospital nurseries are licensed at three different

243

levels of resources; the highest and most centralized of these, the Level III nursery, guarantees maximum long-term intravenous feeding, respirator support, and laboratory facilities, as well as skilled personnel and access to consulting specialists. As a referral system selecting high-risk cases, newborn intensive care costs nationally an estimated 1.6 billion dollars per year, on a par with renal disease treatment and coronary bypass surgery, and affecting about twenty thousand patients annually.

The specific efficacy of new regionalized intensive care units in lowering neonatal mortality rates has been demonstrated in several studies. The argument has also been made that the survival of a greater percentage of infants born at low birthweights is linked to the national increase in newborn intensive care services.

At the same time, the issue of high costs for newborn medical treatment has emerged as a problem. The Florida legislature recently allocated 17 million dollars for neonatal intensive care Medicaid coverage, a bit more than half the amount (30 million dollars) requested by hospitals and physicians. The much publicized result has been a cutback in referrals of infants who would otherwise have received treatment and the death of at least one such newborn. Private insurers of medical services are also beginning to scrutinize the costs of n.i.c. treatment as they weigh against outcome and to subject large individual bills to outside review.

High costs in the category newborn intensive care have several sources. A major one is the recent growth of this type of hospital. In her book *Technology in Hospitals: Medical Advances and Their Diffusion*, Louise Russell outlines the history of the expansion of general intensive care in the 1960s to its present differentiation by medical specialties in the 1970s. The newborn intensive care unit, like other units, has become one of the hallmarks of the modern hospital, to the extent that no centralized facility with a claim to quality service can afford to

be without one. The regionalization of perinatal services, especially in rapidly growing areas of the U.S. South and West, has
added impetus to the development of Level III nurseries as an
area-wide medical resource.

Another factor in the high cost of newborn intensive care
rests on the general tendency for pediatric services to be more
labor intensive than adult services and to rely on more costly
diagnostic and therapeutic techniques designed for adults and
adapted for children. An instance of this in newborn intensive
care is the streamlining of anesthesia, heart and brain surgery,
and renal dialysis to the requirements of the newborn size and
condition.

A third factor, what we call "the latent experiment," lies in
the new approach to the treatment of infants with very low
birthweights. As little as four years ago, the 1200-gram newborn was given a poor prognosis; today, most Level III units
routinely admit and treat infants at this birthweight. The
change in perspective came about as a result of several studies
on neonatal survival and morbidity that indicated good results
from intensive care for this category of patient. Following this
apparent breakthrough, physicians in newborn intensive care
units admit even smaller infants ranging deep into the group
known as "very-low-birthweight" (less than 1500 grams) for
whom outcome is uncertain and treatment costs are higher.
The medical expectation is that eventually neonatologists will
demonstrate their capacity to salvage newborns of 500 grams
or less.

This article will discuss how several systems—professional,
hospital, and social—intersect to generate increasing investment in newborn intensive care and at what junctures it is possible—and impossible—to exert control over costs.

At the end of 1978, with my colleague Lynda Lytle
Holmstrom, I began researching medical decisionmaking in
newborn intensive care, with the aim of discovering the social
context for this kind of hospital work. The main research site

was a regionalized Level III nursery in a large eastern city where, over the course of a year, we did participant observation, interviews, and medical-record coverage. For the last four months of that year a series of 103 admissions to the unit were followed on a daily basis until the latest date of patient discharge in April 1980. In addition, site visits, ranging in length from two days to a week, were conducted at 11 other Level III units in the United States, and visits were made to comparable centers in Europe (London, Amsterdam, Munster, West Berlin, and East Berlin) and South America (Brazil). Our research also included attending courses on transport and clinical work in newborn intensive care and what could be described as a general immersion in the language of neonatology (the pediatric subspecialty pertaining to the first twenty-eight days of life).

The main research site was distinctive in that it selected largely for premature infants and for some infants with multiple congenital anomalies, rather than for a wide range of critically ill newborns. *Spina bifida* babies, for example, were sent to a special neurosurgical unit, and Down's Syndrome infants to an intermediate-care division. In other Level III sites, the premature baby also accounted for nearly all admissions; prematurity was and is the accepted major pathology affecting newborns and is responsible for most deaths in this age category. In this article, low birthweight is used as a general indication of prematurity.

Three major research findings set the stage for a detailed presentation of cost data acquired at our principal site. The first is the paramount importance of specialists in determining case selection and the aggressiveness of intervention for the critically ill newborn. Underscoring this is the affirmative role of parents in supporting medical decisions. The second issue is the importance of institutional interests in competitively defining incentives for the expansion of services. Third, the types of patients recruited by the referral system (the major and minor pathologies and the degrees of severity of illness) need to be descriptively laid out as reflective of physician goals and treatment patterns. Our reference here is to the division commonly found in intensive care patients between the many whose needs are short-term and the few who remain in a critical state for months.

Newborn intensive care begins in the delivery room with the decision of an obstetrician that an infant in poor medical condition is viable enough for intervention. For example, an infant born at 900 grams might be "set aside," a medical euphemism for not using emergency resuscitation techniques and referral to intensive care; or, according to the physician's discretion, the order for intervention might be given.

Specialists and Parents

The working relationship between the obstetrician who refers and the pediatricians who run intensive care units is unique in that both have a vested interest in the event of childbirth, the former with an emphasis on maternal pathology and the latter with an emphasis on fetal and newborn pathology. Within the referral system which directs patients to the newborn intensive care unit (n.i.c.u.), the obstetrician is frequently a community hospital physician who works as a "front line" professional in relation to the neonatologists employed at the major medical center where the unit is located. The neonatologists have the authority of subspecialty knowledge and use it to communicate to obstetricians the standards of medical viability and the specific techniques for transport. Even if referrals are made within the major medical center, from the delivery room to an adjacent or closely affilliated intensive care unit, this knowledge differential obtains. Neonatologists have developed a reputation for a solid research base in biology and biochemistry and a studied familiarity with newborn pathologies to which no other medical specialty can lay claim. Obstetricians, on the other hand, have their own professional struggles as the lowest ranked but most frequently sued of the surgical specialties, working under great pressure to reduce the mortality and morbidity risk associated with reproduction. At present, the incentives for an obstetrician to refer even marginally viable cases to intensive care are enormous. Pressures from the Pro-life Movement have a way of materializing in criminal suits against physicians who do not take extreme measures to rescue critically ill newborns, even when they are medically classifiable as aborted fetuses; the Kenneth Edelin case in Massachusetts was a telling example and others have followed in its wake. In addition, in many states legal redress can later be sought on behalf of an infant damaged at birth by fault of the physician, often up to the age of majority and sometimes beyond. The best evidence an obstetrician has that he or she provided the best care for the newborn is referral to intensive care; the worse the condition of the infant, the more sagacious the decision to refer, given the present climate of legal and moral opinion.

Neonatologists, on their part, support the referral of tough cases, As the subspecialty revises the boundaries of newborn viability, moving from 2500 grams to 1200 grams and progressively downward in birthweight, obstetricians are encouraged to err on the side of optimism in judging viability.

Once an infant is admitted into a Level III intensive care unit, the incentives for aggressive intervention take on new dimensions. Specialists in neonatology are committed to what they construe as scientific-*cum*-clinical progress; that is, improving their capacity to cure the most difficult low birthweight cases. This kind of commitment is an integral part of the professional mission and even physicians not actively engaged in research and working in centers not affiliated with medical schools make clinical decisions in terms of this goal.

The technological means to this end are quite limited and essentially static in their development. The respirator has been fine-tuned for the needs of the very low birthweight infants; intravenous feeding has also been geared to small and fragile newborns. Side elaborations have emerged in antibiotics, phototherapy, and transfusions. The major elaborations over which neonatologists have control are in diagnosis rather than therapy. In many units critically ill infants receive three to five blood gas tests per day, several x-rays, and a weekly ultrasound. The septic work-up—a battery of tests to check for infection—is commonplace, along with tests for sodium, nitrogen, and sugar levels. The reason for all this investigatory activity is that many mysteries about fetal and neonatal physiology still puzzle the physicians who clinically confront the difficult patients they have recruited. The basic patterns of Respiratory Disease Syndrome (RDS), a major lung pathology of premature infants, are recognized by neonatologists, but apart from basic supports, not much can be done to alter the pattern. Other conditions, such as the degeneration of the bowel (necrotizing enterocolitis) and persistent fetal circulation after birth, have unknown etiologies and therefore trial-and-error solutions.

Other newborn problems, especially those related to prematurity, are susceptible to treatment not by neonatologists but by surgeons. Of all the pediatric physicians who consult in newborn intensive care units, cardiac surgeons and neurosurgeons have the most influence on treatment. Due to improvements in anesthesiology and surgical techniques for very small infants, some procedures have become routine for neonates in intensive care. A good example is the closure of the *patent ductus arteriosis* (PDA), a common heart condition in premature infants. Said one resident at a major center, "The PDA ligation is about as risky as putting on a bandaid." Other more risky but still feasible procedures, such as brain shunts and bowel resectioning, are performed with a frequency that varies greatly from one unit to another; but anywhere pediatric surgery is easily available and one or two surgeons are interested in

exploring a new population of patients, the chances are good
that the neonatologists will be persuaded of the benefits of this
kind of intervention. The higher status position of surgeons
over neonatologists within the hospital hierarchy aids in per-
suasion; the main deterrent is the reluctance of neonatologists
to let their patients pass, even temporarily, into the domain of
the surgeons. Even though surgery represents a more radical
intervention than most neonatologists prefer, the combination
of three elements — good results with some procedures, institutional hierarchy, and a shared belief in experimentation — leads
to a potentially high input from surgical specialists.

Newborn intensive care units are hospital areas of low visibility to the public, to use Eliot Freidson's term. Specialists
have been able to control the character of services without in-
trusion from the larger community. Occasionally, because the
Level III nursery serves the general public in a dramatic fashion, the media invades the unit, usually at the behest of the
hospital public relations office. Spot coverage of special programs to help mothers "bond" to their infants, of Christmas
parties for "graduates" of the n.i.c.u., or of miracle cases of
surviving very-low-birthweight infants communicates the
most positive aspects of the service to television, radio, and
newspaper audiences.

The only critical undercurrent in media coverage emerged in
the spring of 1981 when physicians in Illinois, Connecticut,
and Florida simultaneously came under fire for decisions not to
treat certain afflicted newborns, among them a set of Siamese
twins and a severe case of *spina bifida*. Despite one popular article about a case of prolonged heroic intervention that physicians should have stopped earlier, the general thrust of public
sentiment appears to be all-out intervention in every case, lest
the threat of "baby-killer" be leveled at physicians and parents
alike.

In our series of cases, no parents requested cessation of
treatment. To the contrary, several parents were able to com-

pel senior physicians to persevere with treatment after they had (accurately) given up hope of a cure. Ordinarily, parents were guided completely by physician advice on the extent and duration of treatment for critically ill newborns.

Service Expansion and Hospital Interests

The vested interest of hospitals in keeping n.i.c.u. beds full and in utilizing the full spectrum of technical resources is not different than for other in-patient services. Since most neonatologists are hospital employed or at least heavily reliant on the unit to do their work, professional and institutional interests are largely congruent: a steady stream of patients insures the continuity of the unit and the development of the subspecialty. The units we visited between 1978 and 1981 had, without exception, just expanded their bed capacity or were about to do so. Newborn intensive care units were uniformly represented as being a boon to hospital finances. Research grants, special private and public funds for children, emergency medical care allocations, and third-party payments have underwritten the venture with sufficient stability to warrant expansion. Federal guidelines recommend no fewer than fifteen beds per unit; the trend in rural and urban settings alike is for units three and four times this size, whether by affiliations among hospitals or with the building of new centers to compete with existing ones.

To a certain degree, the expansion of newborn intensive care mirrors that of renal dialysis. In the early days of pediatric exploration of therapies for the newborn, physicians selected patients with the potential for best outcome, given uncertainties about experimental techniques and infant physiology. The caution was justified; twenty-five or thirty years ago, for example, the unforeseen iatrogenic consequence of high levels of oxygen for premature infants was blindness. This same hesitancy was characteristic of physicians directing renal dialysis in the 1960s. Patients receiving dialysis were an idealized population, relatively young, at a productive time in their lives, and chosen for the maximum physical benefits they would receive for therapy. By 1979, the population had both increased and broadened in composition. The age span included more older and younger people, more people with complicating diseases, such as hypertension or alcoholism. Many more people from lower socioeconomic and minority groups were receiving renal dialysis. The difference was the mastery of therapeutic techniques, the build-up of institutional facilities, and, most important, the congressional passage in 1972 of the Social Security amendments for Medicare coverage of end-stage renal disease (ESRD) therapy.

Unlike ESRD, intensive care for newborns was never sufficiently extraordinary to compel legislative consideration; hospitals legitimized it as they did other intensive care services. Otherwise, the passage from the mastery of therapeutic techniques to an era of institutional expansion underwritten by federal, state, and private insurers parallels the growth of renal dialysis.

The numerical increase in patients is easier to calculate for renal dialysis than for newborn intensive care. Between 1972 and 1979, the ESRD patient population increased from around 6,000 to 48,000. In contrast, changes in numbers of newborn patients do not always reflect the expanded n.i.c.u. facilities. Designations of types of hospital beds and the unit levels themselves have shifted over the last twenty years. A regional facility could conceivably have lost intensive care beds in absolute numbers while moving from Level II to Level III status. A 1979 survey by the American Hospital Association, for example, showed a decline in number of units in the United States (448) and beds (6,252) from those recorded in 1975 (524 units and 6,602 beds). During this same period, the criteria for neonatal intensive care became more firm, leading to the exclusion of units that could not provide a high level of specialized care.

Adding to the difficulties of calculating present services and their costs is the phenomenon of mixed level units, the combination of Level III and Level II nurseries. In some units, different rooms are devoted to critically ill infants and to those in better condition. In other units, areas within a general space will be informally designated for infants who are "growing" as opposed to those who are being actively treated. The discretion with which unit directors designate bed levels within a unit is an important though elusive part of cost calculations. If an infant moves from the n.i.c.u. front room to the "growing" area, do per diem bed charges (which vary by as much as two hundred dollars) change or remain at the Level III rate? What are the benefits to the unit or the hospital in keeping the rate unchanged? What would be the incentives for adjusting the rate?

The institutional context of newborn intensive care lends it a complexity that goes far beyond the discretion of the unit director concerning bed-type use. There are a variety of ways in which a hospital administration, without reference to unit staffs, can manipulate charges within and among different services to maximize their revenues. One of these is cross-subsidization, the distribution of costs incurred by one patient group by increasing charges for other services. In studies done of reimbursement in newborn intensive care, cross-subsidies prove intimately related to differences between public and private insurance. P. Budetti *et al.* report in *The Cost Effectiveness of Neonatal Intensive Care* (Office of Technology Assessment):

> The major villain in cross-subsidization, as seen by many hospitals, is Medicaid since it reimburses costs rather than charges. It is difficult to identify which is the chicken and which is the egg in the cycle, however. Hospitals adjust charges to cover total expenses; Medicaid and other cost-payers then pay at the level of allowable costs; and hospitals raise charges even more to cover the difference.

The pattern that emerges is one in which Medicaid, accounting for some 15 to 20 percent of patients covered, pays a flat per diem fee significantly under hospital charges. In one study, 51 percent of n.i.c.u. uncollectable bills or write-offs (11 percent of all bills) were attributable to infants on Medicaid. Private insurers, on the other hand, take up the slack by paying more than the average cost per patient.

In their study of n.i.c.u. costs and charges, S.L. Kaufman and D.S. Shepard add another variable to cross-subsidization: length of stay. Blue Cross and charge-payer reimbursements were highest during the first weeks of treatment, in accordance with the initial push for diagnostic information and heroic intervention, and decreased significantly through the fourth week. Medicaid per diem reimbursement steadily reimbursed below costs through the eighth week of hospitalization.

This duality in reimbursement fairly demands cross-subsidization but, more important, if fails to address physician selection for difficult cases and its consequences in a future of declining Medicaid support. Even without the Medicaid shortfall, recruitment of experimental cases forces an increase in hospital charges or other strategies to cover costs: recruiting more healthy, low-cost patients; unnecessarily prolonging stays in hospitals; or juggling budget items. Before we can trace the strain that specialists' goals exert on the hospital economy and insurance coverage, a few empirical facts about case distribution, finances, and outcome need to be presented in detail.

Trends in Care

The kinds of cases admitted to newborn intensive care tend to be skewed between many who are in and out of the unit very quickly and a few whose stays are long and for whom treatment costs are high. At the main unit we studied, 64 percent of infants admitted in 1979 (a total of 342) were discharged in less than a week. Of all mortalities for the year, 75 percent (44) occurred during this same period. In this category, 14 of the infants who died weighed 1200 grams or less and 19 were between 1201 and 2500 grams. Most infants (84 percent) admitted in 1979 had lengths of stay of less than three weeks. A handful, only 10 percent of the total, stayed a month or more. This group accounted for 55 percent of unit bed days for the year. Twenty of these cases were 1200 grams or under and 11 were between 1201 and 2500 grams.

The sample of 101 consecutive cases we followed on a daily basis reflected this distribution. Eighty percent had lengths of stay less than three weeks; 12 percent were in the unit for more than thirty days. Despite the tendency for charges to be higher in the first week of treatment, billing charges for these cases followed the division suggested by length-of-stay. That is, 77 percent of admitted patients had bills under $19,000 and, at the other end of the spectrum, 10 percent acquired bills of $61,000 and more. Those charged at less than $6,000 had an average length of stay (ALOS) of 1.43 days. Of the 17 deaths in the sample, 12 occurred in less than 6 days.

In essence, then, there is a bifurcation of admissions between surviving infants with minor problems and more serious cases. The problem group in intensive care is identifiable by charges and length of stay. It is also identifiable by clinical criteria. The association between high costs and low birthweight has been drawn by other researchers and is confirmed by our data. We can move beyond this association to the broader clinical question: what medical outcome resulted from the recorded investment in treatment? Granting the difficulties that a very-low-birthweight infant presents the clinician, what degree of success can be claimed through prolonged and aggressive intervention? The questions are hard to answer definitively if the criteria for success rests on notions of newborn physical perfection, which no clinician can guarantee. However, there are certain gross measures of permanent damage that, if characteristic of the surviving newborn, would lead to serious questions about the efficacy of treatment. A chronic dependency on a respirator, severe intraventricular bleeding partially remedied by a brain shunt, extensive neurological damage caused by asphyxiation at birth, congenital heart disease—these are some of the major pathologies which can characterize n.i.c.u. patients at discharge and which signal the incapacity of modern medicine to overcome individual problems inherent in extreme prematurity, accidents of nature, and medical mistakes.

We divided the twenty-five highest priced cases into three groups, according to charges. Among these twenty-five cases, there were four deaths; otherwise, all infants were discharged to intermediate level nurseries, whether in a metropolitan or a community hospital, except one, who was taken home by parents.

In the first and largest group of fifteen infants—with an average birthweight of 1244 grams, ALOS of 27.2 days, and average charge of $34,600—there are two deaths represented, along with eight cases in which problems with neurological status are either certain or suggested by test results. Another infant left the unit with the certitude of chronic lung disease. Both deceased infants were one of a set of twins whom the staff made extraordinary efforts to salvage. Though born at 1100 grams and quite frail, one of these infants received a PDA ligation before expiring, as part of the effort to maximize care. Cases such as these two reflect the ability of neonatologists to extend the period of neonates beyond the first six days when the majority of newborn deaths occur. According to M. Hack *et al.* in "Changing Trends of Neonatal and Postneonatal Deaths in Very-low-birth-weight Infants":

> The causes of these "postneonatal deaths" are directly related to known complications of prematurity and intensive care and are especially pertinent to infants with birthweights between 1000 and 1500 grams. These are the infants who may be kept alive with ventilatory assistance, hyperalimentation, and other therapeutic interventions, only

to eventually die from as yet nonpreventable or noncurable diseases, such as broncho-pulmonary dysplasia or necrotizing enterocolitis.

The phase "as yet" in this quote is important because it denotes a pediatric conceptualization of stages in the pathologies of very-low-birthweight newborns. Death is delayed, and in the interim two diseases, one of the lungs (BPD) and the other of the intestines (nec) are configured as soluble problems. Once this is one, it is possible to look at the delay time as a period of potential intervention as a means to a specific though not yet attained solution. Hence a PDA ligation or other procedure can become justified on an infant otherwise in failure, as a step towards a possible medical cure.

In the second group of seven infants, birthweight drifts downward, with one exception, to an average of 1090 grams (excluding the 3800 gram infant from the calculation), and the average length of stay moves from 27.2 days to 80.7 days. The average charge per patient increases from $34,600 to $81,143. The clinical status of the infants at discharge also worsens. Without exception, the infants in this subgroup either expired or left the unit with a questionable neurological prognosis. The one infant who died (after 95 days) was treated aggressively because the parents initially wanted "everything possible to be done." The physicians in charge of the case acquiesced, although they had no firm belief in the infant's being able to survive. The sum of charges uncovered by insurance for this group of seven ($143,900) is greater than the sum which accrued for the fifteen cases in the first group ($128,950).

The last subset is made up of three cases that are extraordinary in the amount of covered and uncovered charges (averaging $190,000), length of stay (averaging 173 days), low birthweight (averaging 797 grams), and poor outcome. The first case was discharged to a Level III nursery with severe neurological impairment and heart disease. The second expired of pneumonia after a long and rocky career of oxygen dependence and a severe brain bleed. The third infant spent 239 days in the Level III nursery and was discharged home with cerebral palsy.

Incentives, Conflicts, and Strains

The variety of incentives for aggressive treatment of a larger and more problematic population of newborn infants was reviewed earlier in this article. Obstetricians feel obliged to turn to intensive care as a response to public and parental pressures. Neonatologists have a vested interest in furthering the techniques of their subspecialty; so do pediatric surgeons. The courts and the Pro-life movement add legal and ethical incentives to expand the service.

In its expansionist phase, newborn intensive care has provided a vehicle for specialists, for hospital economics, and for the public to reap a multitude of rewards. Some have been medical; it is true that a near-term or full-term infant born in critical condition has a better chance of survival, and of survival with normal development, than as little as ten or fifteen years ago. Intervention at the moment of delivery or even before can avert major crises of heart and lung failure, of asphyxia and meconium staining, of hydrocephaly and enzyme deficiency. Once over the initial crisis, the rescued infant transferred to a Level III intensive care unit enjoys the best in technological support.

At the same time, neonatology is supplying more than most patients need to remedy delivery room disasters. The specialty has pushed beyond the mandate to rescue infants with good chances of normal growth to its own brand of "half-way technologies" for the extremely premature newborn. The central question now is whether "latent experiments" in neonatology should be sustained. Costs aside, ought an enormous concentration of human time, energy, skill, and emotion be invested in a premature infant with poor chances of normal development? Nurses and residents in newborn intensive care bear the brunt of clinical work in an area of high mortality and extensive morbidity. The result is increasing evidence of conflict within the n.i.c.u. staff, between neonatologists committed to aggressive intervention without regard for long-term outcome and junior staff lacking credence in the senior physicians' authority. Immediate and lifelong effects of experimental choices on parents remain uninvestigated, in part unquantifiable; yet they must be great.

Costs included, the changing dynamic of hospital-care financing is bound to have its effects on newborn intensive care. The conflict is already apparent. The hospital economy benefits most when there is a high turn-over of cases in need of its resources but only routinely so: patients with unusual requirements raise costs without always guaranteeing coverage. Neonatologists in their clinical mode enjoy the quick victories most of their more healthy patients allow them; in their experimental mode, these specialists cultivate the challenge of extremely premature infants, the very case type that is costly, tends to linger, and upsets the hospital budget.

If hospital reimbursement were completely guaranteed, then hospitals could persist in raising charges as specialists raised costs. In part, this is what has been happening, with cross-subsidization as a compensation for deficits. Many relatively healthy babies paying $600-a-day bed charges underwrite the more costly experimental cases. The actual compensation, of course, comes from private insurance premiums. With foreseeable cutbacks in Medicaid, greater deficits should foment hospital strategies to cover costs. Whether charges are raised or new ways of filling profitable beds with healthy patients or new uses for profitable services are found, hospital costs will be relayed to private insurers and then to the insured via rises in premiums. Ultimately, reductions in Medicaid coupled with physician selection for the most costly cases could lead to a situation where medical coverage for childbirth fits the category of "catastrophe." This would be at the point when the risk of having a baby referred to intensive care for a prolonged stay is so high that extraordinary coverage is justified for women in their child-bearing years. The irony of this development should not be lost. Placing a high value on rescuing all critically ill newborns could lead to disincentives for young people to have children: the costs and the medical risks would be perceived as very high and the effect on the national birth rate would be predictably negative.

The alternate scerario is that social controls external to the intensive care unit and to the hospital might be called into play. Private insurers are capable of tightening review standards for intensive care billing; this is already being done for more expensive cases, with the initial result that payments to hospitals are delayed while n.i.c.u. bills are scrutinized. Any reluctance to pay on the part of private insurers jeopardizes the hospital by increasing the necessary absorption of uncollected bills. Individuals and families would also suffer as if hit by a catastrophic disease or accident. At this juncture, hospital administrations would probably begin exerting pressures on physicians in neonatology and consulting specialists to change case selection and diagnosis and treatment patterns.

A secondary source of control is the government. The initial costs of newborn intensive care are only part of the overall financial picture. Most of the expense of caring for severely damaged infants is assumed by the state government in its programs for the handicapped and in chronic care institutions. With the current shift toward federal block grants allowing state governments to exercise discretion in funding allocations, special review processes could be developed to impose limits on hospital procedures that are both an immediate burden on Medicaid and a long-term burden on programs and institutions. The limits on public monies are obvious enough to dictate caps on hospital payments, as in the Florida example. Fiscal restraints on hospitals and physicians, along with a withdrawal of social welfare support, would demand a reconsideration of heroic intervention in cases with poor prognosis and a careful reassessment of experimentation with very-low-birthweight infants. Yet the state or other agent may not be spurred to exert this kind of external control if the public, parents, and physicians are convinced that newborn intensive care is an unmitigated good. It is quite possible that a confluence of lay and professional beliefs could obstruct even moderate change, simply by giving neonatal care maximum priority in medical expenditures.

There are three basic values underlying the present system of providing high-level intensive care for newborns. Each in its own way represents deeply entrenched beliefs about human life and ethics founded on the most narrow constructions of biology and medicine. The first is the equation of the biological life of the fetus and infant with an idealized and full-blown adult identity. The Pro-life movement bases its arguments on this equation. Parents of critically ill newborns do the same, reacting with guilt and fear toward a dying infant or one who may never cognitively respond to them. From this perspective, the surviving but seriously damaged infants in our sample are the products of morally sound medical judgment, for every organism that is physiologically human has the right to life. The great and unspoken qualification on this dictum is the exclusion of the elderly and senile in chronic care facilities for whom no morally imperious interest group militates and for whom no impressive array of subspecialists and technology is organized, developed, and supported. The human potential we perceive in the infant (and do not see in the elderly) legitimates newborn intensive care to the extent that nearly zero biological potential becomes irrelevant to treatment choices. Equally irrelevant is a broader view of the distribution of resources, medical and social, ultimately troubled by rising costs for this one service.

Fixed Values, Economic Shifts

The second fundamental American value contributing to the expansion of newborn intensive care is the espousal of acute care solutions to health problems. Even in obstetrics and

pediatrics, where human development can be profitably analyzed, treatment for pathologies is often defined by the crisis
atmosphere of the major hospital which, in this country, also
sets the standards for treatment given in the community hospital. Instead of approaching the problem of extreme prematurity as an environmental and developmental pathology, susceptible to diet and housing and prenatal medical management,
the attack is made in the delivery room and in the newborn intensive care unit. Long before childbirth, the high-risk mother
is easily identifiable by objective criteria; yet the American
predilection is for the drama of emergency intervention.

A third and related value is a firm belief in the powers of
specialists. The more fraught with fear and despair the pathology, the greater the impetus to seek out the medical expert.
Curiously enough, the medical management of human reproduction, more in the control of specialists than ever before, has
heightened the perception of childbirth pathologies, coloring
an otherwise normal event with anxiety. Parents need not
specifically choose the services of the neonatologist; the overwhelming choice of American women for obstetricians and
hospital birth involves them and their infants in a well-
integrated system of specialist referral. The aura of risk surrounding childbirth, risks that are economic as well as physical, is already substantial enough for young working women to
feel that specialists alone offer guarantees against the unknown
horrors that can damage the unborn. Specialists in human reproduction, in turn, have elaborated the descriptive categories
of maternal and fetal pathologies and possible interventions to
the point that the percentage of "normal" births drops artifi-
cially every year.

As intractable as this combination of lay and professional attitudes appears, it is also true that the lay and professional experience of this new service has yet to be understood and
evaluated. Certainly, the more neonatologists achieve clinical
victories that are family tragedies, the more negative the lay

reaction to the service will become. Internal to pediatrics, there is already a good deal of soul-searching going on among n.i.c.u. staff who find the immediate and long-term rewards of this kind of work insufficient to its demands. The organizational problems do not stop with a typically high turn-over in n.i.c.u. nurses, but have evolved into emerging patterns of career "burn-out" among senior physicians.

In the latter, the professional realm, lies the most likely source of a restructuring of this service. As long as neonatologists alone define the benefits and deficits of the care they offer, they also control the possibility of innovation. If heroic intervention can be reconsidered as a powerful weapon to be applied with discretion (rather than as a medical benefit applied indiscriminately to an expanding population), the next step could be the development of new, more formalized, and conservative standards of case selection and treatment. The reformulation of medical care for the newborn will be directed by a changing consciousness of the limits of intensive care. Until that change is evident, we can count on heavy and rising costs in the medical management of neonates.

FURTHER READINGS SUGGESTED BY THE AUTHOR:

"Status and Status Strain in the Professions" by A. Abbott in *American Journal of Sociology* 86:819-835.

Profession of Medicine: A Study of the Sociology of Applied Knowledge by Eliot Friedson (New York: Harper & Row, 1970).

"Babies by Cesarean—Who Chooses, Who Controls" by Jeanne Guillemin in *The Hastings Center Report* 11:12-15.

"Ethical Issues in Neonatal Intensive Care: An Economic Perspective by M. Kramer in *The Ethics of Newborn Intensive Care*, edited by A.R. Jonsen and M. Garland (Berkeley, Calif.: Institute of Governmental Studies, 1976).

Technology in Hospitals: Medical Advances and Their Diffusion by Louise B. Russell (Washington, D.C.: The Brookings Institution, 1979).

Health Care and Self-Care: The Genetic Fix

AMITAI ETZIONI

Recent developments in biological and medical science have given man new power over his health and life-span—even the possibility of determining the genetic makeup of his children. Technological developments are transforming death from an unavoidable, natural event into a phenomenon demanding our active participation decision-makers. More and more persons can be kept alive, with the help of machines, long after their consciousness has been lost and cannot be retrieved. This new-found knowledge brings with it new questions. Who has the authority to turn off the machine, to decide to end "life" (if existence without awareness can even be defined as life)? the technocrat-doctor? the hospital-institution-bureaucracy? the guilt-ridden family? the ever-obsolescent legal system? eco-nomic forces which allow fewer heroic efforts to save the lives of ward patients compared to paying ones?

The unlocking of the genetic code and subsequent related developments allow the breeding out of a rapidly growing list of illnesses which are partially or completely genetically determined. A test of the fluid surrounding the fetus (amniocentesis) can diagnose a fetus as defective and permit subsequent abortion. Should we allow such selected breeding for therapeutic purposes? promote it? require it? Should we encourage the development of genetic surgery and manipulation? even if it might open the door to the breeding of "superpersons"?

Beyond that are problems of allocation. If a limited number of hearts are available for transplant operations, who should get them? In view of the fact that hundreds of thousands of persons may eventually need replacement hearts, would it be better to focus research on mechanical devices (artificial hearts) rather than on organ transplants? To what extent should we tolerate research on drugs which modify behavior (for example, anti-aggression powders) and affect thoughts (LSD and beyond)? Should we continue research on subliminal communication, in which messages too rapid to be consciously perceived are flashed on TV screens, commanding persons to buy (or vote) as dictated? If we want to curb such research, how can we do so without violating the freedom of scientific inquiry?

In light of these and many other issues raised by the new biomedical technologies, Senator Walter Mondale has championed legislation which calls for setting up a temporary (two-year) commission to study such questions. The commission would be composed of 15 professionals in fields ranging from law to medicine, from theology to technology, and would be budgeted at about one million dollars a year. The bill was endorsed unanimously by the 92nd Congress in December 1971; "died" when the House did not act on it by the time the session ended; was recently resurrected as Senate Resolution 71, and is again pending. Such a commission would be a first step toward developing the sorely needed tools of effective and responsive societal guidance to biomedical ethics and policies. Even though limited in scope, support, funds and staff, temporary commissions can illustrate both the need for a full-fledged, representative, adequately endowed and staffed permanent commission on biomedical ethics and policies, and the virtue of attempting limited action until such a body is constituted.

The Institute of Society, Ethic and Life Sciences, often referred to as the Hastings Institute, issued a report in the *New England Journal of Medicine* (May 24, 1972) on the ethical and social issues raised by screening large numbers of people for genetic disease. Daniel Callahan, director of the Institute, explained that "the group who formulated the guidelines for mass screening was mostly opposed to the whole idea but favored a cautious and careful approach.

The report's most basic criterion for assessing the merits of genetic screening programs is that no system be set up before adequate testing procedures are available "to avoid the problems that occurred initially in PKU screening." (Mandatory screening for PKU [phenylketonuria], an inherited biochemical malady which, untreated, can result in severe mental retardation and shortened life span, was by 1971 required in 43 states, though the test is not 100 percent reliable. Many children were wrongly identified as having the disease, and quite a few who did have it passed the test as healthy.)

A hastily introduced program to test for the sickle cell trait (carried by about one out of every 500 black children) fails by the Hastings criteria. The program tests either schoolchildren, at an age when the illness very often has already struck, or newborns, a stage at which detection is difficult. Tests of couples considering having a child would make much more sense, although such programs are more difficult to administer than school programs, in which all students can be lined up at will.

Besides asking for safe tests, the Hastings group also called attention to a risk of possible psychological or social injury. The question is, How harmful will the "labeling" of persons be? As the result of mass screening tests, people will be labeled as carriers of sick genes, which may harm their social standing and their view of themselves. Social science data leaves no doubt that at least in some areas, labeling (such as who is branded a criminal and who a law-abiding citizen) has rather serious consequences.

There is little doubt that if children are told that they have an XYY chromosome structure, which occurs in about one of every 1,000 males and which has been repeatedly reported as being associated with a predisposition toward seriously deviant behavior, they could easily begin to assume that a criminal destiny is inevitable. Moreover, parents who are told that their child carries the XYY gene may come to suspect normal assertive moves as being manifestations of their child's criminal potential; consequently, they may push their child—whatever the influence of his genes—into an aggressive, ultimately criminal, personality and way of life.

Beyond parents, teachers and self-image, such labeling is likely to affect the attitudes of practically everyone who knows about a person's genetic test scores. This is no longer a hypothetical consideration. The undesirable consequences which the Hastings group warned were possible have already made themselves felt. In 1971 the state of Massachusetts, responding to the demands of black community leaders and their white supporters, passed a law requiring that all school-age children be tested for the sickle cell trait. A dozen states rushed to follow suit. The trait is harmless by itself, but when both parents have it, there is a one in four chance that their child will have sickle cell anemia, a horrible disease which first causes pain, then deterioration of major organs such as the liver and kidneys.

The results of the tests, presumably kept only on school records, have increasingly been used to brand carriers of the disease as poor employment and life insurance risks. Recently, many black people started wondering whether or not the undesirable consequences of the test outweighed its benefits, especially as there is, so far, no known cure for the illness.

Related questions must be asked about other genetic tests that are being increasingly used, promoted or sought. Screening programs for carriers of the gene for Tay-Sachs disease were started among Jews in Baltimore in 1971. A screening test for Cooley's anemia, most common among people of Mediterranean descent, is being developed, and a new genetic test which will predict people's susceptibility to emphysema, a degenerative lung disease, is being worked on. Tests for dysautomonia (a disease which affects chiefly Ashkenazi Jews) and cystic fibrosis (which hits one out of every 1,500 Caucasian babies) are being actively sought. Dozens of other tests are likely to follow. If they are to do more good than harm, there must be a mechanism for reviewing the programs before they are enacted.

The Hastings report also points out that it is necessary to accompany such a new program with carefully designed and executed public information programs. Experience shows that the public—even some doctors—confuse the sickle cell *trait*, quite harmless by itself, with the disease of sickle cell *anemia*, which is found only when *both* parents have the trait and then only in approximately one out of four of their offspring.

The Hastings report also suggests other criteria for evaluating or designing mass genetic screening tests, including equal access, absence of compulsion and informed consent. The record shows that these recommendations have not often been followed in the past.

This particular Hastings report (other ones are being formulated) is not comprehensive. For instance, it does not deal with the question, How safe is safe?—an essential issue for new tests—or, How can safety be tested before tests are used en masse? In addition, because the report is based chiefly on deliberations and dialogue, it shows little benefit from empirical input to back up its points. Nevertheless, it is of immense value, if only because it provides all those who will listen with a detailed list of what must be taken into account before such programs are initiated. If similar efforts were undertaken by a national health ethics commission, composed of leading authorities in the respective fields, and representative members of the community backed up by congressional status and a staff, they would command an even greater following. Of course, even if such a national body were formed, private groups would still have to continue their deliberations. These issues must be as widely discussed as possible, for a continuous dialogue of many divergent viewpoints is essential if the bases for a new ethic as well as policy guidelines are to evolve. A national body would provide a much-needed focus for such private deliberations, but neither could it nor should it try to replace them.

Patient's Bill of Rights

Another development illustrates how, without benefit of a review mechanism, the nation tries to cope with its need to review and form policy in the health and genetic field. The American Hospital Association first issued a bill of rights for patients in November 1972 and again in January 1973 to its 7,000 member hospitals. Formulated by a committee appointed by the trustees of the American Hospital Association, discussed by its regional advisory boards (which are composed of hospital administrators) and consumer representatives, the bill's 12-point protocol is summarized below:

1. The patient has the right to considerate and respectful care.
2. The patient has the right to obtain from his physician complete current information concerning his diagnosis,

treatment and prognosis in terms the patient can reasonably be expected to understand.

3. The patient has the right to receive from his physician information necessary to give informed consent prior to the start of any procedure and/or treatment.

4. The patient has the right to refuse treatment to the extent permitted by law, and to be informed of the medical consequences of his action.

5. The patient has the right to every consideration of his privacy concerning his own medical care program.

6. The patient has the right to expect that all communications and records pertaining to his care should be treated as confidential.

7. The patient has the right to expect that within its capacity a hospital must make reasonable response to the request of a patient for services.

8. The patient has the right to obtain information as to any relationship of his hospital to other health care and educational institutions insofar as his care is concerned.

9. The patient has the right to be advised if the hospital proposes to engage in or perform human experimentation affecting his care or treatment.

10. The patient has the right to expect reasonable continuity of care.

11. The patient has the right to examine and receive an explanation of his bill regardless of source of payment.

12. The patient has the right to know what hospital rules and regulations apply to his conduct as a patient.

Several hospitals adopted the bill, and at least two (Boston's Beth Israel Hospital and New York's Martin Luther King Health Center) now provide their patients with their own version of it, but most hospitals did not embrace it. Yet, the charter is of great value. Both technological and social developments have rendered the existing hospital structure virtually obsolescent, and there is a particularly great need for a new definition of the relationship between the patient and the institution.

The fact that those who administer hospitals took the initiative in preparing this bill is hardly surprising, since there is no community-based body to assume such duties. However, it must also be noted that the charter, lacking public hearings of the kind a congressional committee would have generated, was not subject to wide discussion or involvement. It is no wonder, then, that the charter is easy to ignore. Moreover, the fact that it was formulated by a board composed chiefly of those in power will hardly reassure the more activist "consumer" groups. (Dr. Willard Gaylin went so far as to indicate that the document "perpetuates the very paternalism that precipitated the abuses.") A more widely representative body would have given the bill more authority.

Like most documents formulated chiefly to express a sentiment and to affirm a position the charter is rather long on general statements, and somewhat short on specifics. For example, the statement, "The patient has the right to refuse treatment," is qualified by the phrase "to the extent permitted by law," as though the law provided a clear guideline. Actually, if the patients themselves have the right to insist, for instance, that life-extending machines be turned off, they must be conscious when they so choose, but their action would be tantamount to suicide. On the other hand, if the patient has to be unconscious beyond recall before the machines can be turned off, the right to refuse service is not his. Who, then, exercises the right? one doctor? two? three? with or without consultation of the next of kin? under what medical conditions?

The Medical Society of the State of New York suggested adding the clause, "irrefutable evidence that biological death is inevitable," but such evidence may come long before a person loses consciousness. The society also suggested using the phrase, "is the decision of the patient and/or the immediate family with the approval of the family physician." But what if there is no family physician? Should not at least one other doctor, not as deeply involved, be consulted? Clearly the Patient's Bill of Rights leaves these and many other issues unresolved.

If the authors of the bill had expressed greater concern with procedure they would have been more aware of the need for local health ethics boards to review decisions made to "turn off" lives; the need for national and international boards to formulate guidelines; and the need for a research staff to study the actual results of various procedures in order to apply them in future deliberations. (There are review committees inside hospitals but these, with few exceptions, are limited to physicians associated with that hospital. Such insularity tends to limit their critical power.)

On January 22, 1973 the U.S. Supreme Court over-ruled all state laws that prohibit or restrict a woman's right to obtain an abortion during the first three months of pregnancy. It is now up to the woman and her physician to decide what course to follow. For the last six months of pregnancy, abortion can be "regulated" by the states to secure maternal health (for example, they can limit abortions to qualified facilities). Only in the last ten weeks of pregnancy, when the fetus is judged "viable," that is, capable of surviving if born, may a state prohibit abortion.

This welcome act also turned a matter that was previously controlled by the government over to individual choice. About 1.6 million American women undergo abortions each year. The risks are not trivial. While an abortion performed by a well-trained physician, during the first 12 weeks of pregnancy, is said to be safer than a tonsillectomy or an actual birth (out of 100,000 patients, the death rate for abortion is two; for tonsillectomy, 17; for pregnancy, delivery and postnatal period, 20).

In the second trimester abortion complications are three to four times more likely to arise.

Arranging the public education campaign which must follow the court's ruling—for instance, advising those who either use no contraceptives or use an unreliable method not to rely on abortion for birth control, or cautioning those who need an abortion not to put it off—is the job of the Department of Health, Education and Welfare. But a public authority could go a long way to see to it that matters the Court leaves undone will be picked up by the appropriate executive agency, and with the desired vigor and scope. Such an authority could also develop and implement a systematic procedure through which the relevant medical data and considerations on this or any other matter are regularly brought before the Supreme Court before it makes a ruling.

Another highly relevant development came in October 1972, when Congress enacted a bill widely referred to as "H.R. 1," a large package of amendments to the Social Security Act. Among the numerous clauses of the bill is Section 249F, barely known to the general public. The amendment calls for setting up "professional standards review organizations" (PSROs) in order to subject hospitals and other health units to outside review, not only of proper use of funds—the typical accountability expected and required of anyone who uses public funds—but also of professional, that is, medical, matters. The main motive seems to be to reduce the number of poor and aged hospitalized charity patients. (The amendment calls for checking non-emergency cases with the PSRO before admission). At the same time, the provision opens the door, in principle, to outside or perhaps even public scrutiny of what doctors are doing.

The law is rather vague as to who is to provide these outside review boards. But the basic assumption is that doctors will oversee doctors. Even this is quite innovative because many doctors feel they need no overseer and that if review is to take place, it should be by their peers. Although peer reviews are often surprisingly strict, the PSROs, which are to be established throughout the United States by January 1, 1976, go one necessary step further, calling for outsiders to review insiders, acting as a kind of medical audit. Above all, it seems desirable that the PSROs should include not only doctors but also community representatives and "specialists" in societal and ethical matters to make sure that consumer, social and moral issues be taken into account, and to counteract any self-serving tendencies of doctors.

The PSROs represent an important spot at which to enter the closed professional system, because, unlike community advisory boards, set up around hospitals or comprehensive health planning agencies, the PSROs will be able to control the main flow of taxpayers' funds to health units.

As the 93rd Congress got underway in early 1973, Senator Mondale reintroduced his 1971 biomedical technology study commission legislation, now numbered "Senate Resolution 71." The Senate may well approve it again, but no one can make any predictions as to what the House will do.

Early in 1973, Senator Edward Kennedy held extensive hearings on an issue that a health ethics commission, had it existed, would have dealt with: the conditions under which experimentation with human subjects can be tolerated. The press was again filled with gory reports about this or that ethical violation, but paid little attention to the more general questions concerning how such regulations could be implemented. Progress was made during the hearing—two expert witnesses called for the establishment of a more advanced, more potent, health ethics commission than the Mondale bill outlines. Dr. Bernard Barber testified before the Subcommittee on Health of the Senate Committee on Labor and Public Welfare that he favored
  . . . the establishment of a National Board of Biomedical Research Ethics. As members of that board I would like to see

not only members of the medical research profession, who are of course indispensable, but also people who are outsiders to the profession and who represent the public. These outsiders cannot be ordinary men-in-the-street or men given to absolute morals; they should be *informed outsiders*, lawyers or social scientists who have the expertise to deal with the fact that medical research ethics are also social and not just medical matters . . . . The Board could define goals, establish institutions and mechanisms, and provide necessary monitoring for standards and practices that are only what the profession rightly values and the public increasingly and rightly demands.

Jay Katz, adjunct professor of law and psychiatry at Yale University, suggested that a permanent body be established to regulate all federally supported research involving human subjects. Such a board, Katz said, should be independent from the government, since much experimentation that requires supervision is carried out in government-owned laboratories. He wanted the President to appoint the board, and suggested that "its members should come from many disciplines, including representatives from the public at large," and that the board should have "regulatory authority," that is, it should formulate policy and set up the needed regulations and mechanisms to promote them.

Note that the concern in the Kennedy hearings focused on those relatively few persons who are subjects in experiments. My feeling is that we are all "subjects"—the millions who take the Pill, the millions who do not receive genetic counseling, the millions exposed to food additives which may well be cancer-inducing and so forth. We need to develop a more effective review mechanism of all illness-producing and illness-preventing forces in our life. The focus on human subjects in laboratories should be the opening wedge, not just a conciliatory gesture that gives reprieve from much-needed nationwide, not just lab-wide scrutiny.

The reforms must not stop here. The efforts to form effective and responsive overview mechanisms cannot be advanced by a few senators and professors. Their future depends on the informed general public, led by active groups of citizens, taking on this issue, as they took on those for peace in Vietnam, civil rights and pollution control.

On the national level, Congress must be urged to set up a permanent national health ethics commission which includes members of a variety of disciplines, not just medicine, and representatives of the public, backed up by a research staff. Locally, each state, city and town needs a local review health ethics board—to oversee its hospitals and clinics, its medical healers and researchers. Individually, citizens and their leaders need to inform themselves about new medical and genetic developments and the public and private issues raised by their effects on matters of illness and health, life and death.

To reap the full benefits of the developments in genetics and medicine—and to be spared the many dangers—individual citizens must be both knowledgeable and aware of the implications of the new technology. A national health ethics commission plus local review health ethics boards would reveal problems and present possible solutions, furthering not only knowledge but also the physical and emotional well-being of the American people.

Chronic Medicare

BARBARA SUCZEK

What is a human life worth? For a people readily moved to personal generosity when catastrophe hits friend or stranger we are strangely reluctant to commit ourselves to the expense of instituting a federally financed health-care policy. One result of this fear of changing the social system is that the life of a victim of a chronic ailment is virtually price-tagged at whatever the cost of treatment is. In the case of renal failure (kidney disease) victims, this figure is at least several thousand dollars a year—the cost of hemodialysis, the process of filtering toxic substances which accumulate in a renal patient's blood. Despite its time-consuming and psychologically demanding nature, dialysis holds out dramatic hope to chronic renal failure victims. But the same society whose technology offers this life-sustaining promise cruelly impedes its fulfillment with random, arbitrary methods of making funds available to those who need treatment.

Regardless of his economic status, the chronic renal failure patient—sick and worried—is forced to chart a perilous physical and financial course. Unfortunately, the physically healthy seem to lack the imagination, the time and the emotional energy to sustain any deep involvement with seemingly interminable medical problems. Bolstered by a proud but largely unexamined assumption that "we," as Americans, are probably doing as well as can be expected in providing for general health care, the chronically sick and those intimately involved with their care are essentially left to cure their own financial ills.

The two major phases of the illness trajectory—the acute, or *rescue* period and the chronic, or prolonged *maintenance* period—are each accompanied by their own special funding problems. Since the latter phase may extend over an entire lifetime, it will almost certainly be accompanied by a sequential depletion of funding sources—each failure initiating a new crisis that propels the patient into a search for new funds.

Without public monies the fund-raising process takes on the ongoing, never-consummated quality of running on a treadmill. A successful kidney transplant may seem the only real hope for escape. Such an escape is not, unfortunately, a panacea. It involves massive problems of its own, such as locating donors, the inevitable risks associated with major surgery and the hovering possibility of organ rejection. Though it is also an expensive procedure, its financial advantage lies in the fact that the costs involved are circumscribed and at least roughly calculable. If it is successful, there is hope for genuine relief at the economic as well as the physical level. If it is unsuccessful, the patient returns to the treadmill.

Originally, at least, the victim of chronic renal failure who has health insurance coverage may be saved from financial worries. Although the costs of the rescue period will probably be higher than those of subsequent phases, the patient may actually experience less financial distress than later in his illness since health insurance generally cushions the initial blow.

Health insurance as it now stands, however, falls far short of meeting the funding needs of dialysis patients. Since health insurance policies are primarily geared to protect the insured against the cost of acute illness, they are rarely adequate for coping with the long-term financial drain associated with chronic illness.

Essentially, health insurance coverage may determine which renal failure victims live and which die. About 80 percent of survivors (those stabilized and on dialysis) carry some sort of major medical coverage at the onset of illness. This figure is higher than the national average. Without recourse to the lifesaving machines or sufficient funds to pay for using the machines, renal failure victims die early in the course of their illness. Many more renal failure victims die than are saved. Of those who die, many could be saved.

Competing for Dialysis

Those who live—even though semi-permanently attached to a dialysis machine—are not randomly selected. As a group they have four outstanding characteristics: urbanity, respectability, affiliation and a record of fairly steady employment.

Urbanity is intended in both its geographical and psychological sense. It takes an urbane, sophisticated know-how to locate sources of funds. Further, dialysis units are almost exclusively located in large urban centers so patients must live in or within commuting distance of the city. Even patients on home dialysis must have some means of reaching the city for the six-week training period, for periodic checkups and for medical and mechanical emergencies. There are, moreover, rural areas that are not suited to the installation or operation of dialysis machinery.

Respectability is less an inherent personal trait than a value judgment made by others who must choose among patients competing for limited medical facilities. Persons who are viewed as "unbalanced" or socially irresponsible are obviously less likely to qualify for selection.

Affiliation, that is, whether the patient has recourse to a social network, will also have bearing on alternatives available to him, especially on the choice between center- and home-based dialysis. Home care is possible only if the patient has a responsible person available to help him use the machine. There are, at present, no trained professional assistants.

A steady employment record is necessary because health insurance policies are frequently sponsored by labor groups or business organizations and are, as such, available only to employees in good standing: and because — regardless of sponsorship — some stable base of income is obviously needed in order to meet a schedule of regular payments.

There is little that can be confidently stated with regard to the overall health insurance picture. Not only do various plans differ widely from one another in the kinds and amounts of benefits they offer, but even within the framework of a specific plan there are wide disparities in coverage, varying according to such criteria as the relationship of the patient to the policyholder (in cases where dependents are covered), type of facility used (many policies will cover hospital treatment but will not pay for outpatient or home care — a source of running dispute, incidentally, between an organization of New York kidney disease victims and New York City Blue Cross), length of time the policy has been in effect (the Kaiser health plan stipulates, for example, that the claimant must have been a member of the plan for at least two years prior to qualifying for prepaid dialysis). Nearly all policies carry clauses that specifically limit the liability of the carrier to prestated amounts. The relationship of the patient to the subscriber, the particular and peculiar conjunction of points in personal, occupational and disease careers, the site and type of available treatment all have their bearing on how the terms of a specific policy will be interpreted.

Coding categorical differences is not the major difficulty, although it is true that here—as in any coding operation—there will be cases whose disposition is not readily clear and apparent. Rather, the major source of confusion stems from a seemingly universal effort to evade the issue of financial responsibility.

Health insurance policies are formulated and contracts negotiated in an atmosphere of uncertainty. One side does not know what reasonably to demand; the other does not know what to refuse. The central issue is the extent to which the surety shall be liable for claims that were unforseeable at the time of contract. Little more than a decade ago the alternative of hemodialysis did not exist in the treatment of kidney failure, and its effect, therefore, could not be anticipated in actuarial calculations. There seems no reason to assume that the present procedure and its attendant costs will long endure; the probability is that any day now some new technological breakthrough will render them both obsolete.

One tactic insurance companies might adopt would be to refuse to honor any claim based on future technological developments. But such a policy could be strategically inadvisable since business competitors might be able to exploit that stand to their own advantage.

Liability Loopholing

Corporate tradition dictates that the problem of competition could be resolved by collusion were it not for the spectre of that anathema to insurance companies—socialized medicine. Certainly it would seem imprudent for anyone with a vested interest in private enterprise to pursue a course that might tip the balance of public sentiment in the direction of state-financed medical care.

The fear of making firm, definitive statements that might inadvertently establish precedents leads both sides to a vagueness of position. The result is that there is a wide area for loopholing for both claimant and corporation.

Further adding to the confusion is that fact that the claimant may be simply and overwhelmingly ignorant. It is a rare person who has the slightest idea what his insurance can be expected to cover. There is simply no way for an individual to be able to anticipate all eventualities and their consequences. Who could have guessed a few years ago that even "forever" might be barely adequate as a time stipulation? Yet this is only a slight overstatement of what has become a fact of life for thousands of victims of renal failure.

A policy carrying a $20,000 liability limitation may seem, to the healthy, more than adequate to protect a family from the costs of even major illness. However, in the case of one young woman—a wife and mother—who was stricken with kidney failure, $13,000 of such a policy was consumed in less than four months. This amount covered only 80 percent of her overall medical expense. Thus, the family was already more than $2,000 out of pocket, the insurance was 65 percent depleted and there was still a lifetime of expense ahead which, for a woman of 27, might be expected to extend for upwards of 50 years. This young and previously prospering family watched a carefully planned insurance program melt away before their eyes, carrying with it many of their hopes and plans for the future.

The simple truth is that, for many individuals, health insurance seems to function like ritual magic: they trust that the powers-that-be, having been duly placated by the proper observances and offerings, will come to their rescue in time of need.

Ignorance of content is often accompanied by ignorance of

procedure. For patients who are unfamiliar with the intricacies of bureaucratic paperwork or for those who are too sick to concern themselves with it, filling out the required forms according to prescribed time schedules may present an almost insurmountable problem. One patient reported:

I owe about $300 in hospital bills that I'll have to pay for myself. I didn't fill out the state disability form so the insurance doesn't cover it. I'm just out of pocket. I was too sick to deal with that, I didn't know *anything* for two weeks and that was when I was supposed to fill out the form. After I was well I called them about it but I found out it was too late . . . .

Diffidence can also limit the patient's knowledge: "I don't know why it's taking so long. I'd kind of like to know, but . . . well, I don't like to call them . . . . Oh, I hate to go causing people trouble."

It seems clear that there are various reasons that patients may need help with insurance formalities. At present, responsibility for assisting patients falls to a motley crew of agents whose efforts are not necessarily closely coordinated.

The hospital employs social workers, administrators and other professionals to recover costs that the institution cannot afford to absorb. There are also unofficial assistants—often nurses and doctors whose work brings them into close and frequent contact with individual patients—who, in addition to their regular duties, may find themselves involved in efforts to unsnarl a patient's financial difficulties. There are two basic reasons for this sort of involvement: first, since effective functioning of the treatment process can be seriously impeded by recurring financial problems, frustrated professionalism may demand their solution by whatever or whosoever intervention seems most expedient; second, the close association between dialysis patients and the professionals who supervise their care often leads to a sympathetic involvement with the patient's affairs. Dialysis room concern often manifests itself in efforts above and beyond the normal call of professional duties. No one, anywhere, serves primarily to help the patient understand and order his financial affairs strictly in accordance with his own needs and interests.

Rejected Claims

The usual procedure followed by insured patients seems to be that of submitting claims on an *ad hoc* basis until such time as payment is refused. If refusal is based on a technicality, a running dispute with the company may ensue:

I had trouble with the insurance company, but Dr. A. finally got it settled. They wouldn't pay for the dialysis unless you spent the night in the hospital and the dialysis unit here isn't open at night. It just didn't make sense . . . all through October and November it was under debate: Dr. A., the hospital and the insurance company. Finally I guess Dr. A. convinced them . . . . since December the insurance company has started paying . . . but I think the hospital took the loss.

If refusal is based on the fact that the company's liability is spent—that the source of funds is exhausted—a new crisis is precipitated. Rarely does a patient make any advance plans for dealing with the crisis. "I just don't know *what* I'll do when the insurance runs out!" is a typical comment. This is undoubtedly because there are few—terrifyingly few—available options. The patient, helpless and bewildered, simply drifts into crisis, hoping that, when the point is reached, some solution will present itself.

Rescue Efforts

Individuals are occasionally rescued by charitable intervention: organizations and groups may have funds available or may undertake fund-raising drives in a patient's behalf. Appeals through the media sometimes meet with surprisingly generous public response. In such cases, however, novelty is a powerful ally. Every fund drive that depends on a human interest motif to insure its success probably serves, in a degree, to desensitize its audience and may decrease the chance that such drives will be similarly successful in the future. A time of increasing need, therefore, may unfortunately be merging with a period of diminishing returns.

It is also true that fund-raising ventures probably do better when it is possible to define a single, specific objective—some indicator that can be used both as the measure of success and the end of the project. Interest and energy flag in confrontation with the demoralizing drain of unremitting need. The renal failure patient thus has a much better chance of receiving aid in some specific amount—the sum needed to defray the cost of a heroic rescue, for example, or to buy a machine for home use—than he has of tapping charitable or voluntary resources for long-term maintenance.

The prolonged maintenance period is one in which the renal failure patient's condition has stabilized. Although it is impossible to keep the body chemistry in perfect balance—there will always be periodic flurries and alarms and medical supervision must be regularly maintained—the physical condition is basically under control and the situation permits some opportunity for predicting and planning of future needs. Despite this, however, the period is characterized by a series of funding crises. While it is presumably true that in California, for example, since the state offers funds under the provisions of MediCal, no Californian need die for lack of money for treatment, there is so much personal misery and financial distress entailed in accepting state medical aid that recourse to public funds will almost certainly be postponed as long as possible.

How early and to what extent an individual will experience the treadmill effect of the prolonged maintenance period hinges on many contingencies. It makes a critical difference, for example, whether a patient is financially dependent, self-supporting or the breadwinner for a family. The most difficult position is that of the afflicted person who must earn a living.

Renal failure is hardest on the breadwinner for three reasons. First, the time needed for dialysis may cut seriously into working hours. Second, physical debility not only hampers productivity and overall efficiency but also limits the sort of work that can be undertaken. Occupations that involve a considerable outlay of physical energy or require extensive travelling, for example, may have to be abandoned. Third, it may be difficult to find any sort of suitable work since employment policies are frequently associated with insurance regulations that will, almost certainly, reject persons suffering from serious chronic disease.

Early retirement is a frequent solution among those whose age and seniority status permit them that alternative. The person who can retire on a pension and is qualified to receive help from Medicare is in a relatively good financial position, providing there are no extraneous complicating factors. Under other circumstances, however, retirement—by cutting down income and changing insurance status—may be extremely threatening. Consider, for example, the plight of a man who had reached the compulsory retirement age but whose wife—20 years his junior—was on hemodialysis that was being funded through his occupational insurance.

Medical Aid

The Californian who is already on welfare at the time of kidney failure—if he survives the many hazards in the path to rescue—will, theoretically, qualify by definition for medical aid from MediCal. Ironically, such patients are often among those whose treatment is the most expensive to maintain since they lack the stable conditions necessary to qualify them for home care.

In California, the whole issue of state-financed medical help is fraught with bitterness and altercation, and the financing of renal failure—because of its chronic nature and its extraordinarily high cost—is a particularly touchy point.

There are three sources of major dispute: welfare restrictions, governmental responsibility and administrative red tape.

Welfare Restrictions. In order to qualify for funds from Medi-Cal, a patient must divest himself of any personal property or income he may have in excess of that permitted to recipients of state welfare. The MediCal plan is apparently so designed in order to insure that an individual will not freeload at the taxpayers' expense—that he will assume liability and share the cost of his illness. In operation it is like a deductible clause that is based on the patient's income. A single person, for example, with an income of $500 a month may be permitted a mainte-nance need allowance of $110 a month (the fact that specifica-tions are subject to unpredictable change is another source of ambiguity and worry); all income above that amount must be used for medical expenses before MediCal will intervene. In addition, according to its policy, MediCal will not assist anyone who owns cash or property in excess of a value of $1,200 (personal dwelling excepted) and /or cash value of life insurance over $100 per dependent. Thus, if the patient has been fortu-nate enough or foresighted enough to be able to provide some security for his family, he is expected to see to the dispersal of that security before he can apply to MediCal for the funds needed to save his life. To lose one's financial foothold is never a happy eventuality, but to do so at a time when the physical realities of illness are making the course of the future extremely uncertain is particularly distressing. Once he has been reduced to the welfare level, there seems little likelihood that a patient can find the means to regain his independence.

To many persons involved in it—patients and professionals alike—the situation seems not only unfortunate but contrary to American principles and goals. Such prescriptions may even be generating a *welfare race* of persons who no longer have any incentive to self-help. That victim of illness through no perceivable fault of his own should be reduced to such a plight is thoroughly unjust. In the words of one administrator:

> Most people are not millionaires. Most people are middle income—six to ten thousand dollars a year. I, myself, just don't think it's worth all that hassle. Especially when you stop to think that these people never feel very good—well, you get accustomed to feeling half-good . . . . But when you work all your life and you pay taxes all your life and taking care of yourself has always been a source of pride to you, and then you get turned down because *you've got too much*! Well, it's demoralizing.

Governmental Responsibility. California's state legislature is caught in a crossfire of constituent demands: reconciliation of public and private interests is not often reached at a single bound. Simultaneously pressured by demands for increased assistance, lower taxes, less governmental intervention and universal health benefits, the result is, not surprisingly, lacking in clarity and direction. The fight over hemodialysis is a case in point:

> The whole dialysis issue is a big problem in Sacramento—an embarrassment. The legislature didn't really want to pay for dialysis. But dialysis, after all, came into being here—here and at a sister center in Seattle. There was a sort of local proprietary pride . . . . And then it turned out there wasn't enough insurance to go around, so great pressure was put on the Reagan administration to accept hemodialysis. This was in 1967. Now they regret it. They didn't know what they

were getting into. The State Department of Public Health estimates that by 1977 there will be 3,000 people on chronic dialysis in California. The money men say, "My God! Who's going to support their habit?"

While the legislature allegedly regrets its decision, lobbies of patients and/or professionals fight desperately to maintain and increase their financial foothold—frustration and exasperation with the ins and outs of bureaucratic evasion sometimes leading to unexpected political and ideological configurations. Because there seems to be no source of funds other than the federal government that is capable of absorbing the potential burden of technological medicine, physicians and other professionals who, in different circumstances, might have been expected to form a bulwark of resistance to socialized medicine may now—for both humane and career reasons—begin to agitate in its favor.

Administrative Red Tape. The organization and distribution of state health-care funds is apparently so tangled in a web of duplication, evasion and conflicting purpose that the overall result is mass confusion. Presumably the outgrowth of legislative ambivalence, the present situation seems to be characterized by overlapping jurisdiction, conflict of policy, bureaucratic shuffling of responsibility, and a general lack of coordination and accountability. The following is a description given by a representative of a community hospital:

We've had reforms and we've reformed the reforms . . . . The providers are so entangled in confusion it is virtually impossible to get reimbursed. Blue Cross pays for MediCal. Welfare establishes eligibility. But the criteria of the Department of Health say *everybody* is eligible. These two agencies controvert each other. So they spend now and eligibility may be established six months from now, but the provider doesn't know whether it will be or not . . . . There's a subtle move—not to *refuse*—but to pressure the provider: 45% of the applications "disappear" or are returned for no valid reason and usually too late to resubmit them. Do you know that there are 218 reasons why a thirty-four item form can be returned? And after that there's "Other"! . . . I think they're deliberately stalling . . . . The provider is caught in a bind . . . . Eventually *somebody* has to reimburse *somebody*!

Loopholing is an informal device whereby officially proscribed actions may be unofficially redefined in terms that permit their accomplishment without open infraction of rules. There is considerable evidence to suggest that—even as lack of clear definition in the private insurance transaction sometimes leads to exploitable loopholes—confusion and ambiguity at the state level inadvertently leaves gaps whereby patients may escape some of the more devastating effects of eligibility rulings.

Paper Statements

Because loopholing must, of necessity, be evasive in method as well as in goal, it entails some special problems. In the case of dialysis patients, for instance, the medical staff or a case worker may point out the possibility of making "paper statements" that will indicate intent but may not be binding in actual commission. This is a task of considerable delicacy: such patterns of evasion are usually couched in subtle terms as a protection against the danger of legal and political repercussions:

    . . . the social workers can't say right out what is going on. They have to hope the patients will catch on when they say things like, "Well, in your case I wouldn't worry too much!" Once in a while but not very often, they'll just come right out with it. But this is dangerous.

Some persons take loopholing easily in stride, seeing it in the light of a sensible and innocuous business arrangement—like maneuvering all possible personal advantages from income tax regulations—or as a more-or-or-less empty ritualistic gesture.

Others view it as simple dishonesty and suffer accordingly—either because desperation leads them to comply with evasionary tactics against the dictates of their scruples, in which case they suffer from the demeaning pangs of bad conscience, or because they do not, and bear, in consequence, the effects of financial anguish.

Patients as Prisoners

Loopholing can sometimes be accomplished by making a change in legal status (a device not infrequently employed by the urban poor). One such case was reported by a social worker:

The husband, who was the patient, was in his fifties but he had a young family from a second marriage . . . . It was a working class family: the mother had a job as a salesgirl and he was a garage attendant. When they applied for MediCal, the welfare guidelines for a family of their size were just impossible—if they kept their combined income they would just be working for the state. It was a total mess! Well, the upshot of the matter was that after he had been on dialysis for a month, the marriage broke up. They got a divorce. It was the only way to save the income . . . . The woman continued to take care of him and was obviously very fond of him.

To be successful, loopholing ususally depends upon an alliance of, for example, patient, case worker and eligibility worker. If participants do not share understandings of need or definitions of loyalty the situation may dissolve into one of personal rancor and agency infighting, with counter-attributions of bureaucratic inhumanity and fiscal irresponsibility being hurled back and forth to the apparent benefit of no one.

The patient, meanwhile, stands helplessly by. He is like a prisoner at the bar waiting for the result of adversary action to decide his fate: in this case, a negative decision will condemn him to the humiliation and distress of ultimate financial wipe-out.

At present several treatment alternatives exist for dealing with chronic renal failure. Chief among these are center-based hemodialysis, home-based hemodialysis and kidney transplant. Each has major drawbacks and each offers its own special advantages. The patient is not likely to have much of a say in deciding on a method, first because he usually inherits certain preselected programs and equipment along with the physician and/or institution which circumstances have assigned him: second, because personal limitations—physical, social and economic—dictate what alternative may be practical or even possible in an individual case; and third, because medical paternalism is such that the situation of the patient as it is perceived by persons in decision-making relationships to him will greatly influence what choices are brought to his attention.

For center-based dialysis the patient comes to a central unit two or three times a week for treatment. There are four major advantages to this arrangement: constant supervision by personnel trained and equipped to deal with emergencies; relief for family members from some of the burden of work and anxiety; availability to many persons who lack a suitable home or who do not have a responsible assistant regularly available; usefulness in transient holding cases—patients awaiting a transplant, for example—where investment for home equipment would be impractical.

The chief disadvantages of center-based dialysis are higher cost, transportation problems and loss of independence. The high cost of center-based as compared with home-based dialysis is an interesting problem. In theory, centralization of services and multiple use of equipment suggest an economic efficiency that should produce the opposite effect. In practice, however, high hospital overhead, inefficient administrative practices (few centers, for example, are operated on a 24-hour schedule), a certain degree of professional and institutional profiteering, and competition among providers combine to make centralization more costly. The fact that dialysis centers have no assurance as to time or extent of reimbursement for their services makes it even harder to cut costs.

Home-based dialysis was initially designed as a program to reduce operating costs and to reach patients otherwise inaccessible for treatment—goals it has achieved with some success. Home dialysis does not eliminate the need for the center, which still provides training, medical—and sometimes mechanical—supervision and emergency care. In addition, it is customary for the patient to return to the center at specific intervals—perhaps four times a year—for a period of followup study and medical workup.

The chief drawback to home dialysis is probably the patient's need for a qualified home helper, one who can bear the physical, emotional and temporal burdens and meet high standards of intelligence, character and training. In addition, even well-qualified helpers are not unfailingly reliable: they fall ill themselves; they leave to get married; they simply grow tired of it all and quit. Their places are not readily filled.

Another problem that may beset the home-dialysis candidate is the fact that his insurance may not cover outpatient care. Unless he can convince his insuror that home dialysis is not in that category, the patient may have no choice but to accpet center-based treatment, with all the irony of its additional cost.

A machine for home use can be either purchased or rented. Unless the patient has reason for anticipating an early release—by transplant, for example—it is cheaper to buy it. Once he has paid for the machine (an expense of, roughly, $4,000) and has completed the launching period of physical stabilization and home training (altogether, perhaps, a matter of $12,000) a patient's home dialysis expenses will probably range from $2,500 to $3,000 a year (as compared with estimates of center-based costs that run from $22,000 to $30,000 annually).

The funding process for home dialysis follows the pattern for center-based dialysis. There is an initial high cost period that may be cushioned by insurance as the patient is rescued and launched into his home-dialysis career. This is followed by a period of somewhat lower and more predictable cost for prolonged maintenance. Treadmilling problems typically attend this situation of continuing need and diminishing supply.

Kidney transplant, the only alternative to dialysis, is the most dramatic and theoretically the most promising of the solutions now available for chronic renal failure. Although an enormously expensive process, like any major surgery, the cost of transplant in no way compares with the financial burden imposed by a lifetime of dialysis. Furthermore, such expenses are often covered by major medical insurance policies, with the unfortunate exclusion of the financial burden of the donor. These latter can be considerable: the surgical process involved in removing a kidney is more difficult than that required for implanting one. However, there are a number of possibilities for defraying donor expenses, including such resources as personal savings, personal loans and charitable subscription.

Unfortunately, the possibility of rejection is high. Figures based on a one-year success rate suggest, very roughly, a 70 percent success with transplants from live donors and a 50 percent or less chance with cadaver kidneys. Further, the antirejection regimen is itself unpleasant and restrictive. If rejection occurs, the patient is once more caught up on the treadmill — searching for funds and probably for kidney donors as well.

Groups of enterprising patients occasionally organize themselves into kidney clubs, which are usually oriented to consumer activities such as group buying in order to reduce the cost of supplies, pressuring insurance companies for certain policy redefinitions, challenging doctors on details of care, small-scale legislative lobbying and fund-raising for specific purposes. (One such project involved an effort to provide flight money for members in the event that an individual awaiting a transplant is suddenly informed, by computerized matching service, that a suitable kidney is available in a distant city.) The effectiveness of such organizations is seriously hampered by basic lack of group cohesion. Since the membership is composed of persons who are chronically ill, there is a marked dearth of the physical energy and stamina needed to sustain a concerted drive towards large objectives. Additionally, members, by and large, are committed to one another only at the financial level. For many, particularly those who exhibit the most vitality and talent for leadership, there seems to be a tendency to disavow the invalid identity and therefore resist any real involvement with persons who are ill, maintaining their own membership only as long as it seems to provide personal, material advantages. Participation in the group is thus apt to be ambivalent and transitory: members who, by good fortune or good management, find better solutions for their problems typically withdraw from the club.

There are some who object to the present emphasis on the treatment of chronic renal failure, arguing that research might more profitably be directed towards prevention than toward cure. A spokesperson for the Northern California Kidney Foundation argues, for example, that a program of periodic urinalysis among school children might provide an effective early warning system, predicting potential renal failure at a phase in its trajectory when it may still be reversible.

Such views are, at present, much overshadowed by public and professional interest in the more dramatic possibilities of artificial organs and transplant. In addition, research findings tend to rule out the effectiveness of any single preventative program.

There is a significantly higher incidence of suicidal behavior among chronic renal failure patients than for the population at large or even as compared with victims of other chronic disease. Suicidal behavior refers both to deliberate action taken by the patient to terminate his own life and to his refusal to undergo treatment with an intent to accomplish the same end.

Over the past few years considerable attention has been directed to identifying predisposing psychological factors that may contribute to the self-destructive impulse. Personality variables such as ego strength and self-esteem have been defined and measured as factors controlling the suicidal tendency. It may be that being in bondage to the machine sends those patients with unresolved dependency conflicts into a state of suicidal despair.

The conditioning effect that circumstance and status can exert on the direction of personal decision is demonstrated in the following examples. The first was reported by the administrator of a dialysis center:

> There are lots of cases where patients just haven't showed up. Patients have been referred to private centers, say, where they demand a deposit of $10,000, and they just toss in the towel. One man I know of personally—thirty-seven years of age with three children and $19,000 in the bank—elected to die. He was perfectly frank. He said if he went into treatment he would destroy his family.

Another patient—a 27-year-old father of two young children—faced a different situation and, in accordance with his perception of it, reached a different decision:

> . . . the way I see it, I'm going to be in the hole all my life. I worry about bills. I worry about a change in the laws that will cut off what we're getting now. Most of my worry is

money . . . . It's my kids. They're forcing me to stay alive. I keep seeing myself caring for them until they're on their own. I imagine what it will be like for them if I die. They'll hardly have anything. My wife didn't even finish high school and she wouldn't be able to take care of them . . . . They'd hardly get anything to eat, maybe. The thought keeps me going. I want to live . . . .

In neither of these cases did the patient—by demeanor or behavior—manifest lack of self-esteem or neurotic fear of dependency. Opposite decisions were apparently reached according to real differences in external conditions.

The funding process pursued by the renal failure patient dramatically highlights, by the urgency of its precarious balance between financial wipeout and death, a course that is probably typical of that to which desperate persons may, in the end, be always reduced—including crisis-oriented, *ad hoc* decision-making and rule-evading loopholing tactics that undermine personal morale, social values and, possibly, in the end, established social systems.

Future Proposals

A number of proposals for alleviating the distress of chronic renal failure patients have emerged from our study of the problem:

- That insurance carriers reimburse claimants for outpatient treatment.
- That unions assign trained persons to act as insurance advisors to their members, on an individual basis.
- That providers of dialysis treatment work together to relieve expensive duplication and overlap that often result from competitive efforts.
- That dialysis centers be operated on a 24-hour basis.
- That paramedical personnel be trained in hemodialysis tech-

niques in order to assist home-care patients, if not on a regular, at least on an emergency basis.

- That prepaid transportation service be provided for center-based patients—urban, suburban and interurban.

- That some relaxation be made in insurance regulations in order to encourage businesses to employ chronically ill individuals who are able and willing to work.

- That state health insurance policies and their administration be completely reorganized in order to cut red tape, to give health care providers a reasonable basis for predicting the time and extent of reimbursement for services rendered, and to remove health care assistance from the restrictions of welfare eligibility rules.

The implementation of any or all of such suggestions would bring some measure of relief to the individual patient. It would not, however, eliminate the basic problem and the crisis-to-crisis course of the funding process. That will happen only when we are ready to take the financial responsibility for our espoused humanitarianism and pay for a federal health care program.

FURTHER READINGS SUGGESTED BY THE AUTHOR:

"Suicidal Behavior in Chronic Dialysis Patients" by Harry S. Abram, Gordon L. Moore and Frederic B. Westervelt, paper delivered to the American Psychiatric Association at San Francisco, May 1970.

"Psychosocial Aspects of Hemodialysis" by George L. Bailey and "Funding for End-Stage Renal Patients" by Margaret B. Wilkins in *Hemodialysis: Principles and Practice* edited by George L. Bailey (New York and London: Academic Press, 1973).

"Help Patterns in Severe Illness: The Roles of Kin Network, Non-Family Resources and Institutions" by Sydney H. Croog, Alberta Lipson and Sol Levine in *Journal of Marriage and the Family*, February 1972.

Chemicals and Cancerphobia

ELIZABETH M. WHELAN

Americans today are nervous. They are worried about funny sounding chemicals in our food, water, and air. It is no wonder people are concerned; the popular press has tolled a litany of potential cancer hazards in our environment. We have heard that hamburgers may cause mutations, that drinking hair dye is no good for us, that saccharin causes cancer in Canadian rats, and that the mild sedative one needs to digest all this good news has just been banned. There are some times when the only solution seems to be a good stiff drink, as long as it is not Scotch—or beer. These may cause cancer, too!

We have become suspicious, and some of us are so jumpy that we are ready to shout "carcinogen" at the merest hint of trouble, or we are simply fed up with warnings on labels. But American industry has responded to our concerns. We are now told that if it is not "natural," it is best avoided. There are natural clothes, natural foods, natural deodorants, and even natural pesticides. And who could forget natural cigarettes with the Surgeon General's warning naturally displayed? The

301

real issue behind this "natural is better than artificial" puffery is not the fact that there *is* concern, but why these concerns exist and what we can or should do about them.

Cancer is an unquestionably serious public health problem in the United States today. In 1980 an estimated 395,000 Americans died from some form of cancer, making it the second leading cause of death behind heart disease. So there is an obvious need for a rational and integrated system to identify and assess cancer risks. This is particularly obvious to those in the chemical or chemical-related industries. But there is substantial disagreement today about the best policy to adopt.

To a large extent, this controversy arises from widespread public misconceptions of cancer and its causes. These misconceptions influence research and regulatory priorities and in some cases divert limited economic and technical resources. A solution to these problems, then, depends in part on correcting these misconceptions through education and research. The problem is a complex one, but in an attempt to simplify this discussion, I have identified seven specific areas of cancer misinformation and confusion among the general public. If we are to have any impact on changing our country's current approach to environmental issues, I think it is critical that we first understand—and then proceed to correct—these areas of misunderstanding.

Prevalent Misconceptions

First, there is apparently a very poor understanding about the relative prevalence of cancer in the United States. Surveys indicate that many Americans assume we have an unusually high rate of cancer here—the implication being, of course, that we are paying for the benefits of technology with poor health. The premise is so widespread that it has become part of the popular wisdom. A network television special opened with the statement, "If you live in the United States, your chances of developing cancer are higher than anywhere else in the world." During the debate with Gerald Ford in 1976, Jimmy Carter informed us we had the highest cancer death rate in the world. And when one hears a statement enough, one tends to believe it and to want to take action on the basis of it. The fact, of course, is that the United States has a cancer death rate which is about average for a developed country. In 1980, Scotland held the dubious honor of being Number 1.

Second, the national surveys tell us that people also believe there is a marked increase in the past few decades in the incidence of cancer—enough to warrant the word "epidemic." In 1975 newspapers around the country carried headlines of a cancer epidemic, referring to the possibility that a timebomb was going off. And again, we are back to the implication that as we have developed as a highly technological nation, we have suffered more and more environmentally induced cancer.

Again, however, the popular wisdom does not correspond to the facts. Data from the National Cancer Institute indicate that the overall incidence of cancer (the number of new cases of cancer per 100,000 population) has declined slightly since 1947. There has been an increase in cancer mortality in the past few decades, but certainly nothing on the order of an "epidemic." Most interestingly, only one form of cancer death has increased significantly for all Americans: lung cancer. At a time when American eaters are particularly nervous about chemicals in their food, it is ironic to note that paralleling the dramatic increase in lung cancer, we have been witnessing a precipitous decline in gastric cancer.

Third, it is common cocktail party chatter these days to acknowledge that 90 percent of cancers are caused by factors in the environment. To most laymen, this conjures up the image of a white-coated evil scientist pouring carcinogens into the air, water, food, and workplace. The origin of the 90 percent figure was an estimate made by an epidemiologist affiliated with the World Health Organization, who compared international cancer rates by site and concluded that simply being human did not explain the majority of cancers, that differences between countries had to be accounted for by different factors in the environment. In making this estimate he was not referring to "chemicals" around us, but rather primarily to differences in lifestyle factors.

Estimates among epidemiologists now vary somewhat, but there is a general consensus that 40 percent of the cancers occurring today in American men are caused by one specific environmental factor—tobacco (25 percent in women). Additionally, there is a strong suggestion that some aspect of nutrition and diet plays a major role in the development of certain cancers—colon, breast, prostate, and stomach, perhaps accounting for one-third of all these diseases. At this point we simply do not have the answer here, but feel that it is some component of the general diet. And there are some other contributors to environmental cancer: excessive alcohol use, especially in conjunction with cigarette smoking, accounts for a substantial number of oral cancers. A few drugs—most dramatically, DES—have been shown to increase cancer risk. Differences in sexual and reproductive patterns influence risks of cervical and breast cancers. Excessive exposure to radiation—background or manmade—has accounted for some of the environmental cancer toll. And, of course, in some specific instances, exposure to occupational chemicals or conditions has led to increased risk of cancer of a number of sites.

But getting back to perspective, the vast majority of that 80-90 percent environmental cancer figure is accounted for by tobacco and the still undefined contribution of diet. The other factors explain only a relatively small amount of cancer mortality in this country. Although there has been considerable controversy about the subject in recent months, it still appears that well under 5 percent of cancer mortality can be related to occupational carcinogens.

There is no question that a number of industrial chemicals

carry potential cancer risks. There is also no question that among them asbestos contributes the greatest risk in terms of exposed populations and widespread use. But if we were to believe Joseph Califano's estimate, there should be an astronomical increase in the number of mesotheliomas, the rare lung cancer almost exclusively related to asbestos. Yet in those states with tumor registries, like New York and Connecticut, these projected increases have not been detected. Perhaps doctors are still misclassifying these tumors as something else, or there is some unknown factor that is delaying their detection. But one thing we do know is that there is a vast amount of difference between the 20 to 40 percent HEW estimate and the 1 to 5 percent estimates of the International Agency for Research on Cancer and another project that reached the same conclusion in a study of the British work force.

There is, however, one point which the HEW paper discussed that has some merit. And that is that we might be misleading ourselves by trying to affix the blame for "X" percentage of cancers to a single chemical or process. The multifactorial nature of cancer seems to argue against this approach. We know, for example, that asbestos is a cancer risk, and we also know that cigarette smoking increases this risk by at least one order of magnitude. Yet it is ironic to read that a court decision declared that a company policy to hire only non-smokers for work with asbestos is discriminatory. It appears that the court has decided that it is better for the company to risk going out of business to comply with regulatory procedures than to deny a worker the right to kill himself by smoking. But the idea that we should consider the interaction of risk factors in a broader perspective is a reasonable one.

Fourth on the list of common misconceptions about cancer—and related to the one just discussed—is the idea that it is industry, particularly the chemical and manufacturing industries, that causes cancer. Under this misdirected reasoning, one concludes that asbestos and vinyl chloride not only do cause cancer in workers, but also become part of a general polluted environment and cause cancer in the residents of the community as well. A case in point here is the state of New Jersey. It is called "cancer alley," and the recommendation is not to live there—and if you must drive through, hold your breath. If you ask a passerby why the cancer rate is so high in New Jersey, he will tell you, "The chemical industries. That's the price I have to pay to live here."

Actually, however, I have never seen convincing evidence to suggest that general air pollution increases the risk of human cancer. Certainly there are other health and aesthetic reasons for cleaning up our air. But again, the popular misconception about cancer does not correspond to the facts. A careful analysis of the statistics in a state such as New Jersey reveals that it has no different cancer pattern than any other urban area. Of interest to some might be the fact that the lung cancer death rate in some of the more polluted areas of New Jersey is about the same as it is in Rutland, Vermont, where the major industry is tourism.

Fifth on my list of points of concern and misinformation is the general concept of the word "risk." When it comes to discussions of cancer and the environment, most Americans have a very poor concept of the nature of the risks we are speaking of. The problem here is twofold: first, extrapolating from one tragic circumstance to all uses of the substance. Thus a poor understanding of risk assessment might make one conclude that if large amounts of inhaled asbestos increased workers' risks of mesothelioma—and if they smoked cigarettes, of lung cancer—then we should tolerate *no* exposure to asbestos in the future, no matter how minute the quantities may be and no matter what the cost, in terms of prices and availability of goods, that this reduction would entail.

The second manifestation of public confusion about risk relates to an apparent inability to distinguish between real and hypothetical risks. A risk is something one can identify and quantify, then either accept or reject. Driving a car and flying in an airplane involve risks. People die. At the end of each year we know exactly what the risks of 12 months of use of these conveniences were. Americans appears to have little trouble accepting these real risks. Similarly, cigarettes pose a known health hazard. Epidemiological studies allow calculations of personal risk assumed here. These are real risks. The use of food additives, pesticides, and low-level exposures to occupational chemicals, on the other hand, pose hypothetical risks. Of course it is possible that they contribute to cancer mortality, but we have no evidence at this point that they do. As a society we seem to be drifting toward a policy which tolerates known, major risks chosen by the individual—and rejects hypothetical risks that might be assumed by industry or society as a whole. This was clear to me last year in New York when nearly a quarter million individuals gathered to protest nuclear power. The newsclippings I saw revealed that a significant number of them were smoking cigarettes.

Sixth, cancerphobia in America and the dozens of environmental regulations which have stemmed from it are very much tied into what seems to be a new philosophy about cause of disease. If indeed there is one classical attitude about human disease and its causes, it is one based on the assumption that most diseases are unexplainably caused by "bad spirits," "bad air," or simply God's will. Diseases, until recently, just happened. But not so today. Instead, now, we are either guilty or angry when someone close to us becomes ill.

An associate of mine was recently diagnosed as having kidney cancer. For three weeks he asked me the same questions: "What caused it? What did I do wrong? Whose fault was it?" The conversations we have had have been tragically frustrating, with my answer always the same: "We have no information on what causes kidney cancer. We simply don't know." He has posed the same question repeatedly to his physician. Last week the doctor gave in to his pleadings, telling my friend that his use of saccharin might be the cause. Presumably the physician knows that even the darkest picture ever drawn on the issue of saccharin's safety has never implicated the sweetener as a cause of kidney cancer. But the doctor was attempting to fulfill a need; my friend desperately wanted to identify a cause and the saccharin explanation satisfied him, allowing him to place the blame somewhere: on the saccharin manufacturers and on himself for using it. My associate's experience is, I believe, characteristic of a major change in attitude noted during the 1970s, and one which resulted from our new emphasis on cancer and the environment and which has major implications for our economy and standard of living.

While I was a guest on a Chicago talk show last year, a woman called in to tell me her four-year-old son had leukemia. "I know the cause," she told me sadly, "I breast fed him, and my milk was contaminated with DDT. We really have got to ban those pesticides to stop this cancer epidemic." This woman's reaction reminded me of an incident which occurred in New Jersey four years ago: two women from the Bergen County town of Rutherford whose sons had died from leukemia within five months of each other began a personal search for other such cancer deaths. They found a number more, and notified the press that they had identified the "cause" of their children's disease: pollution from the chemical companies in the state. They demanded that some major industries in their neighborhood be closed down. Media coverage of the "cancer cluster" was extensive. Follow-up coverage on the findings of the State Health Department that the frequency of cancer deaths in Rutherford was no more than that expected in any population that size was minimal. In many people's minds the "cause" of those leukemia cases is still the New Jersey chemical industry, although the sobering reality is that we do not know the cause of the overwhelming majority of childhood leukemia cases.

Last year in Oregon a group of 14 women who had suffered a

miscarriage or had a child with a birth defect banded together to announce they knew the "cause" of their problem: their area had been sprayed over the past few years with the herbicide 2, 4, 5, T. As a direct result of their announcement, the herbicide was banned, this despite the fact that follow-up reports noted that the miscarriages and birth defects in question occurred in a random manner, with no obvious clustering, within a few months after the spraying. But again, the "cause" of reproductive problems remains in many minds, and again, we simply do not know the real cause of all miscarriages and birth defects. Similarly, Vietnam veterans who now find they have cancer—or children with birth defects—are claiming that this same herbicide, used to defoliate the jungles during the war, is the cause of their problems. And again, the scientific evidence to back up their claims is nonexistent.

In New York City, policemen and firemen have succeeded in passing the so-called "heart bill," which compensates them for any expenses related to the development of heart disease. The assumption here is, of course, that the "cause" of heart disease among these two groups of employees is job stress, and thus the general population of the state should assume all the costs. Actually, however, there is no evidence that "stress" itself is a factor in etiology of heart disease and if, indeed, policemen and firemen do have a higher rate of heart disease than the rest of the New York male population, it is likely to be due to differences in exposure to one established causative factor, cigarette smoking.

We have come a very long way in understanding some of the causative factors in today's major killers. For example, as I have mentioned, we know that cigarette smoking contributes to the causation of one-third of all this year's cancer deaths; that, while the causation of heart disease is complex, cigarette smoking, high blood pressure, and high serum cholesterol are clearly the top three risk factors; that excessive consumption of alcohol increases one's risk of liver and other diseases; that exposure to some occupational chemicals, like asbestos and vinyl chloride, raises cancer risks.

But the fact remains that we simply do not have all the answers. Diseases, and deaths, still occur for reasons unknown to us. Human beings remain mortal. Death and disease are still natural processes. It is unconstructive to blame ourselves in these instances. And it is economically disastrous for a society when there is no proof of guilt.

Seventh, and finally, the cancerphobia which now grips our nation and is dictating federal policy in a number of government agencies seems to be largely traceable to a fear of chemicals. A chemical anxiety. A chemical reaction. Are we eating too many chemicals? Are there too many chemicals in our environment? I met a woman in the supermarket one day who asked me to help her read the label on a box of a low-cholesterol egg substitute. I complied only to have her exclaim, "My goodness, all that aluminum sulfate, sodium and triethyl citrate and emulsifiers. I'd rather keep my cholesterol high than become a walking test tube." Little did she know that the natural organic egg, even if it is laid by a happy hen, contains among other things ovalbumin, conalbumin, globulins, fatty acetic and butyric acids.

Technology and Health

The suspicion over artificial chemicals and complacency over natural ones is silly but seems to be a basis for cancer-chemical phobia. Thus a housewife gets upset about the use of a synthetic estrogen DES sometimes used to stimulate cattle growth and keep prices down, because traces of it have been found in some 5 percent or less of beef livers, and she hears that DES causes cancer. What she does not know perhaps is that any estrogen, natural or otherwise, in high doses will cause cancer, that her body regularly produces it, and that there is 1,000 times the amount of estrogen in a single egg than in a serving of affected liver.

Enough said here. The anxiety, the fear of cancer and its relationship to the environment may be peaking. But misinformation on cancer still abounds. And as it does, and as it directs the policies at the Food and Drug Administration, the Environmental Protection Agency, the Occupational Safety and Health Administration and elsewhere, we are suffering. For businessmen, the implications are clear: more regulation, higher costs, fewer jobs, and limited production. For me as a scientist and consumer the implications are also clear: high prices, higher taxes, fewer products — a diminished standard of living.

When a pesticide is banned, it may make the environmentalists feel good, make them think they are doing something. But as an epidemiologist, I know it is not preventing cancer. And as a consumer it makes me angry that even though the banning has no medical benefits, it means that I will pay more for strawberries and corn next year. Such bannings also serve as a disincentive to an industry that could eventually come up with an even better pesticide — which would help us produce more food, for ourselves and the world. When a food additive is banned, it makes some of the Naderite groups happy, and the government content. But as a scientist I know that, too, will not prevent cancer, but will only serve to remove useful products from the shelves, such as diet soft drinks. When OSHA passes carcinogen standards requiring strict regulation of any occupational chemicals that might cause cancer in laboratory animals, this does not prevent human cancer. That goal could be accomplished effectively and efficiently by giving individual attention to known carcinogens. But what it will mean is that consumers will be paying double or triple for drycleaning in the next few years.

All of us are consumers. All of us are in favor of good health. If a chemical or processing technique, or any other aspect of our environment, threatens our health, we would all be in favor of restricting or curtailing its use. But what a growing number of us are not in favor of is the passage of laws and regulations that do not protect our health and only serve to remove useful things from the market and raise the prices of those that do remain.

What we need, of course, is a new breed of consumer advocate, one who can effectively explode the myth that we have to choose between modern technology and good health. We can have both. Of course we need to keep health-threatening chemicals out of our food, air, and water. However, with today's consumer advocates leading the show, we are heading toward not only zero risk, but zero food, zero jobs, zero energy, and zero growth. It may be that the prophets of doom, not the profits of industry, are the real hazards to our health.

Reducing Environmental Risks

*ROBERT H. HARRIS, ROBERT B. NICHOLAS,
AND PAUL MILVY*

We share Elizabeth Whelan's concern that the public be properly informed about the risks posed to their health by their exposure to chemicals that cause cancer, and that governmental regulatory policies concern themselves first and foremost with those cancer risks the reduction of which will result in the greatest improvement in public health. Where we clearly differ, however, is on the interpretation of the "facts" that underpin the government's current regulatory approach and the "impact" of this approach on the reduction in future cancer deaths.

In the spirit of exposing our "biases," as Whelan clearly does in her article, let us divulge some of ours. We might best do this by discussing how we responded to a recent letter from a consumer whom we will call Mrs. Jones, who worried about her grandson's eating habits. Confused over the recent reports on the cancer hazards associated with charcoal-broiled meat and peanut butter, she related how her daughter became so "panicky" that she did not allow her 12-year old son to eat hot

313

dogs or charcoal-broiled steak and hamburgers at picnics. "If he goes to a ballgame, every kid eats hot dogs. . . . She gives him a peanut-butter-and-jelly sandwich. What is a ballgame without a hot dog? Now a report comes out that peanut butter may be carcinogenic."

What are parents to do? Our response, not unlike Elizabeth Whelan's would likely be, was to begin by placing the problem in some perspective. First, we told her that cancer is not unique to our modern society. The earliest known cancer is presumed to be the tumor discovered in the fossil remains of a dinosaur from the Comanchean Period of the Mesozoic Era of geologic time (ca. 125 million B.C.). Traces of bone cancer were also found in the remains of the Java Man (ca. 1 million B.C.), and bone cancer was identified in mummies in the Great Pyramid of Gizeh (2500-1500 B.C.). Such evidence, together with studies of primitive populations free of industrial pollution, makes clear that a certain amount of cancer is a natural component of all living systems (plants also get tumors). But both the amount and type of cancer is highly variable from one region of the world to the next, largely reflecting the different environments to which the various populations of the world are exposed. For example, populations exposed to excessive amounts of sunlight have a higher incidence of skin cancer. Individuals whose diets are rich in certain natural chemicals run a high risk of cancer, which explains the high liver cancer rates in certain parts of Africa and the high rates of cancer of the mouth in parts of Asia. Thus, nature does tempt us with its "forbidden fruits."

Next we reminded Mrs. Jones that cancer rates are usually higher in the more industrialized countries of the world, such as the United States, and that rates have been increasing fairly steadily since the turn of the century. In addition to sunlight, diet, and smoking, exposure to certain man-made chemicals, such as vinyl chloride, asbestos, and benzene, has been shown to cause cancer in workers. The geographical variation in cancer rates in the United States can in part be explained by the differences in industrial activity such as chemical manufacturing. But much of the growth in the manufacture of synthetic chemicals in the United States has been recent (post-World War II). Since 1940, for example, there has been approximately a 200-fold increase in the production of synthetic organic chemicals in the United States (Figure 1). Because there is typically a twenty- to forty-year latency between first exposure to a cancer-causing chemical and clinical symptoms of a tumor, the impact of this chemical revolution on U.S. cancer rates has probably not yet been fully expressed.

Therefore, we emphasized to Mrs. Jones that our risk of cancer is determined by our exposure to certain of nature's carcinogens as well as to those created by humans. We told her that what was important, however, was that scientists are now beginning to identify just what components of the environment, both natural and man-made, are most responsible for our current risk of cancer. Through such identification, certain types of cancer are now largely preventable. Reduced exposure to sunlight will decrease the risk of skin cancer; avoidance of cigarettes and alcohol will diminish the risks of lung, bladder, kidney, mouth, and certain gastrointestinal cancers; and a reduced consumption of animal fats may lower the risk of bowel and breast cancer.

Herein lies the dilemma: avoiding these risks often involves trade-offs which may conflict with our lifestyles. Mrs. Jones's grandson, for example, like most boys, enjoys going to picnics and ball games. Food served at these events, in the true American tradition, often includes charcoal-broiled hamburgers and hot dogs. We now know that certain ways of cooking food, such as charcoal broiling, create certain cancer-causing chemicals in the food. Hot dogs usually also contain nitrate and nitrite preservatives and coloring agents that can lead to the formation of certain potent cancer-causing chemicals. Hamburgers and hot dogs may be contaminated with pesticides that were used to grow the grains that fed the animals. Both are high in animal fat, a high consumption of which may increase the risk of bowel cancer. The alternative food, a peanut-butter sandwich, is likely to be contaminated with low concentrations of aflatoxin, a fungal toxin which ranks as one of the most potent cancer-causing chemicals known to man.

What are the options? First, hamburgers and hot dogs could be cooked in other ways (not charcoal broiled) and at lower temperatures to reduce this hazard. Hot dogs can be purchased that do not contain nitrites and nitrates, and, in both cases, meats can be purchased that were produced with grains for which pesticides were not used. If these options are inconvenient, or judged to be too costly, his parents may decide that his overall diet is not high in animal fats and that an occasional hot dog or hamburger is not inconsistent with that diet. Or a good education on nutrition at home may naturally lead him to feel comfortable in rejecting these foods at social gatherings.

Our answer to Mrs. Jones, in other words, was not a simple yes or no. Life is full of risks and to suggest that we can avoid them all is patently absurd. But this is not to say that if Mrs. Jones, her children, and her grandchildren were better informed they would not be willing to make some trade-offs in their personal lives that could significantly lower their risk of cancer. We are sure that Whelan would agree with our advice to Mrs. Jones that her grandson's overall lifestyle is one important factor in determining his risk of cancer and that some of these risks can be easily lowered. Some cancer risks are easy to avoid and involve little or no expense or inconveniences. For example, when Tris-treated sleepwear was still being sold after Tris [tris (2, 3-dibromopropyl) phosphate] was shown to cause cancer, it could have been avoided since safer alternatives existed at the same or at lower costs. Avoiding certain foods, however, depends on the availability of safer alternatives and the social stigma attached to refusing these foods at social gatherings. Denying a child an occasional hot dog may not be worth the possible conflict he will experience with his peer group. As we told Mrs. Jones, if a battle must be waged over what he can and cannot do with his life, preventing him from smoking cigarettes clearly has greater benefits than preventing him from eating hot dogs.

On the other hand, many cancer risks, such as those associated with air and water pollution, and contamination of our food supply, are difficult, if not impossible, to avoid. Reducing these risks will depend on the collective actions of our society and is clearly dependent on the extent to which society properly perceives the risks. Herein lies Whelan's greatest disservice to her readership. By distorting, misstating fact, and uncritically echoing arguments made by the chemical industry, she seriously misleads the public by downplaying, and occasionally outrightly denying, the generally accepted risks posed by cancer causing chemicals.

As evidence of governmental and public overreaction to chemical exposure, Whelan, while acknowledging the possibility that exposure may contribute to cancer mortality, concludes that "we have no evidence at this point that they do," and downplays the risk by terming it hypothetical. In making this statement Whelan ignores not only the animal evidence she refers to earlier in her remarks but also dismisses the generally accepted epidemiologic evidence on this point. While it is true that the vast majority of chemicals are not known to cause cancer, at least 26 of the 700 chemicals carefully studied by the widely respected International Agency for Research on Cancer have been shown to cause cancer in humans.

Regulation—Costs and Benefits

The recent attacks on government regulation in general, and the regulation of cancer-causing substances in particular, have usually been accompanied by the arguments that the costs of such regulation are excessive (implying that they greatly exceed benefits) and that government regulation has unncessarily denied the public access to useful products. Whelan embraces this logic when she implies that regulation of carcinogens "only serve[s] to remove useful things from the market and raise the prices of those that do remain." Yet she does not present one single example of a "useful" product that has been banned, leaving higher prices in its wake.

Through a thinly veiled guise of objectivity, Whelan exposes her deeply held prejudices that government regulations are out to get us with statements such as "when a pesticide is banned, I know it is not preventing cancer . . . the banning has no medical benefits . . . I will pay more for strawberries and corn next year." Yet we know of no pesticide which has been banned for its cancer-causing properties (and only a handful have been so regulated) whose cancer risk was anything but irrefutable and whose banning resulted in any significant hardship to either farmers or consumers. Take for example the pesticide dieldrin, which was banned by the Environmental Protection Agency (EPA) in 1974. Numerous scientific studies, including several by industry, demonstrated conclusively that dieldrin causes cancer in animals at extremely low concentrations. In fact, laboratory animals were shown to contract cancer at levels typical of those found in human body fat. Furthermore, during the court proceedings that accompanied EPA's banning of dieldrin, industry failed to demonstrate the efficacy of dieldrin for its intended uses, which might even suggest that banning of this persistent pesticide was an economic favor to farmers.

With regard to other "useful" products, such as food additives, Whelan argues that by banning of such products, " . . . as a scientist, I know that, too, will not prevent cancer, but will only serve to remove useful products from the shelves, such as diet soft drinks." Her target, of course, is saccharin (which has not been banned), and probably other food additives which are only used for cosmetic purposes, such as red dye #2. Cosmetic food additives that are carcinogenic are required to be banned under the Delaney Amendment to the Food, Drug and Cosmetic Act on the logical assumption that the public would rather not bear the cancer risks of continued exposure in the name of enhancing or masking the natural color of foods. Although Whelan's argument assumes that diet drinks and the use of saccharin ward off overweight, the documentation for this simply does not exist. Rather, persuasive studies suggest that no weight reduction results from using saccharin as a sugar substitute. For example, in one careful study obese patients were randomly divided into two diet groups. The diets were identical except that one group consumed artificial sweeteners and the other did not. At the end of the study, those who lost weight, stayed the same weight, or gained weight were unaffected by their use or non-use of artificial sweeteners. Although it is not clear that saccharin as a sugar replacement reduces dental cavities (another of its suggested virtues), it is easy to demonstrate that for most diabetics whose disease is not extreme the condition can be controlled without the use of diet colas, commercial diet desserts, or the use of saccharin.

That saccharin causes cancer in the male offspring of female rats which had been given very high doses for an extended period is not in dispute. Although it certainly has not been conclusively demonstrated that saccharin is carcinogenic to humans, some recent evidence suggests that high saccharin use is accompanied by a statistically significant increased risk of bladder cancer to women. Other studies have not shown this to be so. Thus, in terms of human epidemiological studies, the situation remains equivocal. This does not mean that it does not cause cancer, only that the evidence is not conclusive one way or the other. In epidemiological studies, scientists tried to show statistically that a few excess cancers are present in a population that consumes saccharin when compared to a similar population that does not. With 22 percent of our popula-

FIGURE 1: TOTAL SYNTHETIC ORGANIC CHEMICALS, ANNUAL PRODUCTION (EXCLUDES TAR, TAR CRUDES, AND PRIMARY PRODUCTS FROM PETROLEUM AND NATURAL GAS) TOTAL CHEMICALS AND ALLIED PRODUCTS, ANNUAL VALUE ADDED

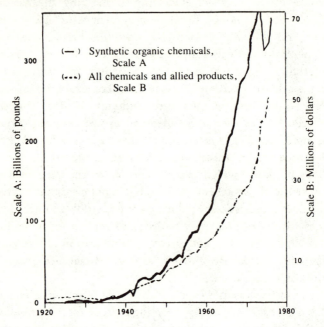

tion dying of cancer, it is extremely difficult to demonstrate that perhaps 0.01-0.5 percent of them have died because of their exposure to saccharin. Human epidemiology may lack the sensitivity to isolate the effects of this very weak (at least in animal studies) cancer-causing agent from the carcinogens to which we are exposed, many of which are much more potent.

As a complement to the "usefulness" argument, detractors of government regulation of cancer-causing chemicals often cite the alleged high cost to consumers that accompanies such regulation. In an effort to accuse government regulators and

"Naderite groups" of overstatement in the name of public safety, Whelan asserts that OSHA's (Occupational Safety and Health Administration) recently developed cancer policy requires regulation of chemicals that "might" cause cancer in animals and " . . . what it will mean is that consumers will be paying double or triple for dry cleaning in the next few years."

First of all, OSHA's cancer policy has a very strict requirement as to what evidence represents an acceptable basis for concuding that a chemical causes cancer and, as Whelan is well aware, the scientific community is nearly unanimous in its conclusion that chemicals which, in well-conducted studies, unambiguously cause cancer in laboratory animals represent a cancer risk to humans. But her main point is that, apart from whether or not a chemical really represents a cancer hazard to the public, regulation is costly and has been bad economic news to consumers.

While it is undoubtedly true that regulation involves direct cost to industry, the costs are frequently overestimated. Whelan's dry-cleaning example is a reference to the efforts by OSHA and by the Consumer Product Safety Commission (CPSC) to reduce the exposure of workers and the public to the cancer-causing dry-cleaning solvent, perchloroethylene. Contrary to the implications of her statement, modern dry-cleaning establishments have installed very tight machines that allow little "perc" to escape. A new line of dry-to-dry machines has been introduced (replacing with a single unit the two separate "washer" and "dryer" units previously used). Although the newer machines are 30 to 60 percent more expensive than the separate units, their use results not only in a much reduced cancer risk to workers but also reduction in the cost of replacing the lost "perc" as well as reduced operating expenses.

Vinyl chloride, a high-volume chemical used in the manufacture of plastics, is an example of a chemical recently regulated by OSHA, CPSC, and other agencies; regulation that had

FIGURE 2: PERCENT ANNUAL INCREASE IN CONSUMER PRICE INDEX WITH AND WITHOUT ENVIRONMENTAL CONTROLS

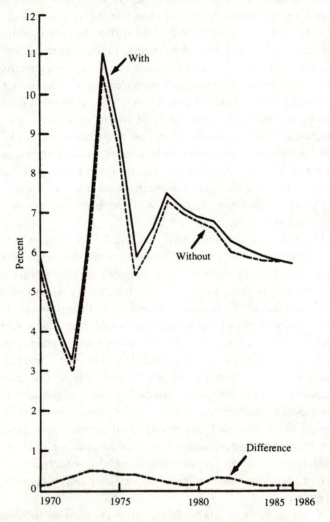

little or no adverse economic impact on the industry, despite its early claims that regulation would produce devastating economic consequences. As has been the case for several chemicals, vinyl chloride was shown to cause cancer in laboratory animals several years before the tragic human evidence precipitated regulatory action in 1975. In opposing the new OSHA standard, the manufacturers of vinyl chloride (V.C.) had argued that they could meet the new standard only through huge price increases that would make V.C. uncompetitive with other types of plastics. In point of fact, V.C. did not increase disproportionately in price (although inflation has modestly raised the price of all plastics) because industry developed two extremely simple methods for reducing worker exposure that have cost very little and allowed the recapture of most of the V.C. vented to the environment—an economic plus. *Chemical Week* headlined an article on this subject in September 1976: "PVC Rolls Out of Jeopardy, into Jubilation." In this instance we see an example of a new regulation forcing the development of a technological improvement beneficial to all society. This experience is hardly unique.

That decreased human exposure to cancer-causing chemicals results in financial savings to industry is not always true, of course. But for Whelan to talk about higher cost, fewer jobs, reduced productivity, and higher taxes, though factually correct in certain instances, gives the impression that these costs are unjustified. Direct costs imposed by regulation are only part of the story. Pollution control adds to our store of healthy citizens, reducing hospital costs and absenteeism, and creating more useful lives.

Although the aggregate costs of regulating cancer-causing chemicals have not been determined, environmental pollution control in general has added only a modest cost (roughly 0.2 percent per year during 1975-1980) to the production of goods and services, as Figure 2 indicates. Similar calculations reveal that these costs have added only about 0.1 percent to the inflation rate this year, while actually creating about 400,000 jobs. In a study which was prepared for the President's Council on Environmental Quality by Professor Myrick Freeman at Bowdoin College, it was estimated, for example, that the benefits from improvements in air quality amounted to about $21 billion in 1978. (Seventeen billion dollars as a result of reduction of pollution-related deaths and illnesses—asthma, bronchitis, emphysema, and lung cancer—$2 billion in soiling and cleaning costs reductions, as well as smaller savings from corrosion prevention, property value increases, increased agricultural yields, etc.) Despite the large uncertainties in this estimate, including omission of a number of important benefits difficult to assign a dollar value, such as improved visibility, this benefit estimate exceeds the nationwide cost estimate of $19 billion to clean up air pollution in 1978.

Cancer Trends

The cancer debate often revolves around discussion of the proportion of today's cancer rate that is due to various activities such as smoking, diet, occupational exposure, and pollution. But because of the 20- to 40-year latency problem referred to earlier, this debate has only limited usefulness in predicting future cancer patterns. However, recent trends in cancer incidence may reveal important clues to future rates. In discussing these trends Whelan erroneously asserts that the National Cancer Institute (NCI) data show an overall slight decline in cancer incidence during the last several decades. In fact, what the NCI data show, to quote the American Cancer Society's *Cancer Facts and Figures, 1980,* is that "the overall incidence of cancer decreased slightly from 1947 to 1970, but has increased between 5 and 10 percent since 1970" (actually from 1970 to 1976, the latest data analyzed). So cancer trends, which had begun to level off (they have been increasing steadily since the turn of the century, although considerably more slowly after the Second World War), have or may have started again to increase. What is of concern to many cancer specialists, of course, is the possibility that this apparent reversal in trend is due to the public's exposure to man-made chemicals which accompanied the significant increase in the production of synthetic chemicals after the War (see Figure 1), and that this is just the beginning of a significant upward trend in cancer incidence.

In the case of occupational causes of cancer, Whelan attempts to downplay this problem by arguing that worker exposure to carcinogens could not possibly explain more than 5 percent of the cancer mortality rate. Although we would agree that much uncertainty is associated with this estimate, a very strong argument can be made that considerably more cancer in the near future will be related to occupational carcinogens. To come up with a reliable estimate is extremely difficult, but to dismiss this possibility and possibly to err on the side of imprudence, seems to us to be ill advised. Five percent of cancer mortality may, when so expressed, seem relatively minor. Yet it represents 20,000 deaths, more than fourfold more deaths than from job-related accidents. If Whelan would vigorously pursue safety-related measures to decrease accidents on the job, she should also consider reducing long-term cancer risks in the workplace.

We would agree with Whelan that smoking is the primary cause of lung cancer. However, her attempt to downplay the potential of chemicals as causative agents in lung cancer is misleading. Whelan seeks to support her position by stating that lung-cancer mortality is identical in the county of Rutland, Vermont, and in the state of New Jersey. The facts are true, but very misleading. Even a state like New Jersey, with its "cancer alley," has large numbers of rural communities which tend to dilute the urban and industrial cancer rates. In Vermont, Rutland's white male cancer rate is more than 20 percent higher than the state average. The explanation for this, according to a representative of the Rutland Hospital's cancer registry, may well be the dust exposure experienced by the large number of men who work in Rutland's important industry, the quarrying of marble, granite, and in earlier years, slate. The wide range of variation among Vermont counties can be illustrated by comparing Chittenden and Essex. Chittenden County, which has considerable industry, has an incidence of lung cancer equally as high as Rutland County's; but rural Essex County has a lung cancer rate 60 percent lower than Rutland's. Similar variations in counties are seen in New Jersey. Nevertheless, it remains true that New Jersey is, in general, more industrialized than Vermont. And, according to NCI, the total cancer mortality during the 20-year period, 1950-1969, was 18.5 percent higher for men and 8.4 percent higher for women in New Jersey than in Vermont. In the case of lung cancer, 24.7 percent more New Jersey men were dying from lung cancer than Vermont men. This is an extremely large differential cancer mortality rate, especially since it reflects exposures to cancer-causing materials that probably occurred during the 1930-1950 interval when "cancer alley" was not yet even a well-beaten path.

"Toxic Chemicals and Public Protection," a recent report to the president by the Toxic Substances Strategy Committee, presents a comprehensive analysis of cancer trends. The report was endorsed by experts from all federal departments and agencies which had major policy, research, or regulatory responsibilities related to control of potentially hazardous chemicals. We hope that Whelan is correct in her belief that cancer trends are not increasing, but it would be unwise and not in the public interest to ignore the more recent data as set forth in this report and in several recent scientific journals.

Lastly, we take strong exception to Whelan's belief, expressed in the final paragraph of a report she prepared for the American Council on Science and Health, *Cancer in the United States: Is There an Epidemic?*, that cancer is due not to "society and the environment, not [to] cells of the body but either [to] an unwillingness to learn or an inability to act." For what she implies, by indicating our lifestyle as the cause of cancer, is that each of us is individually responsible for acts that lead us to get cancer.

It is undoubtedly true that a significant reduction in cancer risk can result from individual changes in lifestyle—reduced smoking and certain dietary changes, for example. But as importantly, strong and abundant evidence implicates exposures deriving from modern industrial processes in the genesis of a significant fraction of all cancer cases. Most, if not all, such exposures are involuntary—frequently we do not even know when or to what we are exposed—and therefore not within an individual's ability to control.

Even in the apparently simple cases involving better recognized risks—smoking, for example—the lines between individual and collective choice often become somewhat fuzzy. Although composition of our diet, and whether we smoke and drink, are clearly within our ability to control as individuals, how we collectively license the public communications network has an important impact as well. Smoking advertisements (a third of a billion dollars are spent on them every year by U.S. companies) bombard us daily with the message that smoking is sexy, stylish, and "with it." There is no doubt that many smokers are, in a very real sense, both psychologically and physically addicted. To call smoking an individual decision that is freely chosen is simply to ignore the effects of advertising on individuals' values and perceptions. In our view the need for collective action is clear. The only question is the manner in which the authority is exercised.

Over the years, society has strongly supported government's authority to act to prevent substantial risks to public health and safety. The more than two dozen federal statutes covering the routes by which certain chemicals or aspects of chemical use can threaten human health and the environment embody a preventative approach, mandating the testing and evaluating of products before they are allowed on the market. These authorities, as well as embodying a precautionary principle, mandate government action when evidence of a hazard is strongly suggestive but not completely certain, and generally provide that the risk of uncertainty—the lack of knowledge about the safety of a product—be borne by the manufacturer and not by the general public. Public experience with DES, Thalidomide, Kepone, and vinyl chloride amply support the rationale of this approach. While government regulation can and must be improved, we do not believe it should be improved at the expense of public health.

Whelan concludes that the regulatory zealots are leading us toward a society that has no food, no energy, and no growth, albeit a society without risk. We do not believe this dire forecast is at all persuasive. Rather we believe that a society with reduced environmental risks is both compatible with economic growth and necessary for the improvement of the quality of our lives.

Cancer and Corporations

ROBERT CRAWFORD

For Elizabeth Whelan, the public's fear of cancer seems to have spawned a new disease, more malignant than cancer itself. This new illness, *cancerphobia*, menaces the social body just as certainly as its progenitor imperils the physical body. Now evidently of epidemic proportions, cancerphobia can be traced to an antitechnology irrationalism, a backwater chemical anxiety, a cold-sweat fear of modern living. Whelan perceives the carriers of this newest social pathology as "prophets of doom," the source of the misinformation on cancer which "directs" the policies of the regulatory agencies concerned with health. The consequences are said to be far reaching. Industry suffers from "more regulation, higher costs, fewer jobs, and limited production." Consumers experience "high prices, higher taxes, fewer products—a diminished standard of living." Aligned against these hazards is a new breed of public-health educator—the scientist-consumer, lending perspective to the uncontrollable mass of public confusion.

Unreasonable fears about imagined threats should be discouraged; the appeal for caution, commended. Everything does not cause cancer. The economy cannot be paralyzed. Media coverage, which feeds the public discrete reports and single points of view released to support one or another side, only serves to confuse. Carcinogen-of-the-day humor has become a public nuisance. If people are to make sense of all that is being said about cancer, the cool, disinterested testimony of scientific expertise is welcome.

The trouble is that the experts do not agree. The search for the "facts" invariably runs into the selective presentation of facts, along with a profusion of nonscientific judgments and interpretations hidden in a jungle of jargon. How is the nonexpert to form a sensible assessment when scientific and political perspectives have become hopelessly entangled? Cancer has become one of the most controversial issues of our time. In such a climate, where charges and countercharges over cause and responsibility are as numerous as the credentials of the adversaries, anxiety becomes almost rational. Matters are further complicated when almost daily one reads or hears corporate advertisements proclaiming the safety of one or another industrial technology and the safety consciousness or record of one or another industry. Why is so much effort being expended, the typical cancerphobe might ask?

While the following is not an appeal to avoid the complex, scientific issues involved, it is an argument that the classical political questions of *who gets what and how* are essential to understanding the cancer issue as well. I have seen credible, opposing perspectives to almost every empirical issue contained (often implicitly) in Whelan's article. Other respondents will address some of these. A political analysis, however, will provide a useful framework, unavoidably entailing a point of view, from which scientific claims and other assertions might be more clearly understood. Attitudes are formed, after all, from experiences which extend beyond the technical discussions of proof, test design and validity, reasonable extrapolations from the data, and perennial questions about the status of

Canadian rats. Are such experiences and attitudes to be discounted as irrational? Should policy makers, while necessarily requiring the guidance of scientific expertise, bypass mass public sentiment which cannot possibly be familiar with the detailed scientific debates?

Whelan denies what I take to be axiomatic when she asserts optimistically that "we would all be in favor of restricting or curtailing" threats to our health (implying that health is simply a matter of pursuing the most rational route to agreed-upon goals). My departing assumption is the opposite—that corporations are willing to tolerate health threats to the public as an unfortunate but necessary byproduct of a perceived higher good. If this is true, how corporations then protect themselves from a health-conscious public, a consciousness which threatens corporate objectives, is an urgent analytical task. But first, it would be helpful to look at how prevention, and thus cancer, emerged as a public issue.

Politics of Prevention

Just a decade ago, the public's fear of cancer was the occasion for a proclaimed war. Federal money flooded into cancer research, a multi-million dollar a year enterprise. Now, at the beginning of the 1980s, another war unfolds: in place of a war on cancer, there is today a war *over* cancer. Instead of seeing the public's fear of cancer as a legitimate concern about a "growing epidemic" and mandating the massive injection of governmental research dollars, the experts now debate whether we are faced with an epidemic at all. It is important to note the two periods because they so clearly illustrate the political nature of the public discussion. In 1971, the primary cancer lobby was the biomedical research establishment. In 1981, there was a different set of political-economic interests mobilized, attempting to define the nature of the cancer problem and shape the direction of public policy. What happened in those ten years to change the terms of the cancer debate?

The short answer is that we have moved into the age of prevention. Certainly, the biomedical research scientists continue to be the masters of publicity, more than willing to appear in white coat, explaining new therapeutic advances and carefully avoiding mention of persisting survival rates. A steady diet of "breakthroughs" stirs the imagination. Nonetheless, during the last ten years, medicine's jurisdictional claims in the war against cancer have been steadily eroded. Even voices from within the medical world have begun to proclaim its limitations.

By the mid-1970s, several forces, each with its own history, converged to make prevention a pressing political and policy issue. One of these was the earlier success of environmental and labor constituencies in creating new legislation and agencies whose mission would be the reduction of environmental and occupational health hazards. Another was the proliferation of American and world-wide scientific studies, both laboratory and human, identifying risk factors associated with the major chronic diseases. Especially with regard to cancer, the studies gave the regulatory agencies the ammunition they needed to act. The activities of these agencies, in turn, sparked a revival of interest in public-health issues. Small environmental and occupational health movements grew in size and visibility. Anti-nuclear protests developed into a mass movement. Social action had become health conscious.

Largely due to all this new activity, a number of public-health warnings and disasters were brought to public attention: PCBs, kepone, saccharin, pesticides, contamination of drinking water, asbestos, vinyl chlorides, DES, Three Mile Island, Love Canal and toxic wastes, and, of course, the accumulation and dissemination of further evidence about three of America's favorite pastimes—the consumption of high fat and high cholesterol foods, tobacco, and alcohol. For still other reasons, to be discussed below, prevention became, by the late 1970s, a widely discussed topic in health policy and medical circles and among the middle class.

The resulting awareness, concern, and polarization over these issues, along with the opening of the new regulatory arenas, politicized health and disease. Prevention became embroiled with other issues and with an array of political tendencies in American life. By 1980, it had become more difficult for the public to think of illness as simply a medical problem. Among growing numbers of people there was suddenly an inkling that vast economic and political forces were at work to shape the course of health and disease. Unlike the relatively stable politics of medical care, prevention emerged as a political unknown — less institutionalized, less amenable to licensed, professional monopolies, and more fractionated by political and economic groups mobilized to protect or extend their interests. Medicine had clearly failed and thus government, industry, and the public, although each manifesting multiple tendencies, began to forge their own health strategies.

Ironically, industry helped create the prevention issue. In the mid-1970s, sectors of the corporate world, along with government officials and the academic policy sciences, turned their attention to the growing problem of medical-care costs. Inflation in the medical sector had become burdensome for everyone; but for government, faced with increasing fiscal pressures, and industry, encountering rapidly rising premiums, medical costs had become critical. A consensus slowly emerged that the medical monolith needed taming, and a broad-based, cost-control coalition began mobilizing to impose reforms. The politics of expansion of medical services, equality of access, and the extension of entitlements, characteristic of the 1960s and early 1970s, was superseded by a politics which would attempt to curb growth, entitlements, and access. The hospital-medical lobby, however, would not be easily dislodged, and thus, direct cost-control reforms were supplemented with intermediate strategems: public hospitals were closed and other government programs terminated; Medicaid benefits were constricted; and Medicare and private insurance shifted more of the burden of payments to workers and consumers in hope that additional personal responsibility for costs would act as a deterrent to utilization. Comprehensive national health insurance became a dead issue.

Following the lead of the Canadian Minister of health, Marc Lalonde, health-policy discussions in the United States turned to the idea of prevention as an antidote to spiraling medical costs. Keeping people out of hospitals by keeping them healthy seemed a promising, long-term solution. Healthier employees, moreover, would help lower industry premium rates, cut absenteeism, and improve productivity.

Health promotion, however, contained an even more important symbolic function. The public discusson of prevention—a prevention campaign—might serve to reassure workers and the general public, who had come to see medical care as a right to be guaranteed by workplace arrangements or government financing, that less medical care is not equivalent to less health. Thus, even though workplace and government entitlements were being eroded, and national health insurance delayed indefinitely, medical benefits would be replaced by a new corporate and governmental commitment to employee and public health. Further, individual responsibility for health, not national health insurance, could be promoted as the optimal solution to both the cost crisis and health maintenance. As of the late 1970s, prevention linked to cost control would become the *cause célèbre* of national health policy.

Of course, prevention is a broad concept. It allows for the possibility of widely differing definitions and directions. In the political context of the last several years, there has been a tendency to define prevention with almost exclusive emphasis as either a problem of industrial hazards, or as a problem of individual lifestyles and at-risk behaviors, especially smoking. In the lifestyle approach, health education and individual responsibility are the means to better health. It is this definition, with environmental and occupational hazards relegated to the status of "also rans," which has, outside the regulatory agencies, become the prevailing understanding. Promotional activities equating preventions with lifestyle changes have become standard fare. For the corporations, the need for such an emphasis is obvious. Prevention, like pollution before it, needs to be portrayed as an individual problem.

For government officials, only slightly more complex considerations need be mentioned. First, if gains in prevention are to be made, simple political calculation discourages policy makers from bothering too much about reforms which would require a political realignment which presently does not exist. Even though the evidence for large-scale behavior change is not encouraging either, at least there are fewer political obstacles, the tobacco lobby notwithstanding, to health-education efforts aimed at individual health promotion. Moreover, as will be discussed below, a new and significant cultural interest in personal health may reinforce efforts to change lifestyles.

Second, in the more practical context of building and maintaining support for policy priorities, holding together the coalition for cost control, not prevention, is most essential. If the entrenched political power of the hospital-medical lobby is to be broken, corporate support cannot be jeopardized. Pressing for environmental and occupational reforms as a primary prevention strategy would undermine an already tenuous coalition, especially with regard to regulatory, cost-control policies.

Finally, at a very general but not-to-be-overlooked level, the fiscal vitality of government as well as both short-term political viability of ruling parties and long-term stability of governments are dependent on the health of the corporate-controlled economy. Even before Reagan, many political leaders were convinced of the industry perspective that more inducements, not more constraints, were necessary in order to stimulate growth and investment. Even the smoking issue could not be pressed too far for fear of the economic and political repercussions. Nonetheless, much to the consternation of those industries which thrive from the at-risk behaviors, prevention has become practically synonomous with the campaign against "sloth, gluttony, alcoholic intemperance, reckless driving, sexual frenzy and smoking." (The words come from the late John Knowles, past president of the Rockefeller Foundation.) Perceived as *victim blaming* among environmental and occupational-health activists and their supporters, this formulation of the prevention problem has itself turned into one of the major issues in the debate over cancer and other health risks.

New Health Consciousness

The interest in prevention, and, in particular, a focus on lifestyle and health, can also be seen at other levels of American society. Not only has there been a surge in popular concern about environmental and occupational health hazards—what Whelan refers to as cancerphobia—but a new health consciousness and health movements are beginning to transform cultural values about personal health. The new health consciousness has generated a vocal and often aggressive anti-smoking ethic, the proliferation of popular health magazines, massive consumption of vitamins and other health aids, profound changes in dietary habits, and a transformation of tens of thousands of sedentaries into marathon runners. If one were to conclude anything about popular health attitudes in contemporary America, it would be that people, especially the middle class, are beginning to take matters of individual health promotion seriously. Contrary to corporate phobias of an aroused, industry-baiting public, Americans are directing their energies toward lifestyle changes.

There is no simple explanation for the current "wellness" enthusiasm. Certainly, as suggested, it has been promoted. The media are flooded with guides to better health, health-related television series, health features in magazines, and health themes in advertising. But this phenomenon must reflect, in part, a perceived interest and demand for such material. The promotion of lifestyle-oriented prevention efforts by both government and private groups has also stimulated the growth of professional and entrepreneurial interests, quick to perceive opportunities for expansion and new markets. The health-education profession and consulting firms specializing in employee health promotion are examples. Hospitals have also discovered the public-relations values of health promotion.

But why has the professional middle class particularly been so receptive? And how does one explain why large numbers of people attempt difficult lifestyle changes, like quitting smoking, or other changes, like diet, which require an investment of time and money? And why are there so many joggers? Understanding the new health consciousness is important if for no other reason than to combat reductionistic characterizations of popular health attitudes like Whelan's visions of cancerphobia and chain-smoking anti-nuclear demonstrators. Causal understanding is extremely complex, but here are a few observations.

First, personal-health promotion is likely to appear to many people as the only possible alternative to a health-threatening environment which eludes control. Both the number of health hazards communicated in the last decade and the seeming intractability of most of them leave people with a sense of having few options. In the absence of a clear commitment by society to health promotion, individual responsibility comes to be seen as a necessity. The most difficult individual adjustments will be attempted. As individuals, we all face the same dilemma: we cannot afford to wait for a political solution, so we adopt health practices which we believe will reduce our risk. The loss of control over health is "eased by its endless pursuit."

Second, much of the new interest in lifestyle and health is

connected with the cultural diffusion of two important health movements—self-care/self-help and holistic health. The growth of these movements (and, I would argue, the spread of the prevention-lifestyle ethic in general) derives, in part, from popular disenchantment with medicine. Tracing the disaffection is, again, complex, but anger about costs and iatrogenesis, the lack of significant therapeutic success for most of the major chronic diseases, and an unhappiness about the experience of the medical encounter and the dependence on drugs and doctors are all important. The holistic health and the self-care/self-help movements have articulated these discontents and communicated them to wider publics.

Third, the enhancement and control of personal health finds fertile ground in a middle-class population which in the 1970s was forced to adjust to a world of increased insecurity and uncertainty. Not only did people experience an assault of health-hazard warnings, but the long wave of post-Second World War economic prosperity began to show the first signs of ebbing. When social life is experienced as eluding control, particularly when people begin to wonder whether a standard of living to which they have become accustomed can be sustained, the need for personal control is often intensified. Personal health has become one area into which people can throw their energies and reassert some sense that they can act on their own behalf. Of course, middle-class people not only have more time and resources for health-promotion activities, they have also acquired fundamental notions about themselves as social actors from work situations and other supporting socializing patterns which predispose them to seeing their achievements as a result of personal effort alone.

Finally, the conception of health which is now applied to prevention retains key medical notions which situate the problem of health and disease at the level of the individual body. In medicine, the individual is the locus of both perception and intervention. Thus, medical perception pushes causal understanding toward the immediate and local, and solution toward the elimination of symptoms and the restoration of normal signs. The new health movements and prevention consciousness modify several important medical concepts, but in one direction only: toward host resistance and adaptation. Social considerations beyond immediate psychological atmospheres are most often neglected. Health promotion remains an individual endeavor.

There are several other explanatory directions one could pursue, connections with social currents both long-standing and recent (e.g., links with the human potential and environmental movements, or cultural traditions about health at least back to the Victorians). What is clear, however, is that the political focus of the environmental and occupational health movements and the public's concern about industrial carcinogens are only part of the total cultural turn toward prevention. Moreover, for complicated reasons, substantial segments of the public, although perhaps holding the more political views as well, have adopted the dominant ideological position that prevention is a problem of lifestyle and requires the assumption of individual responsibility. After all, as we are often reminded, it does make good sense.

Prevention Of Politics

From the foregoing, it can be seen that the age of prevention is evolving and being constructed on several levels. There are powerful forces which converge to define the problem of prevention as a matter of individual behaviors, attitudes, and emotions. Different but overlapping events and forces have given rise to an environmental and occupational understanding of the health problem—a definition which implicates industry. It is difficult to know which way the prevention issue will turn. The ways the public thinks about and acts upon their anxieties and hopes for good health and long life, their understanding of what should be done to promote or maintain health, and their notions of accountability and responsibility are all in flux. The instability of popular perceptions of both problem and solution, especially in a period which will inevitably produce more occupational and environmental health disasters and further discovery of carcinogenic outcomes from industrial products and processes, is the critical ideological and political problem facing the corporations. What is evident is that prevention has become much riskier than corporate executives had ever imagined. The dilemma facing the corporations is that the public discussion and popularity of prevention, even in the form of lifestyle changes and individual responsibility, may reinforce a potentially uncontainable health consciousness. The dilemma cannot be easily resolved since victim-blaming notions of prevention are one of the few ways attention can be diverted from industry. The outlines of an attempted resolution, however, can be seen in Elizabeth Whelan's article. Unlike that of plutonium, the half-life of prevention may have already passed.

Whelan's article contains the classical victim-blaming ingredients: the citation of studies which minimize environmental and occupational health hazards and maximize at-risk behaviors. "As a society," writes Whelan, "we seem to be drifting toward a policy which tolerates known, major risks chosen by the individual—and rejects hypothetical risks that might be assumed by industry or society as a whole." But the real emphasis of her article can be found elsewhere and can be summarized in three points: 1) we are healthier than we think; or certainly, let's not think in terms of epidemics; 2) an irrational cancerphobia—what others sometimes call a Chicken Little syndrome—grips the American public; and 3) we must begin thinking in terms of "acceptable risks"; that is, we must increase our tolerance of an inevitably risky society if we are to continue to enjoy our prosperity. The three are closely linked arguments.

If the primary political concern is to minimize the possibility that the normally quiescent public will become politicized around health issues, the last word one would want thrown about is *epidemic*. It is a mobilizing word, likely to evoke flight or fight. It suggests that all of society's resources and defenses need to be galvanized into action (which is precisely why the biomedical research establishment continues using it). "There has been an increase in cancer mortality in the last few decades," writes Whelan, "but certainly nothing on the order of 'epidemic.'" The fact is that there is no objective way to define *epidemic*: if the "rapidly spreading" part of the definition is emphasized, a usage usually associated with infectious diseases, cancer may not qualify; whereas if the "widespread" or "prevalent" part is stressed, a different determination might be reached. It is not surprising to me that people would assign the term *epidemic* to a disease which, if present trends continue, 25 percent of us will contract and from which 20 percent of us will die. But to Whelan, it is a sure sign of cancerphobia.

Cancerphobia is one of those rhetorical expressions that are clearly designed to stigmatize and belittle political opposition. It is an attribution of both sickness and extremism (combining the best of political slander). Like Spiro Agnew's "nattering nabobs of negativism," cancerphobes are naysayers who neurotically advance the position that "we have to choose between modern technology and good health." Mysteriously, cancerphobia "is dictating federal policy." For Whelan, the source of cancerphobia is a combination of anti-technology sentiment, chemical anxiety, and "a new philosophy" which requires the assessment of blame for disease. The latter, in turn, "resulted from our new emphasis on cancer and the environment." Attached to this circular bit of reasoning is the classic lack-of-proof argument. Since Whelan's definitions of the state of the cancer-research art rarely allows us to attribute cause or probable links, the desire to affix responsibility and to restrict exposure to suspected carcinogens amounts to desperation. After all, we are reminded, "death and disease are still natural processes." Finally, the reader is warned that it becomes "economically disastrous for a society when there is no proof of guilt." The prophecy of economic disaster brings us to the *pièce de résistance* of the new ideology: risk acceptability.

Acceptance of Risk

The discussion of risk and health has several dimensions and can only be touched upon here. The application of risk-benefit analysis to regulatory decisions, for example, would require a thorough discussion of its history and methodology. An excellent critical introduction can be found in an article by David Noble in the July/August, 1980, issue of *Health/PAC Bulletin.* Despite appearances of scientific rationality, risk-benefit analysis is not likely to result in a less political regulatory decision process, since methodologies will inevitably reflect subjective judgments with regard to practically every element in the risk-benefit equation. The determination of an appropriate definition and measure of benefit, for instance, is, at core, a political discussion. Noble argues that risk-benefit analysis shifts the locus of decision making into a mode more clearly dominated by business considerations and makes the decision process even more remote from citizen competence and judgment. I will confine myself to the part of the argument aimed at undercutting public support for *any* effort to force the reduction of industrial hazards.

It is legitimate for a society to ask how much risk is acceptable in relation to expected benefit. Choices are made which have consequences for public health at all stages of research, production, use, and disposal of industrial products. The reduction of risks may involve significant added costs—both in terms of time and resources devoted to researching the question and reducing the discovered risk. The presumption on which the need for regulation is premised is that the rational, private firm will reduce only those risks believed likely to cost the firm more if left unreduced. For corporations, which must continually operate in a social and political environment of actual and potential opposition, economic decisions affecting health risks to workers and the public depend unavoidably on the answers to several political questions. Will existing regulations and the successful enforcement of those regulations result in costly recalls, product removals, burdensome fines, or mandated alteration of manufacturing processes? Will liability suits and compensation claims be successful? Are those costs too high? If disasters do occur, can government be counted on to help pay the costs of cleanup or rectification? Will public anger or perceptions of high risk lead to market sanctions?

These calculations involve every facet of potential regulatory, legislative, legal, and public reaction—including, of course, the political and ideological capacity of industry to weaken or neutralize those threats. Thus, the level of "allowed" or acceptable" risk is best understood as a politically determined outcome. It reflects the relative power of corporations, consumers, workers, and the general public. Risk acceptability, in other words, depends on the success of contending. ideologies and the political-economic power brought to bear to enforce them. The first objective of corporate-risk ideology is to trivialize the public perception of industrial hazards. Unlike the lack-of-proof tactic, which is aimed at minimizing industrial, causal responsibility, the risk argument stresses the insignificance of industrial hazards by presenting them as comparable to mundane and inevitable risks of everyday life.

Modern living, asserts this new ideology, like living in any age, is characterized by inevitable risks. Taking risks is synonomous with being in the world—getting out of bed in the morning, crossing the street, etc. We take risks because we value the activities we pursue. We ride in airplanes; we drive autos; in other words, we make daily choices which involve risks. These choices follow from explicit or implicit calculations which help us determine whether the risk is acceptable. Essentially, the argument goes, we weigh risk against benefit. Likewise, as a society we are confronted with similar choices and calculations. The contention is made that, in principle, judgments about risk acceptability should be no different for valued social activities, like producing chemicals, than for valued activities pursued by the individual. Since people are willing to assume individual risks, they should also accept equivalent risks from industry. People are irrational or "confused" if they seek a lower level of imposed risks than assumed risks. Elaborate calculations are often made to demonstrate, for example, that driving a number of miles to and from work is equivalent to or much more dangerous than the risk of living next to a nuclear power plant. If industrial risks are really no different in kind or degree from the hundreds of risks assumed daily by everyone, then what is all the fuss about?

Many people will find appealing the argument that the risk of cancer from one or another industrial source is no more probable than being killed driving to work or falling off a ladder. Unless burdened with a family history of cancer, people are likely to believe they will win out in the statistical gamble. The belief in the strength of one's resistance allows many people to smoke without fear of cancer, for example. Familiar risks are more reassuring because it seems, at least in the healthy years of life, we almost always are lucky. Judgments about risks on any one day are far different than for the span of a lifetime. People tend to stop thinking about risks taken daily.

Second, assertions about public confusion regarding risks hide an even more fundamental issue underlying the politicization of environmental and occupational health. Public support for controls on industry may reflect not only a perception of unacceptable levels of risk, but a pervasive lack of trust that corporations will place the health of the public and the workforce above considerations of profit. In other words, the issue for many people may not simply be risks to health, but corporate irresponsibility—not a fear of chemicals so much as a fear of chemical *companies*. If an historical mistrust of industry leads to perceptions of negligence, carelessness, or venality, the political issue emerges as very different in kind than if the problem is considered one of acceptable risks and benefits. Is one any less rational than the other? A person need not be an expert in order to reach a conclusion about corporate behavior, whereas risk-benefit assessment is a complex matter more suited to professional policy analysts.

Moreover, most people now seem reluctant to allow any expansion of government power unless some vital aspect of the public's welfare is at stake *and* the institutions responsible for the problem cannot be trusted. Both industry and government compete for lowest ranking in public perceptions of credibility. Issues of credibility have been important in the politicization of almost every major public-health issue. Why did MGM refuse to spend more money on sprinklers in its Las Vegas hotel? Will the utility companies cover up nuclear safety violations or fail to report accidents? Did corporate managers know that asbestos was deadly but continue producing it anyway? Did Ford know about and let stand a Pinto defect that could cost hundreds of lives? What shortcuts were made in the construction or maintenance of DC-10s? Do chemical companies knowingly dump dangerous chemicals, and do they conspire to cover up the evidence? Are the textile companies telling the truth about brown lung disease? Perhaps there would be less of the claimed double standard about assumed and imposed risks if people had more trust. The fact is that they do not. The question of benefit is already on the public's mind, but asked somewhat differently than the corporations would like: Whose benefit is being served when the public is put at risk? The issue is as old as capitalism itself.

The discussion of risk versus benefit bring us to the third, and I think most cynical, objective of risk polemics. In the last decade, so the argument goes, we have been thinking a great deal about risks, but very little about benefits. As a consequence, we are teetering on the edge of economic catastrophe. When everything else fails, the best way to neutralize the public's anxiety about cancer and corporate motives is to introduce into the debate an even greater anxiety. A risk-conscious society and what follows in the form of unreasonable regulation of industry will lead to economic hardship; or as Whelan claims, to "zero food, zero jobs, zero energy, and zero growth." *The prophets of doom, it turns out, are those who see a threat to the profits of industry in a health-conscious public*. America was made great by an entrepreneurial spirit based on risk-taking; and now a public living in morbid fear of cancer and other hazards threatens progress itself. Thus, while the lack-of-proof defense *minimizes* corporate responsibilty for cancer, and victim blaming *shifts* the burden of responsibility to the individual, and the first part of the risk argument *trivializes* industrial risks, now this freezing-in-the-dark imagery *maximizes* the public's acceptance of higher risks through crude scare tactics. Americans must begin thinking in terms of trade-offs.

Americans are used to thinking in such terms. Historically, threats of added hardships have been wielded against workers and communities in order to silence voices opposing existing hardships. People have often capitulated to "we-can't-afford-it" polemics, not because they believed the claim, but because of the willingness of corporations to use economic coercion to achieve their objectives. The near-absolute control over production, the national and international mobility of corporations, and the availability of areas where people are more "willing" to accept industry's terms make the threats believable. Factory closures, including the flight of hazardous industries, are already a stark reality for growing numbers of industrial workers and communities. As unemployment increases and real wages fall, the threat of more of the same is a powerful force for inducing acquiescence. Without the threat of economic coercion, and the willingness of industry to act on that threat, the corporate-risk ideology would fall flat.

Under these conditions, people are more likely to "accept" yet higher levels of risk. But Americans will continue to worry about health. Acceptance of higher risks is not the same as believing that those risks are insignificant. I suspect that people will remain mistrustful or angry, even as they become more resigned. Those who have come to believe in prevention might put in an extra mile on the track. If the stress induced by the entire "reindustrialization" effort is not too great, those who are able will drink and smoke less. Public reaction to the inevitable public-health disasters, however, will continue to pose serious problems for the corporate reindustrialization scenario. Barring the discovery of a cure, cancer will remain a political issue. Thus, we will continue to witness the massive investments by industry in health-related defensive advertising and read articles, like Elizabeth Whelan's, which combine the full arsenal of corporate arguments. For, much to the dismay of some, the profits of industry will remain linked with cancer.

The Price of Survival for Cancer Victims

MORTON BARD

Why is a previously dynamic corporation president confined to a wheelchair, with nurse in attendance—ten years after successful cancer surgery?

Why is a fifty-year-old woman "a prisoner in my bathroom," compulsively (and unnecessarily) irrigating a colostomy for twelve hours every other day—six years after successful cancer surgery?

Why does a thirty-five-year-old mother with three children remain a virtual recluse—five years after the loss of a breast in a successful battle against cancer?

Why did a productive businessman sell his business at a loss, become a non-functioning invalid, and settle down to await death—after successful cancer surgery eleven years earlier?

Tragic stories like these are dramatic evidence of the gap between today's remarkable advances in medical technology and the unpredictable paradoxes of human emotions and

349

behavior. Such stories of "death expectancy" reveal untold suffering for people whose lives have been saved, and for their families. They suggest a disturbing thought—more and more lives are being saved, but *for what?*

Why should the gift of life become so bitter to the survivors of major illnesses who, only a few years ago, would have invariably died?

To find answers to this paradoxical question, a clinical and research team of psychiatrists, psychologists, and psychiatric social workers was organized at Memorial Hospital and Sloan-Kettering Institute for Cancer Research in New York City, several years ago. The group explored the vastly complex interplay of mind and body in the struggle with cancer—a disease which, throughout the history of man, has carried with it a burden of frightening, superstitious, moral, and even demonic implications. Through repeated interviews with patients we probed into their deepest fantasies and feelings to assemble the disheartening picture that follows.

Cancer patients must be regarded as people under a special and severe form of stress. Cancer is commonly perceived as an always-fatal and particularly loathsome disease, not "clean" and uncomplicated like, for example, the frequently more fatal heart disease. In addition to the expectation of prolonged and intense pain, it carries the threat of disability and, even more frighteningly, recurrence and the repeated threat of death. Thus cancer becomes an unusually stressful experience which disrupts the most important lifelong patterns of behavior.

Every individual, throughout his life, develops a system of beliefs and behavior designed to bring his physical and emotional needs into harmony with the demands of his environment. When these patterns of adaptation are threatened or disrupted anxiety is generated, and the individual believes himself unable to engage in the customary activities which have always fulfilled his emotional needs. Each cancer patient's behavior is designed to prevent, avoid, minimize, or repair injury—not merely to a part of the body, or to the psyche, but also to his basic adaptive patterns and all their social implications.

Reactions to cancer and its therapy, then, must be seen as a sequence of related events which proceeds from the first perception of a sign of illness, to the climax of hospitalization and treatment, and then to convalescence and cure, or to recurrence and death. Any behavior or emotional reaction in the sequence can only be understood in terms of reactions earlier in the sequence, and in relation to lifelong adaptive patterns.

For example, one of our patients was an attractive thirty-four-year-old married woman; when admitted to the hospital for a breast amputation (radical mastectomy) she was in a state of agitated depression. During an interview, she hesitatingly revealed the highly charged circumstances of her admission. For about a year before she noticed any disease symptoms, she had been having an affair with the husband of her best friend. They were also next-door neighbors. Burdened by guilt and self-contempt, she felt that her expectation of punishment for wrong-doing had become a dreadful reality with the onset of cancer. Furthermore, the other couple had driven her to the hospital on the day of admission. Being brought to the place of retribution by the objects of her guilt—for a disease and operation directly threatening to her feminine sexuality—proved to be too much for her.

Her reactions are paralleled in other patients through a wide variety of personal, often unconscious, factors: interference with previously important activities; the threat to one's capacity to be loved; conflicts over the dependency imposed by illness; tensions over the handling of hostility; mistrust of medical authority; sexual difficulties; competitiveness; feelings of inadequacy.

How do most people organize their defenses when they first perceive the symptoms of a breakdown in health? Nearly everyone delays taking any action for at least a short time. This period of delay permits adaptation to the threat and a realignment of defenses for coping with it. If the threat is too overwhelming, the period of delay may be so long that the patient's survival is actually endangered. Such cases are a victory for irrational expectation over both intelligence and the normal process of self-preservation. This self-defeating, but emotionally understandable, delay mechanism may go to the extreme of denying the existence of the physical symptom. Such denial, which occurs most dramatically and with great frequency among cancer patients, must be understood in terms of the magnitude of the threat to the individual, and the emotional danger he faces if he admits the reality of the threat.

As one of our studies showed, when first confronted by serious illness, most people establish some sort of belief in order to explain what has happened, even if this belief is not expressed directly. This is an effort to diminish primitive anxiety aroused by a threat of unknown origin. It is an attempt to find meaning and maintain mastery of an otherwise disordered, chaotic situation.

Out of 100 patients with serious illness in our study, forty-eight spontaneously expressed one or more beliefs about the cause of their illness. The beliefs were classified in terms of assigning culpability for the illness. Beliefs were either *self-blaming* (some real or imagined act of omission or of commission by the patient caused the disease), or *projective* (disease was caused by the action of an external agent, human or not). Typical of self-blame were

such comments as, "thinking evil," "didn't take care of myself," or having "pent-up" emotions. Projective beliefs
ranged from the capricious act of a malevolent God to the
concept of the "evil eye." One striking finding was that a
high percentage (37 percent) expressed the deep conviction
that interpersonal relations were stressful enough to cause
serious physical illness.

There is no specific psychology of cancer patients; there
is only the psychology of individuals caught in a special and
severe stress situation. The real problems of the cancer
patient begin early in his experience with the disease, and
a variety of emotional reactions remain associated with
them over its entire course. The emotional reactions vary
in time and in intensity as the "real" (physiological) events
progress. The "reality sequence" consists of four stages:
the onset of symptoms; the diagnosis; the hospitalization;
and the convalescence. Each stage of this sequence contributes to the patient's ability to integrate the total experience, and, modified by his lifelong adaptive patterns,
sets the tone of ultimate post-cancer behavior.

When the first symptom is recognized, the patient immediately begins to anticipate what he thinks will happen
to him during treatment. This anticipation is based on the
generally frightening ideas most people have about cancer. Often, the very recognition of the symptom can produce such acute anxiety that the patient delays going to a
doctor; sometimes, even if medical help is sought, a series
of defensive manuevers follows in order to avoid the inevitable therapy. Fortunately, most people are able to seek
medical care and carry through the necessary treatment.
Highly individual fears and anticipations develop early and
crystallize throughout treatment. For example, patients may
project into the future their concern about recurrence; or
anticipate social rejection if mutilating surgery is necessary;

or develop feelings of unacceptability.

When the diagnosis has been made and the need for therapy established, many of these anticipatory fears acquire a sense of reality. Hospitalization engenders feelings of helplessness. Subjected to awesome and impersonal hospital routines, cut off from the usual sources of emotional gratification, and placed in a dependent, powerless situation, the patient finds his anticipations solidifying.

Some patients interviewed on the day of admission to the hospital express feelings of being trapped and helpless. Some actually telephone their families and ask to be taken home. If they are ward patients, they observe the experience of other patients in a highly selective way to corroborate their fears. The importance of the day of admission cannot be over-emphasized. His very presence in the hospital reinforces for the patient all the fears and anticipations which first occurred at the onset of symptoms and continued through the period of diagnosis.

If surgery is the treatment chosen, as it is for most cancer patients, specific fears concerning anesthesia are expressed immediately before the operation. Most patients state that total anesthesia must be induced before they could possibly submit to surgery. Some ask that they be completely "out" even before leaving their beds for the trip to the operating room. Conversely, others fear a loss of consciousness through anesthetics.

Signs of tension or panic occur immediately after admission to the hospital. Eating patterns are usually disturbed. Even with sedation, sleep becomes impossible for most. Pre-operative dreams, if they are reported, are usually nightmares; they often directly reflect the patient's anticipations. For example, one patient dreamed she was in a butcher shop with female breasts extended from meat hooks all around her, although in the dream her own breasts were still intact.

Post-operative reactions are sometimes even more severe. Horror dreams, excessive perspiration, and rapidly pounding heartbeat are frequent. Most patients have difficulty in eating; they are unable to swallow food or they lose their appetites. Again there are a variety of sleep disturbances. inability to fall asleep, early waking, fitful and restless sleep, and fatigue on rising in the morning. During the day some patients sit quietly, sometimes crying, without participating in any ward activities; others are overactive.

These reactions, with their marked individual variations. may be understood as a watchful mobilization of inner resources to prevent still further injury. They comprise a response to an environment which to the patient seems hostile and injurious. The patient may believe himself to be overwhelmed by the threat to his safety, or be unable to make decisions; he may show signs of actual disorganization. This state of mind is usually accompanied by profound feelings of dejection, a sense of helplessness, a retreat from function, and possibly even suicidal thoughts. When the patient is in this anxiety-ridden state, he tends to turn to other people for help, seeking advice, consolation, and reassurance.

It is important to remember that, although they are commonly regarded as regressive reactions, depression and dependence are both appropriate and temporary for most patients. Often they can be regarded as a prelude to the process of emotional repair. To what extent these feelings persist depends a great deal on the amount of help the patient gets in solving his problems. Unless he has adequate help, the patient may not be able to solve them, and chronic depression, restriction of function, and pathological dependence may persist long after hospitalization.

On the other hand, some people attempt to master their

difficulties by sheer force of will. This is, in effect, a form of denial of the limitations of their own power. When left unguided, it may result in inappropriate solutions which can be bizarre and ineffective, or even result in total failure with subsequent feelings of defeat. Often these enthusiastic attempts to master the situation are closely akin to elation, and are actually a thin veneer for profound depression.

The end of hospitalization heralds the beginning of convalescence. "Going home" is viewed with widely varying feelings. Some patients are eager to see their children and families again and feel that only at home will they be able to recuperate properly. For these patients, family and friends represent the support and warmth they miss in the sterile and symbolically mutilative atmosphere of the hospital. Others, however, are not eager to return home, either because of feelings of weakness or because they feel unable to face people. They are relating the results of their therapy to a social context, and to them the impersonal hospital environment is less threatening than their fears of social inacceptability.

Although the actual surgical experience is over, the feelings it aroused remain. Many patients complain that their families and friends refuse to let them discuss their hospital experiences. These patients are usually resentful; they feel they would be relieved if people would accept the fact that they had cancer, and refer to it as they would to other diseases. However, there are other patients who never want to discuss their experience, fearing they might become depressed. These tend to become hyperactive, doing everything to keep from thinking about it and "feeling blue."

Understanding and support by the patient's family plays an enormously significant part in helping him to resolve his feelings about the whole experience. One woman, who was able to resume full functioning very early, reported that she had never realized how important her family was to her and how deeply they loved her until she became ill.

Of course, the patient's relationship to his family during his illness depends on the nature of the relationship before he became ill. A warm and supportive marriage relationship, with good communication and sexual adjustment between husband and wife, will weather the stormy periods of adaptation. A marriage full of tension, distrust, rejection, and sexual incompatibility will usually deteriorate further under these new stresses.

Cancer presents repeated emotional crises to even a good marriage. A husband may be repelled by the removal of his wife's breast not because of her new physical state, but because of his own unrecognized, long-dormant fears of illness and injury. His uncontrollable withdrawal does not reflect a change in his love for her, but it may nevertheless provoke feelings of rejection in her. Another woman who underwent the same operation may withdraw from her husband because of her feeling that she is no longer acceptable to him.

Not only the family, but the social, economic, and ethnic group to which the patient belongs will influence his view of threatening experiences, determining the confidence he feels in doctors, and defining acceptable ways for him to express his emotional reactions in situations that induce fear and anxiety.

What about the perennial dilemma of "telling the truth?" Nowhere is the anxiety about cancer clearer than in the constantly repeated question, "Should the doctor tell the patient *the truth?*" Plagued by the guilt of bringing bad news, feeling ill-equipped to handle the threatened emotional consequences of the information, burdened by his own confusions about life and death, and often feeling pessimistic even when pessimism is unwarranted, most physicians work out highly personal solutions to this question. The solutions are seldom based on rationality and logic.

As a matter of fact, we have found that in cases where the patient truly trusts the physician's benevolence and skill, the question of "the truth" rarely arises. As for the physician, his decision about what to tell the patient should be determined only by what will help the patient to co-operate in his treatment with a minimum of anxiety. Any other consideration is superfluous. In any case, it seems to me that the question of "truth telling" rests on some highly questionable assumptions—that there is a single disease called "cancer" (that rubric has subsumed under it upwards of 350 diseases) ; that there is a uniform patient; and that there is a uniform physician. In the absence of such constants, the search for a formula is nonsense.

Nowhere is the power of a good relationship between physician and patient more apparent than in those cases where death is imminent. The most frequent problem here is the physician's withdrawal—reluctant to face what he conceives of as his own failure to prevent the inevitable, he finds himself "too busy" to visit the dying patient. Such behavior on the part of doctors or other hospital personnel is *always* interpreted by the patient as an abandonment. This experience is psychologically very painful to the patient, often interacting with the physiological pain of the terminal period, and he tends to become increasingly demanding, querulous, and hostile, or slips deeper and deeper into depressive despair.

At no other time in life is the need for human contact greater than it is as death approaches. Helpless and dependent, the dying patient experiences a reawakening of the feelings experienced in infancy, when he was also helpless and dependent. Often patients would like to speak frankly about their feelings regarding death, but find themselves either alone or with people who refuse to talk with them (usually family members engaged in self-protective evasion). In no other situation is the inherent difficulty of *listening* clearer than it is in communicating with the dying.

On the other hand, no greater evidence of love exists than in the enactment of the "denial charade." Here the patient and his family all behave as if death were not imminent, but the situation is totally different from the self-serving withdrawal from the dying.

In general, then, the problem of emotional adaptation to cancer and its treatment is inseparable from the larger problems of human communication. Anxiety, present in every cancer patient, is a formidable barrier between him and those around him. It causes distortions, shifts in emphasis, indeed, inability to comprehend, to remember, or even to hear. If one wants to be sure communication is successful, efforts must be made to allay disruptive anxiety. More often than not, allaying anxiety rests more on nonverbal than on verbal means: the "how" of communicating is infinitely more important than the "what" communicated.

Finally, it appears that many of the lives saved by advances in medical science and technology are doomed to psychological invalidism—which could be minimized by sound psychological preparation during illness and hospitalization. Perhaps the time is ripe for the introduction of research programs to develop and refine such techniques in order to bring them into line with the advanced technology of the operating room, of radiation therapy, or of medical diagnostics. Psychological preparation units might be established, to prepare the patient emotionally for procedures which might alter his physical state to the point of disrupting his overall adaptation. Is this any less reasonable than the improvements in techniques which have reduced operative deaths? Is it any less reasonable than the remarkable development of recovery units, or intensive care units?

It seems logical to devote as much energy to preserving psychic integrity as we now devote to preserving physiologic integrity. The patient saved from a serious illness should be enabled to live with dignity and self-respect—not merely to exist. We must eliminate the price of survival—the price of misery and unhappiness for those who are saved from death or physical incapacitation by medical progress.

Drugs, Doctors and Junkies

ARNOLD BERNSTEIN and HENRY L. LENNARD

Since the invention of sulfa drugs around 1940, closely followed by the discovery of the antibacterial properties of penicillin, we have been tantalized by the notion that chemical agents are man's companions and can produce medical miracles. Psychoactive drugs, especially, were expected to work wonders for individuals and society in general. The per capita consumption of drugs has been sharply increasing since the early fifties. The production and distribution of psychoactive agents has doubled during the last four years. Physicians wrote 230 million prescriptions for such chemical agents in 1971, but less than 30 percent of the prescriptions were written by psychiatrists. During the same period, probably not by chance, the illegal use of drugs also increased year by year, and we are now faced with an epidemic of illegal drug use, or at least by an epidemic of concern over the illegal use of drugs.

During 1970, five billion doses of tranquilizers, three billion doses of amphetamines and five billion doses of barbiturates were produced in the United States. About one-third of all Americans between the ages of 18 and 74 have used a psychoactive drug of some type. Similar trends have been reported from other countries as well.

Psychoactive drugs are prescribed for most patients in mental hospitals, for most patients attending outpatient psychiatric facilities, to schoolchildren who are behavior problems, to elderly persons in nursing homes, to prisoners in correctional institutions and to persons who are already addicted to drugs. They are prescribed for "psychiatric" conditions ranging from chronic deteriorated psychoses through the psychoneuroses to "nervous" conditions that can only be described as the wear and tear of everyday life. They are also prescribed by internists and other physicians for a wide variety of nonspecific physical complaints. Each year more and more drugs are being used, for more and more reasons, by more and more people, through both legal and illegal channels, and there is more pressure from more and more sources to increase their use.

The rapid development and exploitation of the new biochemical technology can hardly be considered an unmixed blessing for humanity. Every chemical agent introduced into a body, regardless of the specificity of its effects, has a range of side effects. Psychoactive agents (such as stimulants, sedatives, tranquilizers and antidepressants) are no exception to this rule, for their side effects are pervasive and far-reaching, extending from the person who takes them, to his family and others in his social network, as well as to the community at large.

The controversy over what should be done in the drug field revolves around the way drugs are to be seen; the way individuals are to be treated; with what is social and what is medical; with what behavior needs to be defined as illness and what as socially deviant; with what people are like; and finally, with what one can or should do, to whom, in the name of treatment or medicine or social good.

Issues concerning drug use inside and outside the law impinge upon powerful personal, economic and political interests; hence little useful information has become readily available, and meanings therefore remain clouded. Nevertheless, large quantities of potentially toxic chemicals are being introduced into the population of the United States. This phenomenon is being encouraged and supported by a complex of social forces, economic interests and public policies. Contributing to this development is an increasing tendency to medicalize the human condition, the tyranny that ideas about morality exercise upon the community, the metaphor of the body as a machine and the strains that contemporary social problems place upon our social institutions. Many unexplored issues of public policy are involved in the physician's role as society's gatekeeper in the use of drugs.

Medicalization of the Human Condition

The theory used to recruit physicians and deploy chemical technology in the war against deviance, crime, misbehavior, alcoholism, mental illness, drug addiction, overanxiety, overweight, overindulgence, overactivity, underactivity, insomnia, overpopulation, sadness, rage and bizarre ideas, derives from the determination that these conditions are analogous to medical problems and therefore can be solved through medical means. Once a human problem is identified as a disease, the stage is set for mobilizing the technological apparatus for discovering its cure.

The growing inclination to define human problems as medical problems, to medicalize all aspects of human existence, can be observed in such examinations of the state of our mental health as the famous "Midtown Study," which show that 80 percent of the persons interviewed report feelings and symptoms which are classified prima facie by project psychiatrists as signs of "poor" mental health.

The historical developments leading to the present monopoly that modern medicine and modern psychiatry exercise over the affairs of the mind is described in *The Manufacture of Madness*, by Thomas Szasz, and therefore need not be further described here. Instead, we shall address ourselves to some of the social forces at work maintaining and increasing the use of drugs as "solutions" for social as well as personal problems.

Tyranny of Social Prescriptions

The basic secrets of life and health are constantly being discovered and major "breakthroughs" announced by scientists interviewed in the mass media. Yet, despite wonder drugs, new surgical techniques, intracellular manipulations, and a constantly growing technological armamentarium, people continue to sicken and die and hospitals remain overcrowded.

Though the accomplishment of life everlasting, healthy and happy, may be impossible, the fantasy is not, and the main result of such predictions by science has been to convince the public that human suffering is a medical disease. People have become less and less willing to accept pain and anguish as natural concomitants of living, and have come to expect medicine to put an end to all personal suffering.

Approximately 60 percent of the patients who appear in a general practitioner's office or clinic do so for largely nonspecific reasons. Patients seek the help of a physician because they are lonely, depressed, anxious, dissatisfied or unhappy. They are troubled because they find it difficult or impossible to measure up to prevalent social prescriptions concerning what one ought to get out of life. They are not as popular, successful, sweet-smelling, thin, vigorous or beautiful as they have been led to believe that they ought to be and deserve to be. They are in a physician's office because of the premium our culture places upon appearance, mood or performance; they are there because they have been made to feel they should be or feel something other than what they are or feel.

As John Corry says, "there is no end to the ways in which Americans can be manipulated and made to feel that there is something wrong, and that whatever it is, it can be solved by something or someone."

Two sets of ideas are confounded. One has to do with the ideals of health, normality and functioning that members of our society expect to live up to. The second is the notion that failure to live up to these can be remedied through the medium of medical practice or through drugs taken on one's own initiative.

The argument advanced by those who see no problem with widespread prescription and use of psychoactive drugs is that these drugs are prescribed for and used by persons experiencing "psychic distress"; and that, since some persons reporting "psychic distress" are not using drugs, psychoactive drugs are prescribed conservatively by physicians and underused by the public. The proponents of this view further argue that even more persons could profit from the use of drugs for the relief of distress, but, sadly enough, refuse to take them.

If certain human feelings are defined as psychic distress, and if psychic distress, so defined, is further taken as a symptom of indication of a psychological disturbance, and if psychoactive drugs are the treatment of choice for such disturbances, then, the present use of psychoactive agents *is* conservative and should be expected to increase.

Psychic distress most often is a condition of human existence. The intensity, quality and specifics of such distress differ with particular social conditions and circumstances, but human beings incapable of psychic distress would be robots or automatons, devoid of sensibility and responsiveness. It is only too ironic that many persons maintained on large doses of the antipsychotic drugs known as phenothiazines do in fact so behave, and can only be described as having been "zombified."

There can hardly be any doubt that professionals, through their expansion of psychiatric conceptualization to include anxiety, unhappiness, conflict and tension as symptoms of mental disease, have contributed to the rise of psychic distress. The disservice of mental health professionals and the pharmaceutical industry, then, is not simply in the promotion of drug taking, but rather in the promotion of a model which inevitably must lead to the medicalization and technocratization of human existence.

Medical professionals and everyone working in the social and natural sciences must reexamine their definitions of illness, their concepts of normality, the artificial boundaries they have imposed between physical and mental, individual and family, unit and system—and then surrender these narrow theoretical positions. A narrow focus is useless or even harmful. A systems model is the only possible alternative. An ecological model can show how physiology, society and nature can be integrated into a large pattern of interacting systems in delicate balance, demonstrating clearly that interventions at any level disturb the balances and the relations among other parts of the system. One needs to examine the effects upon the whole system from each input. It is one thing to expect a physician to assess the physical effects of a given dose of a particular drug upon a single person; it is quite another matter to rely upon physicians to assess the social consequences of maintaining 500,000 persons on methadone, another million on antipsychotic drugs and untold numbers on a variety of other potent biochemical agents. Such drugs have major social side effects. They dampen, sedate, diminish and dehumanize social interaction and, when directed at old people, women, problem children, prisoners and disturbing people of all kinds, they can become instruments for social control and management.

The Body as a Machine

The metaphor of the body as a machine has profoundly influenced concepts and attitudes toward the human body. This more than anything else can account for certain otherwise inexplicable medical practices. Machines are essentially passive and static and one operates upon them or repairs them when they are out of order. But the human body is a complex and dynamic system in flux. Human beings are active and can operate quite well without having to be pushed or controlled, or having decisions made for them.

Machine operators are separate from and qualitatively different from the machines they control. The functioning of a machine is influenced entirely by physical factors. Although feelings and interpersonal events are real to humans, they have no effect on machines.

Mass-produced machines are substantially identical and perform in the same way. They and their parts are interchangeable. However, each human is unique in respect to his genetic code and history. Human parts are not readily interchangeable, as transplant attempts have demonstrated, and human individuals are not interchangeable in relationship networks. Machines are not affected by their histories in the same way that human beings are. Humans are in a continuous process of growth and historical development, and are at any given time largely a product of this complex historical process. Above all, machines tend to be relatively self-contained. They are not tied into and dependent upon vast social networks for their well-being and survival. The state of one machine does not affect the state of another in the way that the state of one human being affects the state of another. Human beings never exist in isolation from other human beings, and what one does to one human affects many others in significant ways.

Demands of the Social System

The idea that science and technology can provide simple and instantaneous answers to personal and social problems (for example, a pill against war was seriously proposed recently by a nationally known social scientist), is running through our society. No such answers have emerged, and contemporary social systems and institutions (encompassing our educational, health, economic and legal structures) are becoming increasingly inadequate to meet the demands being placed upon them. At the same time many persons are becoming more and more unwilling to accept the limitations of these institutions.

Social unrest and rebellion have created acute and serious problems for these already strained and fragile institutional networks. As a result of population increases, industrialization, urbanization and mobility, the traditional social mechanisms for resolving social problems and dealing with troublesome persons have eroded and are no longer available to provide the means for resolving the rapidly developing crises of living that modern man is subject to. Family, neighborhood and community networks can no longer exert the control, monitoring and healing functions they once exercised. Other institutions have emerged, but they are cumbersome and costly to develop and maintain.

In the light of these phenomena an available scientific technology (i.e., psychoactive drugs) that permits control and management of problems created by social conditions becomes very attractive. Even more alluring is the possibility that the use of such "medication" can be rationalized within the framework of the dominant cultural metaphor—the means are scientific and technological; the problem is medical; and the solution is therapy, that is, in the best interest of the persons on whom they are being employed.

Dr. Henry Brill, a former superintendant of Pilgrim State Hospital, Long Island, New York, recently asserted that much of what is called "crime in the streets" is, in fact, "pathological aggression" and that "there is a considerable body of experience, and perhaps analogy in experience, with various drugs which would indicate that this does fall within the field of psychopharmacology." In this way are dissension, deviance and delinquency annexed to the province of psychopharmacology.

The technology of psychopharmacology is peculiarly functional for maintaining an uneasy and strained social system. Economic forces are also contributing to the gathering momentum of this technological development. Actually, billions of dollars a year are being invested in the manufacture, sale and delivery of psychoactive agents and, paradoxically enough, in the development of still other drugs and programs to solve the problems created by the medical and social "side effects" of the original drugs. Unfortunately, often what is being perpetuated by the use of drug technology are malignant social institutions. The use of drugs thus diminishes the pressure to seek other and more fundamental solutions. We are reminded here of the current attempts in Tokyo to "solve" the problem of air pollution by means of carrying around individual supplies of oxygen in order to make it possible for people to breathe.

Gatekeepers

Drugs enter the human population through two gateways, one legal, the other illegal. Although public attention has been focused on the illegal use of psychoactive agents, by far the larger and more significant problem relates to legal use of such agents. Drugs enter the social body legally through two gateways. Moderately innocuous agents are sold over the counter in drugstores; the more potent and dangerous agents are prescribed by physicians. To a large extent, then, physicians stand between drugs and the public at large; and whether or not drugs are introduced into wide use will depend upon their willingness to employ them.

Many considerations enter into a physician's decision to administer a potent and toxic drug. These considerations always involve some balancing of risks and benefits for the patient. Like the rest of us, physicians are not free agents. They are subject to constraints from social, legal and organizational sources: the absence of other available options for resolving individual distress or social problems; the sharing of the the same dominant conceptual models of illness and health, normality and deviance; and finally, the same forms of mystification.

Physician-patient contacts last on the average of 14 minutes. Two-thirds of these contacts result in the prescription of a drug (one-third of them a psychoactive drug). Physicians who practice in community mental health clinics see patients for even briefer periods of time, and almost all of these contacts result in the infusion of a drug into a patient, and through this route into the community. Some physicians, including psychiatrists, manage to resist these pressures and still refrain from using psychoactive drugs or use them very conservatively, for brief periods, in the smallest possible therapeutic dosage levels.

Many pediatricians still avoid wholesale application of the diagnosis known as "minimum brain dysfunction," a newly discovered "disorder" which according to some estimates, afflicts as many as 5 percent of all children in the United States. Fortunately, such less advanced countries as Great Britain have not yet "discovered" the existence of this syndrome in their children, and are lagging far behind us in the use of drugs for "hyperactive" children.

Physicians are in a uniquely strategic position to limit the flow of drugs into the body social. Part of the unfolding tragedy is that their conceptual model, their training and the contexts in which they practice all conspire to encourage them to open, rather than to close, the main gate through which psychoactive agents are infused into the population.

Within the medical technological model of drug use, the only effects of psychoactive drugs that have been examined are on the "symptoms" or the "diseases" of individuals. Very little detailed information has been gathered on the effects of psychoactive drugs on the everyday interpersonal functioning and social behavior of persons on such drugs—persons who, after all, symptoms notwithstanding, live, love, work, play, make decisions, raise children and have to continue to conduct their lives while under the influence of drugs. Even less attention has been paid to the consequences for social groups when such drugs are introduced into their midst. In our view these effects are serious, manifold and worthy of the closest scrutiny.

When drugs are given to a middle-aged woman who is upset about her child's rebellion or about an unhappy marriage, or to an elderly man or woman who has been isolated from children and community, or to a child who causes trouble in school, the problem is masked. In such cases, the drugs decrease the anxiety or unhappiness of the individual but, more important, they decrease the amount of trouble his anxiety, misery or unhappiness is causing others. The use of drugs makes it easier for others to manage or to cope with the disturbed or disturbing individuals. The drugs do not, however, reach the sources of anxiety or misery—sources which may reside, for example, in an unhappy marriage, in the unfortunate position of the elderly in our society, or in the unsuccessful socialization of many youngsters into group settings.

The use of psychoactive drugs as the main avenue of intervention also tends to atrophy the ability of a group to cope with the distress of its members. Drugs decrease a group's ability to develop and enact strategies of human relatedness in response to particular psychological reactions among its members, such as anxiety, grief, rage or other extreme forms of behavior.

Physicians commonly place individuals who have suffered a loss, such as the death of a relative, on heavy sedation. True, the sedation enables the individual to enact his social obligations during the funeral and the other ritual occasions, but it deprives him of the full experience of grief, which, it is increasingly recognized, fulfills significant psychological functions.

When a family sends one of its members to a physician for a sedative or when a ward psychiatrist prescribes chlorpromazine for an agitated inpatient, both, in effect, amputate the capacity of, or at least render it unnecessary for, respondents in the immediate social environment (the medical and nursing staff) to alter themselves and the pattern of their relationships to deal with extreme or deviant behavior. Drugs alter this basic human function in any group into which they are introduced — families, classrooms, work groups, hospital wards — in the whole array of mental health institutions. Drugs undermine truly therapeutic functions, and the management function is delegated to them, instead of to significant parties in the interpersonal environment.

Psychoactive drugs alter the quality of an individual's relations to the world and to his own body. They do so by impairing his capacities to feel and to perceive. They do this by altering the clarity and capacity of all the senses — taste, touch, sight, hearing and smell. Moreover, they diminish an individual's capacity to feel and control his own body, especially denying him access to sensual and sexual feelings. The interference with many of these normal functions often has profound psychological repercussions.

To the extent that drugs dull the senses, sedate, numb and immobilize, they de-differentiate human experience and behavior. They make persons more homogeneous by restricting variability in sensation and experience; yet it is precisely for this property that many psychoactive drugs are prescribed.

We are not advocating that physicians cease prescribing psychoactive drugs altogether, but rather that they exercise greater restraint and give more careful consideration to other options. Some drugs, when used conservatively, appear to be useful in the short-term treatment of acute psychological disturbances; other drugs may play a role in the long-term control of a few well-defined syndromes.

Implications for Public Policy

Decisions about the distribution and use of drugs are now made by small highly specialized groups, such as physicians, the drug industry, public agencies and the media. These groups are, for the most part at least, as highly motivated by considerations of self-interest as by concern for the future of society and the best interests of the community. The very nature of these groups limits their competence to fully apprehend the far-reaching implications of the decisions they make, especially a full appreciation of the interpersonal, social and ecological costs of drug use. Physicians are locked into a narrow medical or psychiatric metaphor. The pharmaceutical industry is almost totally occupied by a focus on the development, distribution and manufacture of drugs. Public agencies are overwhelmed by law enforcement problems relative to drug-associated crimes and the illegal importation and distribution of drugs. And the mass media are too busy exploiting the drama of drug miracles and drug horrors, their science writers hungry for new materials amply found in the purported advances of medicine.

Decisions relating to the application of drug technology to human affairs give rise to issues and consequences far too important to be left entirely in the hands of the medical profession, the drug industry, the media and public "technobureaucrats." A high priority must be assigned to the immediate public and professional consideration of a number of critical questions that the new drug technology raises.

Public discussion should include, at the very least, a consideration of the moral, philosophical, historical and political implications of drug use. Policies and decisions must derive from these considerations, rather than merely from traditional medical factors. Policies on drug giving and taking need to be responsive to the wishes of those most directly affected, that is, persons defined as patients and their families.

Who should decide on public policy regarding what psychoactive drugs should be administered by whom, to whom and toward what end? We believe that a redelegation of responsibility for decision-making is long overdue!

Should psychoactive drugs be administered only with the consent of those to whom they are given? The larger question is: Under what circumstances and for what purposes should drugs be administered without consent? What information about psychoactive drugs should be disseminated in order that informed decisions can be made by patients, families, professionals and the public? Should all of the information about the side effects and risks available be made public? What social forces and what institutions encourage or discourage the investigation and dissemination of information about drugs?

What kinds of research on long-range consequences of psychoactive drugs (both on the individual and social level) should be encouraged, and who should have the responsibility to chart and support this research? federal agencies? the drug industry? university centers? Within whose province does the exposure of the long-range consequences of expedient short-term "solutions," such as methadone maintainance treatment, fall?

Finally, there is a need to identify more precisely the forces and interests that exert pressure for increased psychoactive drug use, and the mechanisms (many of them covert and not publicly visible) through which this influence is exerted. Guidelines to distinguish between what may be proper influence and what must be rejected as improper influence, are desperately overdue.

Tardive Dyskinesia: An Illustration

The wholesale adoption of the use of phenothiazines (major tranquilizers such as *Thorazine* and *Stelazine*) in the treatment and management of the "mentally ill" provides a recent example of the tragic consequences of a short-sighted medical approach to human problems, a tragedy which touches upon each of the policy questions alluded to above.

Even during the early period of enthusiasm over the application of drugs to the management of psychological disturbances, many clinicians were disturbed about the possibility that psychoactive drugs might have long-range effects on the central nervous system. But these expressions of caution went largely unheeded, and the primary approach to managing severely disturbed patients was shifted to psychoactive drug "treatment." For a time, physicians believed that such side effects as were noticed would subside after the discontinuance of drugs or through administration of other drugs. This view must now be revised. The majority of mental patients in this country are being maintained on drugs, and the long-term effects of the administration of psychoactive drugs are becoming increasingly visible.

A workshop sponsored by the Psychopharmacology Research Branch of the National Institute of Mental Health was convened in 1968 to discuss a new syndrome, *tardive dyskinesia*, which can be recognized in growing numbers of hospitalized mental patients who have been maintained on certain classes of psychotropic drugs over long periods. Tardive dyskinesia is a central nervous system disorder, perhaps with irreversible effects. Its manifestations include involuntary movements especially affecting the lips and tongue, hands and fingers, and body posture. Speech may be seriously affected, the face may become distorted and subject to uncontrolled expressions, and sustained normal posture may become impossible. Aside from the physical limitations this damage imposes upon a patient, the carryover to his human potential is also serious. The dysfunction is twofold: neurological and interpersonal. The chairman concluded the workshop meeting with these remarks:

> During the last fifteen years, drugs have been given to a large portion of psychiatric patients with little thought of what the risks are. The films of this workshop have shown a number of fairly severe cases of dyskinesia. But many such cases can be seen if one takes the trouble of walking through the wards of mental hospitals. I feel that we should revise our therapeutic approach with drugs as the risk seems to be considerable. Twenty to twenty-five percent of the patients are afflicted by this disorder according to our observations; the disorder may last for many years or perhaps indefinitely in the more severe cases. Even if symptoms persist only for months or a few years in the milder cases, the problem still is of considerable clinical importance.

Though reports of tardive dyskinesia have been accumulating since the early 1960s and many hundreds of cases described by 1967, especially by investigators in Western Europe, most psychiatrists were slow to acknowledge its existence. Others went on record as saying that the condition was exceedingly rare. Most of those charged with the care of mental patients either did not recognize the disorder, confused its signs with other drug-induced but reversible neurological conditions (such as parkinsonism), or attributed the emergence of stereotyped or bizarre movements to the patient's "mental illness." Most were not aware of the condition or ignored it completely.

For five years, a number of investigators, foremost among them George Crane, acted as gadflies, calling this syndrome to the attention of the medical profession, the drug industry and the government agencies charged with the protection of the consumer. Only in 1972, after settling a law suit for damages brought by a patient with tardive dyskinesia, did a major drug manufacturer finally include a detailed description of this condition in labeling phenothiazines, the class of drugs mainly implicated in the development of tardive dyskinesia.

Implications of Tardive Dyskinesia

The fascinating and tragic case of tardive dyskinesia illustrates all of the issues of public policy which we have listed and a host of others, as well. What combinations of vested interests, forces, ideological blindness and wishful thinking conspired to keep this problem out of our awareness and under wraps? Where was the leadership from those scientists charged with protecting the public interest in the area of psychoactive drugs? How did they justify then, and how do they justify now, their failure to act or publicly acknowledge the toxic hazards of these drugs?

The issues posed by the physician-induced condition known as tardive dyskinesia can no longer be ignored. There are, at present, many thousands, if not tens of thousands, of patients with symptoms of tardive dyskinesia, exhibiting from slight to serious disfigurement and disabilities. Most of the patients are elderly; the majority are in state hospitals or are receiving drugs from community mental health centers.

As psychiatrists and others become more aware of tardive dyskinesia through belated acknowledgment by the drug in-

dustry and the published efforts of a few stubborn professionals, they will be able to recognize its signs in more and more
patients. The first issue they must face is whether or not a
patient and his family are to be told that drugs administered to
help the patient have resulted in neurological damage which
appears to be irreversible. While it is clear to us that the
patient and his family must eventually be told about the effects
of the drug, it is also clear that this is not yet being done.

We have listened to discussions in which dissemination of
information about tardive dyskinesia to patients' families was
opposed on the grounds that it might tend to decrease the
employment of neuroleptic (psychoactive) agents because it
would tend to make physicians more conservative about the use
of these agents! We hold no brief for this position. It is surely
unethical and most definitely unwise at this juncture. Some
patients and families may undertake unpleasant legal actions
against physicians, hospitals and drug companies, but the outcome of such legal actions is unpredictable, since treatment can
be rationalized on the basis of accepted medical practice undertaken in the best interest of the patient and with good intent,
weighing risk and benefit. Only the professional's resistance to
recognizing the condition and procrastination in acting re-
sponsibly may cast doubt on both his competence and his
concern for his patient.

Once it is agreed that the prolonged administration of a
potent psychoactive agent poses a serious risk to a patient, risks
must be weighed against benefits. Should this task be restricted
only to the professionals directly engaged in the patient's care,
who are deeply committed to drug treatment and working
within medical and mental health organizations, systems which
often do not allow for different strategies?

A number of strategies have been recommended to minimize
the risk of tardive dyskinesia; all of them are sensible and long
overdue. They include discontinuing the administration of

phenothiazines to perhaps half of the patients now maintained on them, suspending medication periodically for others, and lowering the maintenance doses for still others.

Even such conservative suggestions are not likely to be heeded because psychiatrists fear that some patients will relapse (in terms of the psychiatric criteria employed), and some will become more troublesome, creating additional work for hospital staffs. Paradoxically, therefore, policy-making should not be left entirely to those too closely involved in the giving of drugs, but rather to persons outside the system who could represent the interests of patients as well, and who could bring to bear other perspectives. Such outsiders would be less constrained to maintain the status quo.

With the emergence of tardive dyskinesia, another unforeseen but nonetheless disastrous effect must be added to the long list of drug-induced conditions. Surely one must raise the issue of whether drug treatments should remain the main avenue of treatment for even the most severely disturbed and disabled mental patients. As Crane puts it:

> Clinicians feel that the massive use of drugs is necessary because responders cannot be differentiated clinically from non-responders. Nor is it possible to predict when a relapse will occur in a well-compensated individual. This practice would be justified if neuroleptics were low toxicity agents. While a single dose of any neuroleptic is seldom dangerous, the administration over a period of weeks or months causes a variety of side effects and complications. Parkinsonism, acute dystonia, akathisia, hypotension, drowsiness, leukopenia, jaundice, galactorrhea, photosensitivity, excessive weight gain occur with a certain frequency, but are generally reversible upon drug withdrawal. The only lethal effect is agranulocytosis, usually due to chlorpromazine. It seems to be a rare complication, most likely to occur in the elderly during the first few months of therapy . . . . More

disturbing was the discovery of changes in the electrocardiograms, particularly in subjects taking thioridazine. This discovery was followed by the report of serious cardiac complications, and the possibility of sudden death . . . .

The variety and number of side effects would suggest a certain caution and selectivity in the use of neuroleptics.

Considerable problems will be engendered by abandoning the prevailing drug strategy, especially for groups of disturbed, disturbing and disabled individuals (and of course for physicians, hospitals, staffs and social agencies). It will become necessary to seriously consider the development of a network of new arrangements and more imaginative strategies; for example, residential centers, halfway houses and other protected settings, well staffed with professional and nonprofessionals who can offer social and human support.

Drugs offer a simpler, more efficient and less costly way of managing large groups of disturbing persons, but it now appears that this strategy has become self-limiting, self-perpetuating and highly destructive. Heavy reliance upon the drug "solution" has already eroded support for many other more benign possibilities which exact considerably lower social and human costs. These other options demand to be reconsidered.

Reason for Alarm?

Tardive dyskinesia is only one example of many. The new drug technology is a hydra-like creature. Consider only the potential growth in the use of psychoactive drugs for children, the rapid acceleration of interest in the use of methadone and narcotic antagonists for persons already addicted to drugs, or the use of intravenous *Valium* and *Demerol* now being promoted as a routine dental procedure in such scientifically sophisticated areas of the country as Southern California.

We have been accused of being worriers and alarmists who do

not sufficiently acknowledge and appreciate the benefits of scientific progress and of overestimating its darker side. But shall we agree with Archie Jumper, philosopher and acrobat, a character in a play by Tom Stoppard, who allays our fears thus?

Do not despair—many are happy much of the time; more eat than starve, more are healthy than sick, more curable than dying; not so many dying as dead; and one of the thieves was saved. Hell's bells and all's well—half the world is at peace with itself, and so is the other half; vast areas are unpolluted; millions of children grow up without suffering deprivation, and millions, while deprived, grow up without suffering cruelties, and millions, while deprived and cruelly treated, none the less grow up.

Modern technology is changing life on earth in ways not yet even remotely perceived by the architects of that technology. In all phases of modern life man now is faced with problems created by the remoteness of his actions from their visible consequences. This antihumanistic model of behavior, more than anything else, makes possible actions such as high-altitude bombing or the dumping of poisonous wastes into rivers and lakes. It also facilitates the new psychoactive drug technology.

Author's note:

On July 1, 1973 new provisions for funding hemodialysis went into effect under Medicare. Such provisions offer some hope for easing the financial burden of many chronic renal failure victims. What the actual effect will be, of course, nobody knows, but professionals with whom I have spoken are cautiously optimistic. At the very least this sort of funding proves that efforts *are* being made in response to lobbying pressure.

Despite the fact that this article was written prior to the new rulings, none of its basic points has been invalidated. The new guidelines simply demonstrate the ongoing struggle over funding which will not, I am convinced, reach any satisfactory resolution until we face the need to socialize medical services for all.

FURTHER READINGS SUGGESTED BY THE AUTHOR:

Mystification and Drug Misuse by Henry Lennard *et al*. (New York: Harper and Row, 1972).

Patterns in Human Interaction by Henry Lennard and Arnold Bernstein (San Francisco: Jossey-Bass, 1969). An introduction to clinical sociology.

"Competitive Problems in the Drug Industry," United States Senate hearings before the monopoly subcommittee of the Select Comittee on Small Business, chaired by Senator Gaylord Nelson (Washington, D.C.: Government Printing Office, 1969). Also highly recommended are all of the volumes of testimony before this committee which deal with antibiotic and weight-reducing drugs as well as psychoactive drugs.

The Making of a Counter Culture by Theodore Roszak (New York: Doubleday, 1969).

"The Chemical Comforts of Man" in *Journal of Social Issues*, Vol. 27, No. 3, 1971. See especially the article by H. Nowlis.

The Mirage of Health by R. Dubos (New York: Harper Bros., 1959).

Part V
Queries about Medical
Competence and Morality

Malpractice and Medicine

DAVID MAKOFSKY

The malpractice crisis in medicine has continued for more than two years. Its immediate cause was the decision of the major national malpractice carrier, Argonaut Insurance Company, to increase premiums for malpractice insurance by 196.8 percent. Present reports indicate that the rates may be four or five times as high in the near future but, at the time of their increase, Argonaut simply intended to leave the field of malpractice insurance and never expected the doctors to pay these new charges.

During this crisis the public has seen and learned a great deal about medicine as it has been practiced in the United States. It is now apparent that incompetence is a fairly widespread problem. It has been estimated that 5 percent of all practicing doctors— roughly 16,000 out of 320,000—are unfit for practice, being mentally ill, addicted to drugs, or ignorant of modern medicine. Thirty thousand Americans die yearly from faulty prescriptions, and ten times that number suffer dangerous side effects. Incompetent and unnecessary surgery is now a serious problem. But despite this situation, state and local medical societies are reluctant to act against doctors, and consumers are often too ill informed to separate good from bad medical service until it is too late.

Care, Salaries, Profits

Two questions can be asked about the turmoil. First, has American medicine been getting worse? Malpractice settlements in New York State doubled from 1,174 in 1967 to 2,085 in 1974, and malpractice awards went from $3.4 million in 1967 to $21.8 million in 1974 (see Table 1). The trend has been nationwide. One conclusion might be that patients and the public have not been satisfied with health care. Insofar as the doctors are concerned, the public is being misled. Bernard Hirsch, general counsel for the American Medical Association (AMA), has said that "when God put you on the face of the earth, he did not mean for you to receive compensation for every distress that occurs. The rule of sympathy is no substitute for the rule of law" (*New York Times*, 7 May 1975).

Without invoking the intent of the deity, doctors have concurred. The president of the Kings County (Brooklyn) Medical Association has stated that most malpractice suits have no merit, and that the best doctors are being sued since they take the most risks. Other high medical officials have said that we expect too much from doctors, that we have been watching *Marcus Welby* and reading books like *The Making of a Surgeon*, and that we expect doctors to be too good. In this view the doctors, not the patients, are the victims of malpractice.

Second, have the large salaries and profits to be made in the field of medicine played a part in harming American health care? The salaries are there—for the last twenty-five years doctors have outdistanced the average income of all male professionals. The issue of profits is more crucial. Argonaut first entered the field of malpractice insurance in 1971 and, by 1974, had driven most of its competitors out of the field and become the major national carrier for this type of insurance. What attracted Argonaut was the fact that premiums paid by doctors generate an enormous fund of cash, and claims often take seven years to settle. In the seven-year period the money — Argonaut collected $70 million in New York State alone in 1974, paying no claims — can be used interest-free for investment purposes.

The rosy visions of 1971 were not borne out in 1974. Stock market difficulties resulted in an investment loss for Teledyne, Argonaut's parent company in the conglomerate, of $21 million, and the company lost interest in malparactice coverage. Although Argonaut precipitated the crisis when it chose to enter malpractice insurance as a field of speculative investment. American doctors did not complain about the evil effects of capitalism. Even so, the issue remains: has profit-making potential hurt American health care?

American Doctors

American citizens spend more money on medical care — both in absolute and proportioned terms — than the people of any nation in the world. But we do not receive the best care. The United States has an infant death rate that exceeds that of fourteen other nations, and a male life expectancy that is shorter than that of nineteen other nations. American nonwhite rates are much worse than the national average for both categories.

Part of the problem results from the efforts of doctors to maintain their high earnings. In 1959, after expenses, the average yearly income of all doctors was $22,000; in 1970 it was $41,500; in 1974 it was $50,000. For each year cited doctors have earned five times the average male income and 3.5 times the average professional income. Someone, of course, must be at the top; but the high income has been achieved in two ways.

First, there has been an effort to limit the number of physicians admitted to practice to a number below public need. In 1964, for instance, the United States had fewer physicians per one million population than Russia, some Western European countries, and even fewer than Bulgaria and Argentina. The scarcity of doctors has led to the demise of the home visit and the growth of its substitute, the crowded waiting room. On a more fatal note, it has left a sizeable proportion of families with no medical attention, even for the care of children.

Second, the type of doctors has changed as well. There are fewer primary physicians, those who treat general illness. The number of general practitioners, pediatricians, and internists (internal medicine) has been declining since the Second World War even though the population has grown. Medical geographers estimate that, in proportion to its population, the United States has less than half the number of primary physicians it needs to provide adequate treatment. The shortages have been felt almost entirely in rural areas and in the poorer sections of urban areas. Doctors earn a great deal of money because, given the shortage of physicians, the American public is forced to accept any medical care it can get on the doctors, terms.

Despite the public need for primary care, doctors were being drawn into high-paying specialties. To earn the high fees they were demanding, doctors needed referrals; and between 1945 and the advent of Medicare a wide variety of schemes appeared that met the specialists' need for patients—kickbacks to general practitioners, unnecessary operations (such as many of the tonsillectomies and hysterectomies that were performed), and the padding of Blue Cross and Blue Shield bills with undelivered services and extensive hospital stays. To accomplish this end the doctors needed the help of lax enforcement by the American Hospital Association and Blue Cross. All these practices would be magnified enormously under Medicare.

Growing Scandals, Public Control

The American medical profession has not been publicly concerned about the growing scandals in health care delivery. In June 1975 a New York State Assembly committee led by Andrew Stein estimated that $300 million fraud existed in the Medicaid operations in New York State; Stein's committee simply read computer printouts which listed that general practitioners were charging Medicaid for "psychiatric consultations," that pediatricians were charging for electrocardiogram tests (usually given to middle-aged men), and the like. The man in charge of supervising Medicaid matters. Deputy Health Commissioner Morton A. Fischer, was quoted in the *New York Times* (15 July 1975) as saying that he "was surprised to hear of doctors performing services of which they are not really qualified."

In May-June 1975 it was also revealed that nursing home operators were gaining millions of dollars through fraudulent claims, while elderly patients were being starved, ignored, and shipped against their will to other empty nursing homes on the demands of paid recruiters. The AMA, meanwhile, was announcing that America's number one medical problem was the size of malpractice premiums.

American physicians have been concerned about the threat of socialized medicine and public control over health care delivery. As a check against congressional activity the AMA created a well-financed political front, the American Medical Political Action Committee, whose extensive activities eventually brought the AMA under charges of tax evasion for violating its status as a tax-exempt organization. To deal with the problem presented by the Department of Health, Education, and Welfare, the AMA developed plans for a priority system to staff every one of the 315 health advisory panels of the department with AMA-approved physicians, and replacements for these physicians filled every vacancy by specialty and by region of the country.

To deal with the public's demand for medical insurance, the AMA kept the public at arm's length by insisting on "fiscal intermediaries" as a means of answering the problem. Blue Cross was created during the depression to help people pay for doctor and hospital bills, but in the postwar period it became the AMA's response to proposed government-supervised socialized medicine for the elderly. American doctors announced that if the government did not cooperate with Blue Cross, it could not predict that hospitals and doctors would participate in the program.

In medicine, in the words of Malcolm X, "the chickens have come home to roost." Practices begun on a small scale have become major problems. Rural areas and older urban areas were ignored by affluent young doctors, and those that had customarily treated people in these regions eventually retired. Doctors abandoned family practices for lucrative specialties, and the kickbacks and bill padding that occurred did not appear dangerous or even remarkable until the 1960s, when the situation became more serious.

Profit Making in the Blood Market

In 1971 Richard Titmuss, the British scholar and Labor party advisor on welfare, published *The Gift Relationship*, a well-received book on blood collection. By comparing the

British and American systems the issue was put before the American public: irrespective of whether the state or the individual pays for medical insurance, is a system based on profit making better or worse than a socialized medical system?

After the Second World War modern surgical techniques developed to the point where demand for blood increased rapidly. Red Cross blood drives were not sufficient to meet greater needs, and American hospitals were forced to rely on replacement obligations and commercial blood banks. In Britain, in a socialized system, the government made greater efforts to increase voluntary donations.

The American medical profession was less hostile toward private enterprise than toward the federal government. Hospitals charged patients $50 for a pint of blood during the 1960s, and they paid commercial blood banks $35 to supply them with blood. In skid row areas donors would be found for as little as $5 to $15 per pint; and skid row blood, collected at storefronts, became a major factor in the American blood market.

The principle medical danger in commercial blood transactions is that of infected blood. In a survey of all patients who received blood transfusions at the clinics of the University of Chicago, 11,382 patients in eleven years (1946-57), cases of postoperative hepatitis rose as the proportion of blood from paid donors increased. In 1946 no paid donors were used, and of the approximately 500 patients transfused none contacted postoperative hepatitis. In 1954-55, 50 percent of the blood was obtained from paid donors; and of the approximately 1500 patients transfused, 42 contracted the disease (3 percent of the total group). Experts estimate that the risk of infection to the patient is ten times greater from blood collected from commercial blood banks than from voluntarily donated blood.

Thus the commercial market possibilities in blood offer no

great benefit to the patient; in fact, they offer just the reverse. Between 3 and 4 percent of transfused patients are dead or seriously ill because of the profit-making possibilities in blood.

Medicare and Medicaid

Hospitals, doctors, and health entrepreneurs, recognizing the support for socialized medical care for the elderly, accepted it as long as the role of the government was limited to the provision of funds. Medicare operated through fiscal intermediaries such as Blue Cross and private insurance groups, and the government provided these intermediaries with funds for buildings, computer installations, and the apparatus necessary to run such a program. Originally this insurance was to cost $2 billion per year, but costs escalated. In 1969 the Medicare program cost $6.6 billion and Medicaid (public assistance-vendor medical payments) cost an additional $4.6 billion. Costs for both programs increased at a rate of over $1 billion per year, and by 1974 the programs cost more than $16 billion. Obviously the demand for services was much greater than Congress had envisioned, but other factors contributed to high costs.

Corruption by doctors seems to have played a role in the high cost of the programs. By 1975 there were extensive reports of Medicaid mills operating in New York City, and the following practices were disclosed: ping-ponging (sending patients from one doctor to another for unnecessary examinations and shots, the fees being charged to Medicare and Medicaid); unnecessary medication; unqualified practice; no services; and first-visit claims (doctors are allowed to charge higher fees for first visits). The Stein committee estimated that over $300 million per year has been paid to doctors for these fraudulent claims. In the past year a sizeable number of doctors have been arrested for Medicare fraud, but no one knows if this enforcement will prove to be a deterrent.

Nursing Homes

An elderly person or couple may receive housing allotments, food stamps, and SSI-public assistance in addition to the $2,000-$3,000 per year available from Social Security, but it is a sad fact that many elderly cannot care for certain specific needs because they lack funds to hire help for a limited time. If an individual is sent to a nursing home, the operators—under Medicaid provisions—are eligible to receive a large sum of money. In 1975 the state of Connecticut paid a flat rate of $23/day to homes ($8200/year). Florida nursing home operators refused to take new patients unless they could receive $615/month ($7200/year). The average payments of the state of New York to nursing home operators under Medicaid was $41.25/day ($15,000/year).

Once Medicare was established, the number of nursing homes increased so rapidly that new homes were forced to hire recruiters, and social administrators transferred patients from homes that had not paid a recruiters fee to those that had done so. Three illegal practices have been found in the nursing home industry: double billing, falsifying claims (dummy claims), and fraudulent cost estimates. Federal officials are aware of these abuses, but have not pressed charges.

Malpractice

In the early 1950s malpractice claims were numbered in the hundreds; by the late 1960s they were being filed at the rate of 7,000-10,000 a year. In 1970 it was forecast on the basis of current trends that at least one physician in four could expect a claim to be filed against him before he retired from practice. The pessimism of this report was easily borne out in the mid-1970s, at least in New York State.

The malpractice problem leads to medical practices that are harmful to the patient. There is increased inclination to give tests, to practice "defensive medicine," which is hardly what the patients need in order to become healthy. Much of the substance of defensive medicine, unnecessary tests and operations, was already being done by doctors in order to increase their yearly income.

The profit potential in medicine has begun to hurt doctors as well as patients, and the problem has been aggravated by the legal profession. Legal firms have developed a contingency fee system that is extremely lucrative for successful lawyers. They receive 50 percent of the malpractice settlement; but in the 70 or 80 percent of the cases that the patient receives nothing, the lawyer receives nothing as well. The average monetary settlement, excluding "zero" cases, now averages $25,000; thus lawyers stand to earn a great deal of money from the best cases. Since cases commonly last seven years, there is considerable risk in entering this field of law. But it obviously attracts many—in the Detroit area malpractice claims rose 27 percent per year from 1970 to 1974, and when "no fault" legislation passes the number of malpractice claims rises.

What Doctors Want

What doctors want is embodied in a piece of legislation passed by the state of Indiana and subsequently called the Indiana Plan. Parts of this plan are being adopted by New York State. The following outline of the Indiana Plan shows that doctors see malpractice as a legal, rather than a medical, problem.

There should be a limitation on the right of patients to sue doctors. Typically, although this factor varies, the statute of limitations is reduced from three to two and one-half years and from eighteen to ten years for infant cases. Claims that are otherwise perfectly legitimate would then have no legal standing.

Those people who sue should face a critical audience. The plan holds that the finding of a panel of doctors should be binding on the court, Jurors, perfectly capable of deciding cases of murder, robbery, and rape, are not satisfactory for judging malpractice. The AMA feels that a panel of doctors will be less sympathetic to patients. Legislators in New York State have been reluctant to accept the idea that doctors should hold exclusive legal judgement on physician-defendants, and the Special Advisory Panel on Medical Malpractice has proposed that a workman's compensation model, where injuries receive specific, listed compensation, be substituted for the jury process. One panel member, State Senator John Dunne, warned that any savings on legal fees and public sympathy for the victim would be offset by an increased number of claims.

People who sue should not win very much. The plan proposes that a state ceiling of $500,000 be set on plaintiff awards, with the state paying all damages over $100,000. The New York state legislature is limiting to $100,000 the amount that can be awarded for "pain and suffering," but this ruling avoids the major problem: the cost of future treatment. Robert Lerner, an official of the American Arbitration Association, has suggested that award damages for negligent care might not serve patients as well as a contract promising appropriate medical care. Excluding socialized medicine under federal supervision, it is not evident that any doctor or hospital would be in a position to honor such a contract.

The major problem in malpractice, therefore, is legal, not

medical. The Indiana Plan suggests that the contingency fee of lawyers should be limited to 10 percent of all awards over $100,000. Without entering into a discussion of the ethics of the legal profession, the plan is designed to allow lawyers to absorb all the risk of malpractice litigation without an opportunity for substantial gains. To limit the benefits of lawyers under the current system is tantamount to limiting the right of patients to press this type of case.

What We Need

What we need depends on how much we are willing to accept the proposition that there is something seriously wrong with American medical care. The evidence shows a substantial number of corrupt and incompetent doctors and, at the same time, a serious shortage of doctors. We need more doctors, ones who are willing to serve the public when and where medical service is required.

The private, professional administration of health care, and the reliance of the government on fiscal intermediaries to police and carry out health care, has had major failings. The health care delivery system is incompetent at the very top—the heads of hospitals, health commissioners, nursing home operators, Blue Cross officials—because it has not been able to control well-known and medically dangerous, fraudulent practices.

Finally, if we accept the fact that doctors are experts at curing people but that they cannot run a competent medical system, then what we need is socialized medicine. In clinics doctors would work fixed hours for a fixed salary, and the staff of the clinic would be adjusted to the size of the population served.

Many doctors recognize the problems of health care. The measures taken to police doctors are ineffective because they harm only honest physicians, making them submit to long bureaucratic delays. Dishonesty itself has not been punished. In malpractice claims themselves an important principle is at stake. Victims hould have the right to sue; no one should suffer medical mistakes without some form of compensation. Let them sue the state. While the Indiana Plan limits individual rights, a socialized system would advance them.

FURTHER READINGS SUGGESTED BY THE AUTHOR:

Duffy, John. *The Rise of the Medical Establishment.* New York: McGraw-Hill, 1976.

Ehrenreich, Barbara and John Ehrenreich. *The American Health Empire.* New York: Random House, Vintage Books, 1971.

Law, Sylvia A. *What Went Wrong.* New Haven, Conn.: Yale University Press, 1974.

Titmuss, Richard. *Commitment to Welfare.* New York: Pantheon Books, 1968.

Titmuss, Richard. *The Gift Relationship.* New York: Pantheon Books, 1971.

Dead on Arrival

DAVID SUDNOW

In County Hospital's emergency ward, the most frequent variety of death is what is known as the "DOA" type. Approximately 40 such cases are processed through this division of the hospital each month. The designation "DOA" is somewhat ambiguous insofar as many persons are not physiologically *dead on arrival,* but are nonetheless classified as having been such. A person who dies within several hours after having been brought to the hospital might, if upon arrival he was initially announced by the ambulance driver to be dead, retain such a classification at the time he is so pronounced by the physician.

When an ambulance driver suspects that the person he is carrying is dead, he signals the emergency ward with a special siren alarm as he approaches the entrance driveway. As he wheels his stretcher past the clerk's desk, he restates his suspicion with the remark, "possible," a shorthand reference for "possible DOA." (The use of the term *possi-*

399

ble is required by law, which insists, primarily for insurance purposes, that any diagnosis unless made by a certified physician be so qualified.) The clerk records the arrival in a log book and pages a physician, informing him in code of the arrival. Often a page is not needed, as physicians on duty hear the siren alarm, expect the arrival, and wait at the entranceway. The patient is rapidly wheeled to the far end of the ward corridor and into the nearest available foyer or room, supposedly out of sight of other patients and possible onlookers from the waiting room. The physician arrives, makes his examination, and pronounces the patient dead or not. If the patient is dead, a nurse phones the coroner's office, which is legally responsible for the removal and investigation of all DOA cases.

Neither the hospital nor the physician has medical responsibility in such cases. In many instances of clear death, ambulance drivers use the hospital as a depository because it has the advantages of being both closer and less bureaucratically complicated a place than the downtown coroner's office for disposing of a body. Here, the hospital stands as a temporary holding station, rendering the community service of legitimate and free pronouncements of death for any comers. In circumstances of near-death, it functions more traditionally as a medical institution, mobilizing life-saving procedures for those for whom they are still of potential value, at least as judged by the emergency room's staff of residents and interns. The boundaries between near-death and sure death are not, however, as we shall shortly see, altogether clearly defined.

In nearly all DOA cases the pronouncing physician (commonly that physician who is the first to answer the clerk's page or spot the incoming ambulance) shows in his general demeanor and approach to the task little more than passing interest in the event's possible occurrence and the patient's biographical and medical circumstances. He responds to the clerk's call, conducts his examination, and leaves the room once he has made the necessary official gesture to an attending nurse. (The term "kaput," murmured in differing degrees of audibility depending upon the hour and his state of awakeness, is a frequently employed announcement.) It happened on numerous occasions, especially during the midnight-to-eight shift, that a physician was interrupted during a coffee break to pronounce a DOA and returned to his colleagues in the canteen with, as an account of his absence, some version of "Oh, it was nothing but a DOA."

It is interesting to note that, while the special siren alarm is intended to mobilize quick response on the part of the emergency room staff, it occasionally operates in the opposite fashion. Some emergency room staff came to regard the fact of a DOA as decided in advance; they exhibited a degree of nonchalance in answering the siren or page, taking it that the "possible DOA" most likely is "D." In so doing they in effect gave authorization to the ambulance driver to make such assessments. Given that time lapse which sometimes occurs between that point at which the doctor knows of the arrival and the time he gets to the patient's side, it is not inconceivable that in several instances patients who might have been revived died during this interim. This is particularly likely in that, apparently, a matter of moments may differentiate the revivable state from the irreversible one.

Two persons in similar physical condition may be differentially designated dead or not. For example, a young child was brought into the emergency room with no registering heartbeat, respirations, or pulse—the standard "signs of death"—and was, through a rather dramatic stimulation procedure involving the coordinated work of a large team of doctors and nurses, revived for a period of eleven hours. On the same evening, shortly after the child's arrival, an elderly person who presented the same physical signs, with —as one physician later stated in conversation—no discernible differences from the child in skin color, warmth, etc., arrived in the emergency room and was almost immediately pronounced dead, with no attempts at stimulation instituted. A nurse remarked, later in the evening: "They (the doctors) would never have done that to the old lady (attempt heart stimulation) even though I've seen it work on them too." During the period when emergency resuscitation equipment was being readied for the child, an intern instituted mouth-to-mouth resuscitation. This same intern was shortly relieved by oxygen machinery, and when the woman arrived, he was the one who pronounced her dead. He reported shortly afterwards that he could never bring himself to put his mouth to "an old lady's like that."

It is therefore important to note that the category DOA is not totally homogeneous with respect to actual physiological condition. The same is generally true of all deaths, the determination of *death* involving, as it does, a critical decision, at least in its earlier stages.

There is currently a movement in progress in some medical and lay circles to undercut the traditional distinction between "biological" and "clinical" death, and procedures are being developed and their use encouraged for treating any "clinically dead" person as potentially revivable. Should such a movement gain widespread momentum (and it, unlike late 19th-century arguments for life after death, is legitimated by modern medical thinking and technology), it would foreseeably have considerable consequence for certain aspects of hospital social structure, requiring perhaps that much more continuous and intensive care be

given "dying" and "dead" patients than is presently accorded them, at least at County. (At Cohen Hospital, where
the care of the "tentatively dead" is always very intensive,
such developments would more likely be encouraged than
at County.)

Currently at County there seems to be a rather strong
relationship between the age, social background, and the
perceived moral character of patients and the amount of
effort that is made to attempt revival when "clinical death
signs" are detected (and, for that matter, the amount of
effort given to forestalling their appearance in the first
place). As one compares practices in this regard at different
hospitals, the general relationship seems to hold; although
at the private, wealthier institutions like Cohen the overall amount of attention given to "initially dead" patients
is greater. At County efforts at revival are admittedly superficial, with the exception of the very young or occasionally wealthier patient who by some accident ends up at
County's emergency room. No instances have been witnessed at County where, for example, external heart massage was given a patient whose heart was stethoscopically
inaudible, if that patient was over 40 years of age. At
Cohen Hospital, on the other hand, heart massage is a
normal routine at that point, and more drastic measures,
such as the injection of Adrenalin directly into the heart,
are not uncommon. While these practices are undertaken
for many patients at Cohen if "tentative death" is discovered early (and it typically is because of the attention
"dying" patients are given), at County they are reserved
for a very special class of cases.

Generally speaking, the older the patient the more likely
is his tentative death taken to constitute pronounceable
death. Suppose a 20-year-old arrives in the emergency room
and is presumed to be dead because of the ambulance

driver's assessment. Before that patient will be pronounced dead by a physician, extended listening to his heartbeat will occur, occasionally efforts at stimulation will be made, oxygen administered, and often stimulative medication given. Less time will elapse between initial detection of an inaudible heartbeat and nonpalpitating pulse and the pronouncement of death if the person is 40 years old, and still less if he is 70. As best as can be detected, there appeared to be no obvious difference between men and women in this regard, nor between white and Negro patients. Very old patients who are initially considered to be dead solely on the basis of the ambulance driver's assessment of that possibility were seen to be put in an empty room to wait several moments before a physician arrived. The driver's announcement of a "possible" places a frame of interpretation around the event, so that the physician expects to find a dead person and attends the person under the general auspices of that expectation. When a young person is brought in as a "possible," the driver tries to convey some more alarming sense to his arrival by turning the siren up very loud and keeping it going after he has already stopped, so that by the time he has actually entered the wing, personnel, expecting "something special," act quickly and accordingly. When it is a younger person that the driver is delivering, his general manner is more frantic. The speed with which he wheels his stretcher in and the degree of excitement in his voice as he describes his charge to the desk clerk are generally more heightened than with the typical elderly DOA. One can observe a direct relationship between the loudness and length of the siren alarm and the considered "social value" of the person being transported.

The older the person, the less thorough is the examination he is given; frequently, elderly people are pronounced dead on the basis of only a stethoscopic examination of the heart. The younger the person, the more likely will an examination preceding an announcement of death entail an inspection of the eyes, attempt to find a pulse, touching of the body for coldness, etc. When a younger person is brought to the hospital and announced by the driver as a "possible" but is nonetheless observed to be breathing slightly, or have an audible heart beat, there is a fast mobilization of effort to stimulate increased breathing and a more rapid heartbeat. If an older person is brought in in a similar condition there will be a rapid mobilization of similar efforts; however, the time which will elapse between that point at which breathing noticeably ceases and the heart audibly stops beating and when the pronouncement of death is made will differ according to his age.

One's location in the age structure of the society is not the only factor that will influence the degree of care he gets when his death is considered possibly to have occurred. At County Hospital a notable additional set of considerations relating to the patient's presumed "moral character" is made to apply.

The smell of alcohol on the breath of a "possible" is nearly always noticed by the examining physician, who announces to his fellow workers that the person is a drunk. This seems to constitute a feature he regards as warranting less than strenuous effort to attempt revival. The alcoholic patient is treated by hospital physicians, not only when the status of his body as alive or dead is at stake, but throughout the whole course of medical treatment, as one for whom the concern to treat can properly operate somewhat weakly. There is a high proportion of alcoholic patients at County, and their treatment very often involves an earlier admission of "terminality" and a consequently more marked suspension of curative treatment than is observed in the treatment of nonalcoholic patients. In one case, the decision whether or not to administer additional blood needed by an alcoholic man bleeding badly from a stomach ulcer was decided negatively, and that decision was announced as based on the fact of his alcoholism. The intern in charge of treating the patient was asked by a nurse, "Should we order more blood for this afternoon?" and the doctor answered, "I can't see any sense in pumping it into him because even if we can stop the bleeding, he'll turn around and start drinking again and next week he'll be back needing more blood." In the DOA circumstance, alcoholic patients have been known to be pronounced dead on the basis of a stethoscopic examination of the heart alone, even though such persons were of such an age that were they not alcoholics they would likely have received much more intensive consideration before being so decided upon. Among other categories of persons whose deaths will be more quickly adjudged, and whose "dying" more readily noticed and used as a rationale for apathetic care, are the suicide victim, the dope addict, the known prostitute, the assailant in a crime of violence, the vagrant, the known wife-beater, and, generally, those persons whose moral characters are considered reproachable.

Within a limited temporal perspective at least, but one which is not necessarily to be regarded as trivial, the likelihood of "dying" and even of being "dead" can be said to be partially a function of one's place in the social structure, and not simply in the sense that the wealthier get better care, or at least not in the usual sense of that fact. If one anticipates having a critical heart attack, he had best keep himself well-dressed and his breath clean if there is a likelihood he will be brought into County as a "possible."

The DOA deaths of famous persons are reportedly attended with considerably prolonged and intensive re-

suscitation efforts. In President Kennedy's death, for example, *The New York Times* (Nov. 23, 1963) quoted an
attending physician as saying:

Medically, it was apparent the President was not alive
when he was brought in. There was no spontaneous res-
piration. He had dilated, fixed pupils. It was obviously
a lethal head wound. Technically, however, by using
vigorous resuscitation, intravenous tubes and all the
usual supportive measures, we were able to raise the
semblance of a heart beat.

There are a series of practical consequences of pronouncing a patient dead in the hospital setting. His body may
properly be stripped of clothing, jewelry, and the like,
wrapped up for discharge, the family notified of the death,
and the coroner informed in the case of DOA deaths. In
the emergency unit there is a special set of procedures
which can be said to be partially definitive of death. DOA
cases are very interestingly "used" in many American hospitals. The inflow of dead bodies, or what can properly
be taken to be dead bodies, is regarded as a collection of
"guinea pigs," in the sense that procedures can be performed upon those bodies for the sake of teaching and
research.

In any "teaching hospital" (in the case of County, I use
that term in a weak sense, that is, a hospital which employs
interns and residents; in other settings a "teaching hospital" may mean systematic, institutionalized instruction)
the environment of medical events is regarded not merely
as a collection of treatable cases, but as a collection of ex-
perience-relevant information. It is a continually enforced
way of looking at the cases one treats to regard them under
the auspices of a concern for experience with "such cases."
That concern can legitimately warrant the institution of a
variety of procedures, tests, and inquiries which lie outside

and may even on occasion conflict with the strict interests of treatment; they fall within the interests of "learning medicine," gaining experience with such cases, and acquiring technical skills.

A principle for organizing medical care activities in the teaching hospital generally—and perhaps more so in the county hospital, where patients' social value is often not highly regarded—is the relevance of any particular activity to the acquisition of skills of general import. Physicians feel that among the greatest values of such institutions is the ease with which medical attention can be selectively organized to maximize the general benefits to knowledge and technical proficiency which working with a given case expectably affords. The notion of the "interesting case" is, at County, not simply a casual notion but an enforced principle for the allocation of attention. The private physician is in a more committed relation to each and every one of his patients; and while he may regard this or that case as more or less interesting, he ideally cannot legitimate his varying interest in his patients' conditions as a basis for devoting varying amounts of attention to them. (His reward for treating the uninteresting case is, of course, the fee, and physicians are known to give more attention to those of their patients who shall be paying more.)

At County Hospital a case's degree of interest is a crucial fact, and one which is invoked to legitimate the way a physician does and should allocate his attention. In surgery, for instance, I found many examples. If on a given morning in one operating room a "rare" procedure was scheduled and in another a "usual" procedure planned, there would be no special difficulty in getting personnel to witness and partake in the rare procedure, whereas work in the usual case was considered as merely work, regardless of such considerations as the relative fatality rate of each procedure or the patient's physical condition. It is not uncommon to find interns at County who are scrubbed for an appendectomy taking turns going next door to watch a skin graft or chest surgery. At Cohen such house staff interchanging was not permitted. Interns and residents were assigned to a particular surgical suite and required to stay throughout the course of a procedure. On the medical wards, on the basis of general observation, it seems that one could obtain a high order correlation between the amount of time doctors spent discussing and examining patients and the degree of unusualness of their medical problems.

I introduce this general feature to point to the predominant orientation at County to such matters as "getting practice" and the general organizational principle that provides for the propriety of using cases as the basis for this practice. Not only are live patients objects of practice, so are dead ones.

There is a rule in the emergency unit that with every DOA a doctor should attempt to insert an "endo-tracheal" tube down the throat, but only after the patient is pronounced dead. The reason for this rule (on which new interns are instructed as part of their training in emergency medicine) is that the tube is extremely difficult to insert, requires great yet careful force, and, insofar as it may entail great pain, the procedure cannot be "practiced" on live patients. The body must be positioned with the neck at such an angle that the large tube will go down the proper channel. In some circumstances when it is necessary to establish a rapid "airway" (an open breathing canal), the endo-tracheal tube can apparently be an effective substitute for the tracheotomy incision. The DOA's body in its transit from the scene of the death to the morgue constitutes an ideal captive experimental opportunity. The procedure is not done on all deceased patients, the reason apparently being that it is part of the training one receives in the emergency unit and is to be learned there. Nor is it done on all DOA cases, for some doctors, it seems, are uncomfortable in handling a dead body whose charge as a live one they never had, and handling it in the way such a procedure requires. It is important to note that when it is done, it is done most frequently and most intensively with those persons who are regarded as lowly situated in the moral social structure.

No instances were observed where a young child was used as an object for such a practice nor where a well-dressed, middle-aged, middle-class adult was similarly used. On one occasion a woman supposed to have ingested a fatal amount of laundry bleach was brought to the emergency unit, and after she died, several physicians took turns trying to insert an endo-tracheal tube, after which one of them suggested that the stomach be pumped to examine its contents to try to see what effects the bleach had on the gastric secretions. A lavage was set up and the stomach contents removed. A chief resident left the room and gathered together a group of interns with the explanation that they ought to look at this woman because of the apparent results of such ingestion. In effect, the doctors conducted their own autopsy investigation without making any incisions.

On several similar occasions physicians explained that with these kinds of cases they didn't really feel as if they were prying in handling the body, but that they often did in the case of an ordinary death—a "natural death" of a morally proper person. Suicide victims are frequently the objects of curiosity, and while there is a high degree of distaste in working with such patients and their bodies (particularly among the nursing staff; some nurses will not touch a suicide victim's dead body), "practice" by doctors is apparently not as distasteful. A woman was brought into the emergency unit with a self-inflicted gunshot wound which ran from her sternum downward and backward, passing out through a kidney. She had apparently bent over a rifle and pulled the trigger. Upon her "arrival" in the emergency unit she was quite alive and talkative, and though in great pain and very fearful, was able to conduct something of a conversation. She was told that she would need immediate surgery and was taken off to the operating room; following her were a group of physicians, all of whom were interested in seeing the damage done in the path of the bullet. (One doctor said aloud, quite near her stretcher, "I can't get my heart into saving her, so we might as well have some fun out of it.") During the operation the doctors regarded her body much as they do one during an autopsy. After the critical damage was repaired and they had reason to feel the woman would survive, they engaged in numerous surgical side ventures, exploring muscular tissue in areas of the back through which the bullet had passed but where no damage had been done that required repair other than the tying off of bleeders and suturing. One of the operating surgeons performed a side operation, incising an area of skin surrounding the entry wound on the chest, to examine, he announced to colleagues, the structure of the tissue through which the bullet passed. He explicitly announced his project to be motivated by curiosity; one of the physicians spoke of the procedure as an "autopsy on a live patient," about which there was a little laughter.

In another case, a man was wounded in the forehead by a bullet, and after the damage was repaired in the wound, which resembled a usual frontal lobotomy, an exploration was made of an area adjacent to the path of the bullet, on the forehead proper, below the hair line. During this exploration the operating surgeon asked a nurse to ask Dr. X to come in, and when Dr. X arrived, the two of them, under the gaze of a large group of interns and nurses, made a further incision, which an intern described to me as unnecessary in the treatment of the man, and which left a noticeable scar down the side of the temple. The purpose of this venture was to explore the structure of that part of the face. This area of the skull, that below the hair line, cannot be examined during an autopsy because of a contract between local morticians and the Department of Pathology to leave those areas of the body which will be viewed free of surgical incisions. The doctors justified the additional incision by pointing to the "fact" that since he would have a "nice scar as it was, a little bit more wouldn't be so serious."

During autopsies themselves, bodies are routinely used to gain experience in surgical techniques, and many incisions, explorations, and the like are conducted that are not essential to the key task of uncovering the "cause" of the death. Frequently specialists-in-training come to autopsies though they have no interest in the patient's death; they await the completion of the legal part of the procedure, at which point the body is turned over to them for practice. Mock surgical procedures are staged on the body, often with co-workers simulating actual conditions, tying off blood vessels which obviously need not be tied, and suturing internally.

When a patient died in the emergency unit, whether or not he had been brought in under the designation DOA, there occasionally occurred various mock surgical procedures on his body. In one case a woman was treated for a chicken bone lodged in her throat. Rapidly after her arrival via ambulance a tracheotomy incision was made in the attempt to establish an unobstructed source of air, but the procedure was not successful and she died as the incision was being made. Several interns were called upon to practice their stitching by closing the wound as they would on a live patient. There was a low peak in the activity of the ward, and a chief surgical resident used the occasion to supervise teaching them various techniques for closing such an incision. In another case the body of a man who died after being crushed by an automobile was employed for instruction and practice in the use of various fracture setting techniques. In still another instance several interns and residents attempted to suture a dead man's dangling finger in place on his mangled hand.

What has been developed here is a "procedural definition of death," a definition based upon the activities which that phenomenon can be said to *consist of*. While in some respects this was a study of "dying" and "death," it might be better summarized as a study of the activities of managing dying and death as meaningful events for hospital staff members. My attention has been exclusively given to the description of staff behavior occurring in the course of doing those things which daily ward routines were felt to require.

It was in the course of these routines—handling bodies, taking demographic information on incoming and outgoing patients, doing diagnosis, prognosis, medical experimentation, and teaching—that certain patients came to be recognized as persons legitimately accorded special treatments—the "dying" and "death" treatments. In the hospital world these treatments—organized to fit institutionalized daily ward routines built up to afford mass treatments on an efficiency basis, to obtain "experience," avoid dirty work, and maximize the possibilities that the intern will manage to get some sleep—give "dying" and "death" their concrete senses for hospital personnel. Whatever else a "dying" or "dead" patient might mean in other contexts, in the hospital I investigated, the sense of such states of affairs was given by the work requirements associated with the patients so described. For a "dying" patient to be on the ward meant that soon there would be a body to be cleansed, wrapped, pronounced dead, and discharged, and a family to be told. These activities and the work requirements they entailed provided the situational frame of interpretation around such states.

At least one question that has not been directly addressed is that which would ask why hospital personnel feel treatments must be organized on a mass basis. Its answer, I believe, is to be found in a historical analysis of the development of the medical ideology toward the nonpaying patient and in the peculiarly impersonal environment of the charity institution I examined. I decided at the outset of my investigation to leave unexplained general matters of ideology about patient care and to proceed from there to learn something about the ways in which existing practices were organized and what these practices entailed as regarded the occurrence of "dying" and "death."

While hospital personnel managed, on the whole, to sustain a detached regard for the event of death, it occurred, on occasion, that routinely employed procedures and attitudes became altered and upset. The successful daily management of "dying" and "dead" bodies seemed to require that patients have a relatively constant character as social types. So long as the patient whose death was anticipated or had occurred was an elderly, poor, and morally proper person, the occasion of his "dying" and "death" was treated with little notice and in accord with ordinarily enforced routines of "death care." On critical occasions, however—when, for example, a child died or a successful, middle-class person was brought into the emergency unit as a DOA—ordinarily employed procedures of treatment were not instituted, and special measures were felt to be necessary. Nowhere was this disruption clearer than with the deaths of children. Nurses have been known to break down in tears when a child died, and in such cases, particularly, "dying" and "death" temporarily cease to have their firmly grounded, organizationally routinized meanings, activities, and consequences. When an intoxicated or suicidal or "criminal" patient was treated, these persons' moral characters intruded as prevalent considerations in the way in which they were regarded, providing a special frame of interpretation around the way care was organized over and above that which the category "patient" established. In key instances, patients' external attributes operated to alter the institutional routine in significant ways, causing vehemence, disgust, horror, or empathetic dismay, and—particularly in the case of children's deaths—a radical though short-lived movement entirely out of role on the part of staff members. No matter how routinized an institution's methods for handling its daily tasks, those routines remain vulnerable at certain key points. No matter how nonchalantly staff members managed to wrap patients' bodies for discharge to the morgue, taper off in the administration of drugs and care to the "dying," pronounce deaths, and return to other tasks, special circumstances caused these routines to be upset—either made more difficult to carry off, more interestedly attended, or substantially revised.

In regarding these special cases—those persons deemed particularly obnoxious or particularly worthy—perhaps insight may be gained into the requirements for usual, orderly ward activities. On those occasions when a nontypical death caused staff members to step outside their regularly maintained attitudes of indifference and efficiency, one could glimpse a capacity for emotional involvement which ordinary work activities did not provide proper occasions for displaying. The maintenance of appropriate impersonality in the hospital requires an enforced standardization to the types of events and persons which personnel confront. This work of *affect* management is aided by staff-held theories of proper fate, proper deaths, proper persons, and notions regarding the appropriate role of medicine and surgery in prolonging life and delaying death. These theories are invoked on a daily basis to support the patterns of care given the dying, the tentatively dead, and the decidedly dead, but they can be employed only as long as the patient in question can be construed to fit the categories for which the theories are relevant. I made every effort to construct classifications of patients so as to provide for the propriety of treating them in organizationally routine ways, but occasionally there was a case which resisted that classification. The death of a child, a young adult, or the deaths of those persons who were regarded as morally imperfect stirred a noticeably atypical degree of moral sentiment.

This class of atypical deaths, those occurring for atypical persons or in atypical ways, became set off as the specially noteworthy events of hospital life, the cases which staff members recounted for long periods of time and built into stories that were frequently retold when death was made a specific topic of conversation. In selecting certain cases to invest with special meaning, staff members demonstrated that despite their work involvements in matters of life and death and their routinely casual attitude toward such events, death nonetheless was an event which could call forth grief and empathy.

"Dying" and "death" are categories that have very broad currency, being variously used in many settings throughout the society. I have examined only one setting, only one locus of meanings and associated activities. The use of the categories in the hospital is to be regarded as hospital specific, although in other domains their usages may share features in common with those found in the hospital. While clinical death occurs, in American society at least, chiefly within the hospital setting, that setting provides only one of a variety of socially organized worlds within which its meaningful character is provided. What "dying" and "death" procedurally entail among staff physicians within the hospital would seem to share little in common with those activities anticipatorily organized by and consequential for the patient himself and members of his family—those for whom doing autopsies, handling the census of a hospital ward, cleaning up dead bodies, and the rest are not relevant considerations. My restricted interest in death in the hospital requires that the formulation of the notions "dying" and "death" given here be clearly confined in generality to this highly instrumental domain of technical activity.

FURTHER READING SUGGESTED BY THE AUTHOR:

Awareness of Dying by Barney Glaser and Anselm Strauss (Chicago: Aldine Press, 1965).

Death, Property and the Ancestors by John Goody (Stanford: Stanford University Press, 1962).

The Meaning of Death by Herman Feifel (New York: McGraw-Hill Book Co., 1959).

Contributors

George W. Albee is professor of psychology at the University of Vermont and author of *Mental Health Manpower* (1959).

Natalie Allon is assistant professor of sociology at Hofstra University.

Morton Bard is professor of psychology and director of the Psychological Center of the City College of the City University of New York.

Arnold Bernstein teaches psychology at Queens College of the City University of New York.

Robert Crawford is on the faculty of the department of political science at the University of Illinois, Chicago Circle. He is the author of two articles on the politics of prevention, "You Are Dangerous to Your Health: The Ideology and Politics of Victim Blaming" and "Healthism and the Medicalization of Everyday Life," both in the *International Journal of Health Service*.

Ernest Dernberg is a psychiatrist in a private practice in San Francisco.

Amitai Etzioni is professor of sociology and chairman of the department at Columbia University, and author of *The Genetic Fix*.

Shizuko Fagerhaugh is a research nurse affiliated with the department of social and behavioral sciences in the School of Nursing, University of California, San Francisco, and is co-author (with Anselm L. Strauss) of *The Politics of Pain Management*.

Florence Galkin is a participant in the CORO Foundation's Public Affairs Leadership Training Program for Women. She was previously the founder and director of Community Action and Resources for the Elderly, a consultant to the Community Council of Greater New York's Nursing Home Ombudsman Project, and a staff associate at the United Hospital Fund. She has published several monographs on long-term care and articles in *Congress Monthly* and *New York Affairs*.

Jeanne Guillemin is associate professor of sociology at Boston College. She is the editor of *Anthropological Realities: Readings in the Science of Culture* (Transaction).

Robert Harris is a member of the President's Council on Environmental Quality. He was formerly associate director of the Toxic Chemicals Program for the Environmental Defense Fund and is the co-author of *Malignant Neglect*, which deals with the risks posed to humans from exposure to cancer-causing chemicals.

Martin Hochbaum is director of the Commission on Urban Affairs at the American Jewish Congress, professor of health advocacy at Sarah Lawrence College, and chairman of the New York State Council on Shared Health Facilities. His publications have appeared in numerous journals and newspapers and he is co-editor of *Poor Jews: An American Awakening*.

John Krizay is a writer and independent consultant specializing in the economics of health care. He is the co-author of *The Patient as Consumer*, winner of the Norman B. Welch Award for the outstanding contribution to the economics of medicine.

Henry L. Lennard is a medical sociologist at the University of California, San Francisco.

John Luce is associate editor of *San Francisco Magazine* and public affairs director of the Haight-Ashbury Free Medical Clinic.

Elizabeth Markson is director of the Mental Health Research Unit of the New York State Department of Mental Hygiene.

Dorothy H. Miller is director of the Scientific Analysis Corporation in San Francisco.

Paul Milvy is a member of the President's Council on Environmental Quality. He was formerly a member of the Environmental Sciences Laboratory of New York's Mount Sinai Hospital, working on aspects of environmental and occupational cancer.

Charles Nanry is vice-dean of University College, Newark Division, of Rutgers University, and co-editor of *Journal of Jazz Studies*.

Jacqueline Nanry is a graduate student in social work at Rutgers University.

Robert Nicholas is a member of the President's Council on Environmental Quality. He was formerly deputy attorney general for the Commonwealth of Pennsylvania, with responsibilities for consumer and environmental law.

Julius A. Roth is professor of sociology at the University of California, Davis.

David E. Smith is assistant clinical professor of toxicology at the San Francisco Medical Center and medical director of the Haight-Ashbury Free Medical Clinic.

Anselm L. Strauss is professor of sociology and chairman of the graduate program in sociology, University of California Medical Center, San Francisco, and author of numerous books, including *Professions, Work and Careers* (Transaction, 1975) and *Chronic Illness and the Quality of Life*.

Barbara Suczek, a sociologist, is a lecturer at the University of California, San Francisco.

David Sudnow is assistant professor of sociology at the University of California, Irvine.

Elizabeth M. Whelan is executive director of the American Council on Science and Health and a research associate at the Harvard School of Public Health. She is the author of numerous books, including *Panic in the Pantry: Food Facts, Fads, and Fallacies* (with F.J. Stare).

Carolyn Wiener is a sociologist affiliated with the department of social and behavioral sciences in the School of Nursing, University of California, San Francisco.

Irma G. Zuckermann is a doctoral candidate in sociology at the University of California, San Francisco and a registered nurse and social worker.